Praise for Susan

"I love reading about women who continue to challenge themselves on trails. In *Walk, Hike, Saunter*, 32 women, all over 45, openly share their stories of the rewards and challenges of hiking. This is one book you will want to sit down and savor for the inspiration and wisdom."

— **Jennifer Pharr Davis,** Appalachian Trail record holder, motivational speaker, National Geographic Adventurer of the Year, critically acclaimed author of *The Pursuit of Endurance.*

"Thank you very much for the opportunity to read *Walk, Hike, Saunter.* I'm only a few years away from the 45 and up age group, and it was personally encouraging to read so many stories from women who are hiking strong well into their seventies!

"*Walk, Hike, Saunter* will take 'I'm too old to hike' out of your vocabulary! These profiles of women who are hiking and backpacking from 45 into their seventies will leave you inspired to get off the couch at any age."

— **Heather 'Anish' Anderson,** 30,000 miles hiked including the Appalachian, Continental Divide and Pacific Crest Trails three times. National Geographic Adventurer of the Year. Author of *Thirst:2600 Miles to Home.*

"Long-distance hiking is one of the world's great challenges. More people have successfully climbed Mt. Everest than have completed the 'Triple Crown' of hiking — thru-hikes of the Appalachian, Pacific Crest, and Continental Divide National Scenic Trails. But at the same time, long-distance hiking can be enjoyed by anyone, regardless of age or gender.

"Women, especially older women, will find inspiration and advice in these pages as their peers share their experiences on everything from attitude to equipment, challenges to triumphs. So pull up a comfy chair, light a fire, open these pages and let these remarkable women spin their tales of their adventures — and inspire yours."

— **Karen Berger,** author, *America's National Historic Trails a*nd 18 other books.

"Both inspirational and reassuring, Susan Alcorn's *Walk, Hike, Saunter* provides a wealth of encouragement for any woman. These thoughtful interviews, made up of tales from real women, in their own voices, will find a home on your bookshelf and in your heart.

"Whether you aspire to long distance wilderness hiking, prefer the historic byways of Europe or enjoy a gentle stroll around the neighborhood, you will respond to the diverse personalities and likeable personas of the author's many female protagonists.

"*Walk, Hike, Saunter* is full of pearls of wisdom from women who actually walk the walk. It will remind you that each walk has its own reasons for being special, and it may just inspire you to take your own next step."

— **Amy Racina**, hiker, speaker, adventurer, author of *Angels in the Wilderness: The True Story of One Woman's Survival Against All Odds.*

"A uniquely entertaining look into the lives of 32 dynamic women hikers—their vulnerabilities, harrowing escapes, and funny experiences. In addition, their practical tips on how to plan ahead—from what to eat to how to face your fears—are all quite valuable, so get your highlighter out.

'The mere act of hiking can guide us to living in the present. Readers will no doubt be inspired to take to the trail with an eye to the horizon, the mind set on the now, and feet lightly on the ground ready for that next step!"

— **Karen Herzog**, President Adco Marketing. Post-50, hiking and meditation enthusiast.

# WALK, HIKE, SAUNTER

## SEASONED WOMEN SHARE TALES AND TRAILS

### Susan Alcorn

Shepherd Canyon Books
Oakland, California

Shepherd Canyon Books
Oakland, CA 94611, U.S.A.
backpack45.com

Published in the U.S.A. by Shepherd Canyon Books and printed in multiple countries. See last page for point of manufacture.
ISBN 978-0-936034-07-2
Library of Congress Control Number: 2020915563

Publisher's Cataloging-in-Publication data

Names: Alcorn, Susan, author.
Title: Walk , hike , saunter : seasoned women share tales and trails / Susan Alcorn.
Description: Oakland, CA: Shepherd Canyon Books, 2020.
Identifiers: LCCN: 2020915563 | ISBN: 978-0-936034-07-2
Subjects: LCSH Hiking for women. | Hiking for women--Anecdotes. | Backpacking. | Backpacking--Anecdotes. | Women travelers--Biography. | BISAC TRAVEL / Special Interest / Hikes & Walks | SPORTS & RECREATION / Hiking | BIOGRAPHY & AUTOBIOGRAPHY / Sports | BIOGRAPHY & AUTOBIOGRAPHY / Women
Classification: LCC GV199.58 .A53 2020 | DDC 796.51/082--dc23

27 26 25 24 23 22 21 20    1 2 3 4 5

# Dedication

For the women who have conceived of, designed, built, maintained, and otherwise fostered hiking trails for our public use and enjoyment.

# Contents

# Preface

*The most difficult thing is the decision to act, the rest is merely tenacity.*
~ Amelia Earhart

This book is to support, encourage, and provide a source of information for women who want to walk, hike, or backpack. Whether you prefer to walk in your neighborhood, hike short paths while on vacation, or set out with a pack on long-distance trails here or abroad, you will find inspiration and advice in the collection of stories that follows. The 32 women in this book have shared many delightful tales—and based on their extensive hiking experience, you'll find much of their wisdom can be useful with planning and setting out on your future adventures.

This book has something to offer any hiker, but its primary focus is on, and for, women 45 years of age or older. Whether you define a hiker as someone who finds hiking to be a rewarding part of their life or as a lifestyle, there are differences between hiking when you are 20 and when you are 60.

Although there are some exceptions (some quite startlingly so), generally women who began hiking or backpacking when they were in their 20s or 30s may find that when they reach 45 or so, they are unable to hike the distances or at the speeds they used to handle with ease. However, there are many women now entering their 40s, 50s, 60s, and older who hardly hiked at all when they were younger—and they have discovered that they now have more discretionary time, more endurance, and more perseverance than they had when they were younger.

We are all at different points in our lives facing different circumstances, so one size does not fit all. As you read the stories of the women of the book in the following chapters, you'll no doubt identify with the goals and interests of some of the women, be in awe of many, and learn or be reminded of important skills throughout.

As you read, let yourself dream a bit, too. If you were able to hike as often as you'd like, with whomever you wish (or solo), and as far and as fast as you'd like, where would you go? No matter your age or ability now, if you want to enjoy being outdoors more—whether in forests, deserts, plains, or mountains—we'd like to inspire and support your efforts.

— *Susan 'Backpack45' Alcorn*

# Acknowledgments

When I began this project by sending a cover letter and questions to a group of women hikers I'd selected, I had no idea how it would go. There were a few who I figured would answer because they were good friends and would want to support me if nothing else. But from the rest, especially those who didn't know me, I didn't know what to expect.

It has been an incredibly rewarding experience to receive their outpouring of stories meant to not only share with me but to benefit women everywhere. Some responses made me laugh out loud, others almost brought me to tears, some made me search online for trails and peaks I had never heard of, and still others convinced me I should add new destinations to my hiking list. I hope you have the same experiences!

When the coronavirus raged its ugly head, the back-and-forth emails to collect more information or to get permission to use quoted material lifted my spirits because of the open, creative, and thoughtful ways that so many of the book's contributors were spending their time. Most of the women (including me) had to postpone or cancel travel plans for the year and had to deal with those disappointments as well as the changes that everyone has tried to manage. When they wrote me to say they were finding ways to continue to hike (but generally more locally), volunteering for various causes, and tackling projects at home, it lifted my spirits because it reminded me that we were all in this together—and would get through this!

I was struck by the humility of many of the women; some were initially hesitant and asked if there might be other women more qualified than they are. They were proud and confident about their accomplishments and didn't want to brag about themselves, but participated to help others.

When I reached out to get permission to use copyrighted material, I was again unsure about the degree of help I would get. However, because of their generosity, I was able to include quotes from Elizabeth Vasquez (Outdoor School instructor at the REI Southlake store near Dallas); Thomas Armstrong, Ph.D.; and Cam 'Swami' Honan of The Hiking Life. Stephanie Elizondo Griest, I appreciate your sharing your photo. I greatly appreciate the help from all of you.

Many thanks to the friends who read the manuscript and helped catch my many errors. Tom Coroneos, you did some very helpful fine-tuning—and gave me an 'aha' moment when you suggested that all section quotations should be from women. Linda Grayman, I am grateful that you have a keen eye for catching left-out words and confusing sentences. Rachel Makool, thanks for asking insightful questions to keep me on track. Mary Nowee, I appreciate your input.

Bob Cooper, thanks for your thorough copy editing; I know you improved things manyfold. I appreciate your patience and advice.

And to my husband, Ralph Alcorn, many thanks for reading and commenting on my many drafts. Your patience at working with me when I was blocked or stressed with how the project was going was amazing and much appreciated.

Liz 'Snorkel' Thomas, I am grateful to you for suggesting women I might interview. I would have loved to include your story, but because you were not yet 45 or older, you became a prime example of why it was hard to stick with my age criteria.

Thanks also to Scott Williams for providing the names of several women to consider including. You were right; they all had great stories to tell.

And lastly, to the 32 women who shared your stories here, I want to express my deepest gratitude for your generosity.

# Introduction: *It's Your Time!*

I started writing my first hiking book, *We're in the Mountains not over the Hill: Tales and Tips from Seasoned Women Backpackers*, after coming off my first backpacking trip in 1989. We had come over Kearsarge Pass in the Sierra Nevada to meet the John Muir Trail and to continue on for several days to reach our ultimate goal—the 14,505-foot peak of Mt. Whitney.

Though I was determined to reach the summit—even stating that I would crawl to the summit if required—I wasn't all too sure that it was a realistic goal. No one I knew was doing this sort of thing, but I figured if I could walk, I could keep taking step after step until I reached the top. Though I hadn't done much research on our upcoming hike, I did know that Whitney was a 'walk-up' peak, not a mountain-climbing adventure (at least during late summer and early fall when there was no snow).

I was 48 at the time. Some of my friends and acquaintances liked to hike, but like me, hadn't gone on any long-distance hikes much less backpacking trips. However, I felt that there had to be other women of my age doing such things, and I was curious how many actually were. I decided to try to collect their stories. I fairly arbitrarily set 45 years as my lower age limit and went in search of women who fit that description (with a couple of notable exceptions—Jenny Jardine and Isabella Bird). I ended up interviewing 31 remarkable hikers and backpackers for my earlier book.

I am now 79. Turning 45 seems so long ago and so young compared to where I am now. My friends and I now laugh about how young it really was and is. In the intervening years, I have met many women in their 40s, 50s, and older who are now able to start or continue to take long-distance hikes. As my husband Ralph and I have continued our hiking through the years, our network of hiking friends has expanded, and our lives have been enriched by hearing about their adventures and learning from their wisdom. For years, I have dreamed about writing a new book about women hikers in order to bring their stories to light and to inspire others.

We all experience stages in our lives. We progress through childhood, adolescence, and young adulthood pursuing an education and/or learning a trade, and then perhaps establishing and growing a career and family, and then for most of us eventually—retirement.

Most people set off on their wildest and craziest explorations, if they do so at all, in their late teens and early twenties. Some grab a backpack and set off for Europe or elsewhere to see the world. Others may take a 'gap year,' a yearlong break between high school and college or between college and a career start. But then, most of us settle down and truly become 'adults.' During those adult years, many take on the responsibilities connected with raising children, and the trips and vacations are more often friend- or family-oriented rather than solo treks.

As the children mature and are able to be left home with other responsible adults or on their own, many women find that they are finally able to take some time for themselves. Some, and I speak from personal experience, may continue to shoulder responsibilities caring for their own children, grandchildren, ailing spouses, mates, or aging parents, but generally speaking, a new stage—with more discretionary time—opens up.

As we age and seek to find ways to fill the time that work and perhaps family life once occupied, we *can* decide to start or continue caring for family members or engaging in volunteer work, but we can also choose to develop new interests: establish a new career or business, travel, or pick up hobbies, new or old—and exercise.

In our mature adulthood, we can continue to participate in activities that we have enjoyed for decades, and we also have a new opportunity to make more time for ourselves—whether hours, days, weeks, or months at a time. These years can be great ones for trying new things and reinventing ourselves.

## More women are on our trails

The enactment of Title IX in 1972 encouraged and supported women's participation in sports. James Fixx's *The Complete Book of Running*, published in 1977, promoted acquiring a 'natural high' and popularized that sport. Women found that putting on their sneakers for runs on a regular basis helped with stress relief, weight management, endurance, and self-esteem. The women of that generation who took those changes to heart were able to envision greater freedom to pursue loftier goals and aspirations.

However, while tremendous strides have been made toward overcoming barriers that have blocked women from participating in sports as both recreational and professional athletes, obstacles linger. Women are more likely to be reminded of societal expectations. They are warned, "It's not safe for you to go alone" or "You're needed at home" or "People will 'talk' if you just take off."

In an article by Thomas Armstrong, Ph.D., entitled *The Human Odyssey: Navigating the Twelve Stages of Life* (published by Ixia/Dover), he summarizes the later years as follows: "Mature Adulthood (Ages 50-80). Benevolence – Those in mature adulthood have raised families, established themselves in their work life, and become contributors to the betterment of society through volunteerism, mentorships, and other forms of philanthropy. All of humanity benefits from their benevolence. Moreover, we all can learn from their example to give more of ourselves to others."

What Armstrong doesn't delve into, but I'd like to add, is that we have paid our dues. During these years, we can adjust or change the priorities in our lives. When women are told that they must behave in certain ways or are bombarded with messages telling them that they should put other people's needs and wants first, it takes more strength to step out the door for a walk, much less a long journey.

Women, by and large, do put the needs of others ahead of themselves. And often this is regarded as the way things *should* be. We are told that doing things for ourselves is selfish, disregarding the fact that 'A pitcher must be filled with water before it can be used to fill the glasses.' It is not selfish to take care of yourself. Exercise—as well as good nutrition, plenty of sleep, community, and spiritual care—is beneficial to us as well as those who count on us.

Even women who manage to work around expectations that they will always be the ones to care for others can run into barriers. They are too often treated as if they are too old, too inexperienced, or too weak to operate on their own. Many complain of feeling invisible—that younger people do not value their contributions and strengths as much as they should.

Unfortunately, when we take in these messages, we start doubting our own abilities, strengths, value, and rights. We may worry too much about what other people will think—especially if we try things that are new to us and our families.

**There are realities**

Indeed, there are realities about aging, but the stories that follow should demonstrate how you can set your own goals and empower yourself to set forth on your next hike. Don't let others tell you what you can achieve or discourage you by making ageist remarks. Negative comments such as "You're too old for that" or "Are you still doing that?" can be demoralizing. Look for friends, family members, and community members who 'get it' and will support you. Avoid those who make self-serving comments. Above all, allow your own confidence, dignity, and feeling of self-worth to propel you toward your goals!

Of course, with age comes decline—but despite accrual projections, not everyone should be lumped into 'declining' at the same rate as they pass through various age categories. When I was in my 50s, I went to my doctor (who was then in her 40s) about some ache or pain, and her response was, "My mother told me that at her age [presumably in her 60s or older], something always hurts." I changed doctors immediately; I wanted my symptoms to be evaluated, not to receive a dismissive, ageist remark.

Healthcare providers and insurance companies all too often make arbitrary decisions about treatments. Perhaps you have heard, "Oh, that happens to everyone by 'X' age." Or maybe you've noticed that your medical plan, rather than considering your overall health and personal fitness, makes judgments about your need for various annual screening tests based *strictly* on your age. I urge you to challenge and question this mentality when appropriate.

Some people see the empty nest or retirement stages as a time when they are ready to physically slow down. They want to take it easy—so watching TV or playing on the computer may take precedence over more demanding activity. But others prefer to keep physically challenging themselves—and in so doing, may well be adding three to 15 years to their lives over their inactive contemporaries.

### Hike because it's fun!

Exercise is good for us—*very* good! In fact, increasing physical activity during midlife has been found to be "associated with 32% to 35% lower risk for mortality."*

The American Cancer Society recommends that adults get at least 150 minutes of moderate-intensity or 75 minutes of vigorous activity each week (or a combination of these). You can do this by walking during your lunch break or after dinner for 30 minutes, five days a week. If you're not currently active, you can check with your healthcare provider to plan reasonable starting goals.

However, I also hope that you will adopt or continue the hiking lifestyle because it can be fun and rewarding in other ways—as a way to make friends, experience the wonders of nature, and help discover your inner and outer strength.

In this book, I hope you will find the support and inspiration you need to start or continue your healthy hiking lifestyle.

*Saint-Maurice PF, Coughlan D, Kelly SP, et al. Association of Leisure-Time Physical Activity Across the Adult Life Course With All-Cause and Cause-Specific Mortality. *JAMA Netw Open*. 2019;2(3):e190355. Published 2019 Mar 1. doi:10.1001/jamanetworkopen.2019.0355.

# The Women Adventurers

"Women make awesome backpackers because we're well-equipped biologically and physically: We're built for endurance, have high pain tolerance, store fat better than men, are stronger in the hips (which is great for carrying packs), and are more in tune with our bodies so we know when to rest. And, women excel at creating community on the trail, at supporting each other." — Elizabeth Vasquez, REI Outdoor School instructor, rei.com/learn/expert-advice/backpacking-women.

# Inga Aksamit

**Susan:** Inga is an accomplished hiker, backpacker, writer, skier, and kayaker/paddler (she once did a paddling trip of 500 miles on the Yukon River). When the trim 62-year-old is not on a major long-distance trail, she's enjoying challenging shorter ones near her home in Sonoma County, California. Not content to keep all of this rewarding activity to herself, she regularly volunteers to lead hikes in the region's state parks.

I first met Inga at a meeting of Bay Area Travel Writers (BATW). I was immediately drawn to the animated woman who shared my interests in the outdoors and hiking. Most of the members I had met before that time were writing for magazines and other media about travel destinations that interested me, but involved staying in comfortable hotels and eating at local restaurants. While we enjoyed that kind of travel, both Inga and I also liked to challenge ourselves by roughing it in the mountains.

**Inga Aksamit:** I've always loved the outdoors. When I was younger, I was more involved with running, mountain biking, and rock climbing. I started hiking more regularly when I was forty-five. My husband Steve and I have hiked mostly in California, but we've also enjoyed our big hikes in the Coast Mountains of Alaska and British Columbia, the Cordillera Blanca in Peru, Tour of Mont Blanc, and Alta Via 1 in Italy.

## Proudest moments

However, I am proudest of doing the John Muir Trail, the 211-mile hike through the Sierra Mountain Range of California ending with the climb of Mt. Whitney, which I did when I was 56.

It was my first long backpacking trip, and I proved to myself that I could do it and more. I think backpacking is 50-percent physical and 50-percent mental. You need a certain level of fitness to enjoy the steep passes in the Sierra, but it's not just physical. You need to have some skills, experience, and a can-do attitude. I learned so much on my first long hike about how much more I can do than I ever thought possible, and part of the learning involved is taking things one step and one day at a time, and figuring out how to handle each challenge as it came.

**New worlds open**

And it led to my first book, *Highs and Lows on the John Muir Trail*, which was completely unexpected and not on the radar at all when I started. That led to two more books, the *Hungry Spork* series, which focuses on meal preparation for long-distance backpacking and a whole lot of recipe testing.

Now hiking has become a way of life for me. We live in a rural area close to three state parks, so it's my daily exercise. I do it to stay in shape, but it's also important to my mental health to get outside and be in nature. Hiking in more remote areas is rewarding because of the fitness that I develop and the opportunity to be in nature where I can spend time appreciating the beauty of natural settings. I've been able to accomplish more than I ever thought possible, and hiking reinforced the ability to overcome adversity by taking a hike or life one step at a time.

**Sharing with the community**

I'm very involved as a volunteer for Sugarloaf Ridge State Park and the Sierra Club and am passionate about teaching and encouraging others to get outside and overcome barriers. I helped with the initial planning and lead hikes for Sugarloaf's 'Hiking for Fitness' program, an eight-week progressive hike series where we do a slightly harder hike each week. We weren't expecting people to repeat the series, but it has become a bit of a social group, and some do it every time we offer it. I also teach beginner backpacking classes and lead backpacking trips for the Sierra Club, SF Chapter.

## Thoughts on solo hiking

I do day hikes on my own unless I'm guiding and generally prefer it as it's my time to decompress. As far as overnights—I've done it and appreciate the extra confidence and competence it takes, but I know that I am a sociable person who likes having company in the evenings.

There's no reason to be critical of going solo; I support it 100-percent. I'm a big believer in 'Hike your own hike,' and not everyone is fortunate enough to have friends who like to hike. And some are introverts and may prefer being on their own. I don't mind backpacking alone during the day but prefer to have dinner and camp with others.

## The challenges

When my head and/or body is begging me to stop, I generally do need to stop at least for a short period of time, anywhere from 15 to 60 minutes, and a sagging attitude often has to do with a need for food and water. For one thing, no matter how blasted I've been, I've noticed that after we set up camp and I've rested and had some food and water, all of a sudden I'd pop up and start scrambling all over the place exploring where we were. That taught me that there were some strategies I could take to recover from the doldrums.

In addition to learning what works for Steve and me with food and hydration, I've had to learn about gear. Currently, my favorite piece of gear is my Gossamer Gear Mariposa Pack because it's so comfortable that I barely feel like it's there.

## Overcoming fears

However, I've also needed to learn how to manage fears, some realistic (exposure, heights, river crossings) and some unrealistic (a general fear that I couldn't do anything like a long hike). Before doing the John Muir Trail, I read accounts of the four or five most challenging passes. Ticking them off, one at a time, taught me that most of the perceived dangers could be managed.

Perhaps the scariest time was descending from Mt. Whitney. We were camped at Trail Camp (located at 12,000-ft. elevation and six miles from the endpoint of the JMT) and were woken in the middle of the night by thunder. It was so beautiful and unique to look down on the thundercloud and see lightning discharging all over the place below us, like looking at a movie from behind the projection screen, and so scary as we understood and then experienced the thundercloud move up the mountain, envelop us, and continue to the summit.

After the initial terror, I became calm as I realized that we would either survive or not, but we had no control. It was just luck that lightning didn't strike us, and we lived to hike another day.

All of this has taken a period of years to learn what worked for me.

## Changes ahead

At this point, Steve and I are feeling stronger than ever but recognize that the day is coming when we'll need to make adjustments, likely in the daily mileage and overall length of trips. This puts pressure on us to do as many adventurous things as we can, while we can. I'm 62 and Steve is 71, so we probably have 10 years or less to do the most adventurous activities, but hopefully, we'll still be able to get out there for more gentle trips after that.

## Encouragement and advice for other women

To other women who are uncertain about their ability to hike long-distance trails, just start doing it if you can, find someone to do it with you if you can't or won't do it solo, or join a group if that's more appealing. Educate yourself by attending backpacking, navigation, and wilderness first-aid classes as information is empowering. Some people even become hike or backpack leaders so they can be with others.

Women excel at endurance activities and long-distance hiking is such a good endurance activity that blends fitness with nature. The mental and physical health benefits are immeasurable. If you're not fit now, you can get stronger by simply hiking more, especially on hills. If you don't have the skills to be confident operating a stove or setting up a tent, you can learn in a class or on a guided backpacking trip.

## Not all advice is good

The worst advice I've heard is to not do it because it's danger-ous out there. It's not. I hear bad advice all the time, including people telling others that you don't need to acclimate for high elevation, that you don't need a map in the Sierra, or that you don't need to train to do a long hike. All of this can be true for some but not all.

## In the future

I've been enjoying long hikes in other countries because there are the added elements of cultural exchange and trying new foods. At some point, we hope to hike Japan's Nakasendo Trail as well as trails in Patagonia and the Himalaya.

**Susan:** Inga lives in Sonoma County, California, with her hus-band Steve Muller, their cat, and chickens. Her books, *The Hungry Spork Trail Recipes: Quick Gourmet Meals for the Backcountry* (2019); *The Hungry Spork: A Long Distance Hiker's Guide to Meal Planning* (2017), and *Highs and Lows on the John Muir Trail* are available in print and eBook.

Her site, ingasadventures.com, is a rich depository of back-packing tips, trip reports, gear reviews, and other resources. On social media, she is administrator for the John Muir Trail and Healthy Gourmet Backpacking Food and Altitude Acclimati-zation Facebook groups.

Though Inga is generally busy with hiking, volunteering, writing, and cooking up healthful and tasty foods, she took a bit of time to share one of her trail recipes here. It can be enjoyed during either day hikes or longer treks.

## Vietnamese Cabbage Salad and Peanut Dressing
~ Inga Aksamit

A salad can be a welcome change of pace, especially if it has some crunch from peanuts and fresh cabbage. Fresh cabbage keeps pretty well for a couple of days, but for longer trips, use the dried cabbage. I couldn't eat a full serving for lunch at Lassen

Volcanic National Park, so I saved it and enjoyed the leftovers in a tortilla for dinner. It made a delicious filling for the tortilla.

### The salad ingredients
- ¼ cup dehydrated shredded cabbage (or fresh cabbage on a short trip)
- ⅛ cup chopped peanuts
- ¼ cup dehydrated shredded carrots
- 1 teaspoon minced dried onion
- 1 teaspoon dried cilantro or mint
- 2 tablespoons peanut dressing (recipe follows)

### Peanut Dressing
- ¼ cup (4 tablespoons) peanut butter, creamy or crunchy
- 1 teaspoon rice vinegar
- ¼ teaspoon fish sauce
- ⅛ teaspoon ginger
- Pinch of cayenne (optional)
- Pepper to taste

### Add on the trail [or at home for a day hike]
- 1 tablespoon olive oil
- A few drops sesame oil (optional)

### At home:
- Combine the dry salad ingredients into a bag.
- Combine the Peanut Dressing ingredients into a small, leak-proof bottle.

### On the trail:
- Add ⅛ - ¼ cup cold water and a few drops of oil, enough to cover the dry ingredients if dehydrated.
- Stir well to moisten throughout.
- Rehydrate for 10-20 minutes until softened. Water may be added several hours earlier (e.g. add water at breakfast to be ready by lunch).
- Add dressing to taste.
- 1 serving. Calories 537; Carbohydrate 24 g; Protein 30 g; Fat 40 g; Sodium 319 mg

### Variations
- This can be a vegetarian/vegan dish if you omit the

fish sauce or substitute vegetarian or vegan fish sauce (search online for recipes or purchase). Add bean curd stick pieces, freeze-dried tofu (known as koyadofu in Japanese), dehydrated tofu, or dehydrated tempeh for extra protein.

- Add ¼ - ½ cup freeze-dried chicken to create a hearty meal.
- On a short trip, use fresh shredded cabbage, carrots, and herbs instead of dehydrated. Cabbage can last a couple of days in mild temperatures on the trail.
- Substitute powdered for jarred peanut butter.

**Inga Akasamit — Echo Lake, Desolation Wilderness**

# Barbara Anderson

**Susan:** I met Barbara in 2014 at a Camino gathering in Berkeley. She was there to meet or reconnect with others who were interested in hiking or who have hiked the ancient pilgrimage trails of Europe. I was drawn to her because she had just published an attractive book, *Letters from the Way*, which takes readers on her 600-mile solo walk on the GR 653 (Grande Randonnée—a marked hiking trail) from Arles, France to Puente la Reina, Spain. While on her walk, she wrote letters to family and friends about the world around her, and as these letters got in the hands of more people, the new number of readers grew. Engaging color photos accompanied the story of her journey—and reminded me how much I loved walking this route myself.

Since that time, Barbara has taken several other impressive hikes—including the South West Coast Path, England's longest waymarked long-distance footpath—630 miles from Minehead in Somerset, along the coasts of Devon and Cornwall, through Poole Harbour in Dorset, to Bournemouth.

**Barbara Anderson:** As a child, I was a Girl Scout from grade school through high school, and I was given "camperships" to attend summer camps. Working at Girl Scout camps was part of the way I worked my way through college. I loved everything about being outdoors, and I will forever be grateful to scouting for introducing and encouraging me to be a part of nature.

During my working career, I traveled the world and hated to drive, so much of my walking was in towns as I walked from hotels to my workplaces. I hate to say it, but in America, there are many towns where walking is almost impossible.

I enjoy hiking on the San Francisco peninsula on an every-day basis; hiking near where I live has been a great luxury. From home, it is a very short drive to beautiful county and state parks with magnificent trails, so I enjoy a great deal of day hiking. Everyone knows about Muir Woods, but our redwood forests, coastal hikes, wildflower hikes, and Santa Cruz Mountains make the peninsula a gem for fabulous hikes. When I retired in 2012, I finally had the time to undertake long-distance hikes.

For continuous hiking, I love France and Britain. France has a myriad of Grande Randonnées (GRs) with gites (shared sleeping accommodations), beautiful villages, and very good food. Britain has two miles of footpaths for every one square mile, so there are endless wonderful hikes on their National Trails. Some are leisurely and filled with interesting sites like Hadrian's Wall, the West Highland Way, and the Cotswold Way. Others like the Southwest Coast Path, the Pembrokeshire Trail, and the Coast to Coast are challenging but gorgeous. One big difference is that Britain has the 'Right to Roam'—that means one can roam through cow and sheep pastures filled with, well, cows and sheep. In England, one shares the pasture with animals, but in France, the cows are on the other side of barbed wire.

**Why I hike**

Honestly, I hike for my sanity. It not only keeps me physi-cally healthy, it keeps me mentally healthy. I write short stories and plays, and when I walk, I create. In my book, *Letters from the Way*, I wrote: "I am a walker, and a walker walks. A walker walks when they are happy, when they are sad, when they are bored, when they are busy. A walker walks because there is noth-ing that offers more pleasure, sweeps away the cobwebs, frees the soul, grounds the body, or relaxes the mind. A walker walks to resolve problems, to forget problems, to understand problems. A walker walks for no reason and for every reason."

I don't walk to prove anything. I rarely keep track of how far I walk unless I need to know to be sure I am correctly following trails. I never know nor care about how fast I walk, though oth-ers complain that I walk fast. Walking is not my best time for social interaction as I have few friends with whom I truly enjoy walking, but those I treasure. The reason I find it difficult to walk with most people is that I like to be present when I walk. I am not walking and talking about other places and other people. A friend who will be present in the moment with you is the greatest gift I can imagine.

I am renewed mentally and physically after every walk, long or short. I am at one with my surroundings whether I am on a city walk or visiting a foreign city or in the mountains, a forest, or the desert. It is that overwhelming sense of being connected to the earth and to others. That sounds strange coming from someone who loves walking solo, I know, but when walking I feel as though problems, disagreements, and fears slough off like dust, and a sense of belonging overwhelms.

I have realized that though we talk about hikers and backpackers, some of us are really just walkers. Yes, sometimes it's a 600-mile walk or a 30-mile day, but in many ways, I can enjoy 15 miles on a city or village walk such as in Portugal or a forest walk in the Santa Cruz Mountains as much.

### Accomplishments to be proud of

This is a difficult one for me to answer. I suppose because it became a book, I could say that walking the GR65 and GR653 across France (each 600 miles) were my biggest accomplishments. From my book: "The walk was not to prove anything, to lose weight, or to get in shape. The walk was not a lifelong dream or an entry on a bucket list. In fact, I don't believe in bucket lists, at least not ones that are somebody else's list of things you should do before you die. Those lists are about the end, not about the doing. They're about ticking off where you got to, not about the getting there. No, the walk was definitely not a checkmark on a bucket list."

But every walk has its own reasons for being special. A short walk where I solve a problem can be remembered fondly. The Yosemite High Sierra Camp walk was an accomplishment of exciting beauty, and a challenge to complete the day's walk by 2 p.m. when the daily thunderstorms began.

Certainly, the South West Coast Path in Great Britain was something I am proud of. It's a great hike. It's the farthest south, farthest west, and has more ups and downs than one can imagine. It's 630 miles and equal to scaling the world's tallest mountain four times—115,000 feet of ascent and descent.

## On solo hiking

People are not so much critical as worried [about solo hiking]. I did fall once and knocked myself out cold. Fortunately, I was rescued by a cow-herder. I carry all sorts of first aid and a fully charged phone, etc., but I never considered being knocked out. Now I keep a few friends informed about my daily walks and check in at the end of the day. I can do that as I am not walking the Appalachian Trail or the Pacific Crest. To be honest, if I walked those I would prefer to walk them with another person or a small group.

I think American women are needlessly afraid of gites and hostels and being alone. They think people are going to accost them. Generally, except for city hostels, everyone hikes in. Everyone is tired. Most everyone has an interesting story to tell. Meeting people you share sleeping accommodations with can be the highlight of the trip.

I am often asked what I think about spending so many days solo. Again from my book: "A friend asked, 'What on earth do you think about?' Well, if I were Benjamin Franklin, Ludwig von Beethoven, Gustav Mahler, Erik Satie, Pytor Tchaikovsky, Søren Kierkegaard, Immanuel Kant, Ludwig Wittgenstein, or any of the other great walkers, I might have truly great thoughts. I'm not them, so here is what I think about.

"Some days I think about blue skies, billowing clouds, rainbows, bird songs, soft breezes, colorful flowers, undulating hills, shifting shadows, dappled leaf patterns, Technicolor butterflies, cowbells, meandering sheep, and cuckoo songs. Some days I am completely content.

"Some days I think my pack is too heavy, my foot hurts, I am thirsty, tired, too hot, too cold. I wonder how far I have walked and if this trail can continue uphill forever. Can I make it to the next town before I need the toilet? Some days I think this will never end.

"Some days I think how to solve a problem, what a character should say, what I should do. I write scripts and stories, create lists, make decisions. Some days everything becomes clear.

"Some days I think what I should have said, what I could have done. I would have if only, but now it's too late. He died before I could say goodbye. Did I do enough? I never said, I would have said, I should have said. I should have been there. Some days I cry.

Some days I think nothing, nothing at all.

Some days I think all of these things and more."

What I do believe is that if I am too bored to be alone with myself then why would anyone else want to walk with me?

## What it takes

To be a successful long-distance hiker is not about fitness or athleticism. It is the ability to be completely present and to appreciate what one is experiencing. I hiked with a woman who kept her nose buried in her phone taking photos, and whenever she got a signal, texted those photos to friends. Soon she was bored and tired.

We were walking the Southwest Coast Trail in England and for her, it was just too much sameness, but had she opened her eyes and looked around, she would have seen the pewter grey of the Bristol Channel give way to the startling blue of the Atlantic. She would have heard the rippling of the tides over rocks give way to crashing waves. She would have seen fields of flowers and butterflies and colorful moths changing every day.

But she wasn't there. Not really. She was too interested in what others thought of her hike, and a hike is not something where every moment can be posted. If what one wants is to impress others with minute-by-minute excitement then long-distance hiking is not the right activity.

I am fairly crazed on this point. I don't believe in using earbuds to listen to podcasts. I take days off from taking any photos.

I am a writer, but I do not write a daily or even weekly blog. I turn off my phone to save its battery in case I need it but also because I don't want to be taken away from where I am.

I also think people may walk for the wrong reason. When I was out speaking about my book, I found the questions to be very interesting. Men asked, "How far did you walk each day? How fast did you walk?" Women asked, "Did you lose weight?" (Sigh.)

## Self-care

I sing—especially when I am very tired. I sing my way up hills and over the last few miles. I sing when I reach the crest and before I begin going down. Now, I am not saying that everyone else appreciates my enthusiasm for singing, and perhaps this contributes to my hiking alone so often. Hmm...

One time in Yosemite I walked with two women from the SF Opera Chorus who sang all through our hike. As I passed other hikers who couldn't believe I was being trailed by opera singers, I told them that others merely bring a radio but I bring my own backup singers.

## Challenges

I have the worst sense of direction in the universe. I am often 'lost.' I probably liked the Southwest Coast Path and the Pembrokeshire Trail so much because I just needed to keep the water on my right. Have I overcome my bad sense of direction? No, I have accepted it as part of the challenge. I now consider being lost as an opportunity for new adventures and to meet new people...

I vividly recall falling and ending up unconscious and being stranded in France with a concussion bad enough that I couldn't continue hiking and I couldn't fly or take a boat home. So, one thing I learned, of course, was to let people know where I was supposed to be.

More importantly, it was being stranded for months in France that was a challenge. The concussion left me confused and finding it difficult to make decisions. I have been poor (financially), but I have never been unable to form a plan, decide what to do next. I grew to have great empathy for others who mentally or financially just cannot think of what to do next. I now know what it feels like.

## Advice?

My advice for women who want to start hiking or backpacking regularly, or who are nervous about hiking on a new and more challenging trail, is to *walk*. Not all hikes have to be on trails. Simply walk out the door to get where you need to go. Walk to the store. Walk to meet friends. Walk to yoga class. Walk around the block. Once you start walking, you will keep walking.

If you don't enjoy simple walks, it's possible you won't enjoy long-distance trails. And find what works for you. Some amazing women backpack alone over long-distance trails. I am not one of them. I sleep in gites and hostels and inns. I wouldn't enjoy sleeping alone in a tent on a trail. I have talked to other women who wouldn't enjoy sleeping in a bunk bed in a room full of strangers. We are all different.

When I first started sleeping in gites, I was 60. Gites are coed, so I tried desperately to change clothes inside of my sleep sack. It is almost impossible to put on a bra inside a sleep sack. One day, a French woman sat down on my cot and spoke with me. She asked how old I was. I said 60. She said, "Look you're 60 years old; just sit up and change your clothes. If anyone wants to stare at you, be proud."

## Gear

This is just me, and no, it's not risky except to one's self-esteem. I was advised not to carry cosmetic creams, etc., to avoid the weight. I lasted about four days before I found a shop and purchased some. A few ounces of sunscreen, moisturizer, and a good soap I find to be a necessity. But like I said before, everyone is different

As far as what works for me, I have an exceptionally wide (and damaged) foot. My foot is narrow at the heel and wide in the toe, so men's boots do not work for me because they are cut more as a rectangle, wide at the heel and the toe. I find Solomon hiking boots work for me because they fit my foot. The important thing is that boots are cut in so many different ways, so trying them on and *wearing* them before one takes off on any long-distance hike is essential. One should never accept blisters as a part of hiking.

I like Icebreaker [Merino wool] socks cut for a right foot and a left foot even though I have to put on my glasses to read the L and the R to be sure I get them on the correct feet. Other people swear by liner socks and over socks. Socks, like shoes, should be chosen for the individual and worn before embarking on a long hike. I went on a multi-week hike with a woman who had never tried out her socks and only realized that she was allergic to them once we had set out. She hiked for the next ten days with a rash on her feet.

Finally, I love Arc'teryx rock-climbing jackets and pants. I only rock-climbed once, and it terrified me, but I find those clothes to be perfect for long journeys. The pants are made with fabric that is impossible to tear; the knees are made with darts so there is no sagging, and they are breathable yet waterproof, and hand- or machine-washable. The jacket is cut in at the waist, and like the pants, there is no sagging or bagging or excess fabric. It looks good out and about as well as while hiking. Admittedly, I must wait for sales to purchase Arc'teryx, but I am a patient woman.

**Final thoughts**

Since I started long-distance hiking late in life, I have not faced adjustments due to age. I have been thinking a lot lately about climate change, though. I hiked through a terrible drought in England, and a year later those same trails and villages were washed away in fierce storms. As the weather becomes more severe, I am more aware that there needs to be a backup plan if I choose a time for hiking that is going to be dangerous.

I haven't decided what kind of trip I want to do next. I may choose more trips where I stay in one place and do day hikes as I did recently while staying in a hostel in Madeira. I don't mind hiking in the rain, not at all, but I won't hike when it is dangerous. I know I want to return to hike sections of the Southwest Coast Path. I have hiking friends in Europe and Britain I want to visit and hike with. I don't usually go with hiking groups, but there are countries where a woman hiking alone is not a good idea, so I may go on a hiking tour.

This year, I have other issues to deal with and of course the pandemic makes a long distance hike impossible so I might be enjoying the splendors of the U.S. West Coast. I don't normally set mileage goals, but I am making a 2020 resolution to hike 1500 miles this year, so I will keep a daily track to meet that goal.

It might not be exotic as past hiking, but as long as I am putting one foot in front of the other and experiencing the beauty of my surroundings, I'm happy, whether it is close to home or exotic. I have a great deal to look forward to.

After considering it, I realized what a difference there was between hikers and walkers. I am definitely a walker. Even when I was working as a consultant, I always tried to get hotels where I could walk to the office. When I lived in Italy, I walked everywhere and drew pictures everywhere, and eventually exhibited an art show of my drawings.

If I have a choice between an escalator, elevator, or stairwell, I always take the stairs. I walk through towns as often as I walk through forests. I think that does make me more of a walker than a hiker.

### And as COVID-19 sent us reeling

[May 10, Santa Cruz, California]: I am surviving quite well. My life is Zoom meetings, gardening, walking, daily drawing, and writing. Also, given the circumstances and no possibility to do a long-distance walk, I am growing not only flowers and roses but lettuce, herbs, and tomatoes. I don't expect to make much of a change to this lifestyle for another six months. So, I am committed to the garden. The saddest part of this is that I no longer employ my gardener because I simply have no need for one.

Every morning begins with going out into the garden with my coffee and wearing pajamas with the intention of simply relaxing and smelling the roses, so to speak, only to find myself three hours later still pruning, weeding, and digging, and in need of throwing that pair of PJs into the wash.

I am walking but rarely on trails. I am thrilled that so many people have discovered trails, but it makes social distancing very difficult. Of course, as for exercise, those of us in the Bay Area usually face walking challenges when we walk out the doors of our homes as we must either walk uphill or down.

I often virtually 'walk' with a friend who lives in Detroit. We chat by phone and generally just have a grand old time while we are both exploring our neighborhoods. And of course, the clear unpolluted skies have been amazing. The quiet, and the clarity of vision, has been incredible. I will miss it if we decide to go back to what it was.

Writing was at first a challenge because my plays are usually about social issues of today and the near future. But I have no idea what the near future will bring. I take up writing challenges and have begun writing specifically for Zoom.

For example, I wrote several three-page duologues [plays with speaking roles for only two actors] about life during the pandemic, which were 'produced' in London. The prompt arrives Friday morning and the play is turned in by Friday night, and the Londoners create the play on Zoom. I find that I cannot go back to writing about the reality that I knew before this began.

A huge benefit of Zoom is my playwriting group from London, which is actually folks from Ireland, Denmark, Spain, England, New York, Washington, and me here in the SF Bay Area. Another playwright group from the peninsula can meet easily since no one need face Bay Area traffic.

My Zoom folk-singing group is like bad karaoke because we cannot sing together. I once snuck out to meet a couple of friends to sing harmonies—masked and socially distanced in an open-air amphitheater. It makes me happier than I can express.

But, then we read how very dangerous singing is. Who would have guessed that group singing, church and bars, would be the trifecta of pandemic danger.

I have been drinking Zoom cocktails with friends from SF and also friends from NYC. This is interesting because I doubt there would ever be another time when these folks were all home on the same evening. (After all, it's NY City!) So, we have gotten to do something that won't exist after this is over.

**Susan:** Barbara Anderson is the author of *Letters from the Way*. From Amazon: "The letters are her musings about fellow pilgrims, vultures and butterflies, the endless rain, lessons to learn, and spiritual questions to answer. Her often humorous and always honest reflections make a good resource for anyone wondering what it would be like to set out on their own very long journey."

Moreover, Barbara's talents extend beyond hiking, art and writing. In January 2020, her plays *The Piazza* and *An Empowered Woman* were produced in New York City. Several of her plays have been produced at the Pear Theatre in Mountain View, California, including *The Wedding* and a monologue *Billie*, recently produced on Zoom by that theater.

Barbara Anderson — Bournemouth 600-mile SW Trail

# Beebe 'Jack from Ireland' Bahrami

**Susan:** Though I have not met Beebe, I've read her newest book, *Moon Camino de Santiago—Sacred Sites, Historic Villages, Local Food and Wine*, which is an excellent guide to the Camino Francés. Beebe's background as a professional writer and anthropologist is reflected in her work. Not only does the book contain practical information and fine maps, but it also delves into the rich culture and history of the route. The generous descriptions include "The best detours, festivals, and villages along the way."

**Beebe Bahrami:** I've had many trail names, most recently, "Jack from Ireland"—thanks to being discovered by a fellow pilgrim as a travel writer. The original "Jack from Ireland" was one of the four main characters—the travel writer character—in the Martin Sheen movie, *The Way*. Home is in southern New Jersey for most of the year, but I also am often in Boulder, Colorado, where I am from, and also annually in southwestern France and northern Spain.

I am a Colorado native, born and raised in the Rocky Mountains, and hiking was a normal thing and thankfully quite accessible from the beginning. My parents loved to make big picnic expeditions into the mountains with friends, and these would involve a good hike and then a good feast, usually alongside a river or glacial lake. I really began taking hiking seriously, though, in college, when I would go for restorative and head-clearing hikes with a friend between classes or on the weekends. (I attended the University of Colorado in Boulder, which made heading to the trail easy.)

Beyond Colorado and hikes in other parts of the USA, such as Northern California, Lake Michigan, and the Pine Barrens and Jersey Shore of New Jersey, my main hiking destinations, and where I work and do extensive anthropological research and writing, is in Europe, especially France, Spain, and Portugal.

### The hiking lifestyle

Hiking is my life. I am a writer and anthropologist by profession, and walking and hiking are how I gather information about and experience a place, culture, and people. I learned long ago when doing ethnographic fieldwork in Spain, Morocco, France, and Portugal that to slow down, walk, and talk to people was the best way to learn about the realities of each culture. It is as important to my professional toolkit as are copious field notes and learning the languages, histories, and prehistories of the places I visit and live in.

I like going and soaking up life at the pace of footfalls. It slows me down so that I notice things—small details that often carry big secrets. I witness the earth's beauty more fully and stop taking it for granted. I fall in love with our earth all over again, something our modern world and all our news, devices, and media detract from so often.

### Solo hiking

I especially fell in love with southwestern France and northern Spain because these were the regions where I hiked solo as a woman. I had read rich ethnographic literature about the cultures of these areas and discovered that the women there have a long history (and prehistory) of greater self-determination than in other parts of Europe. As I hiked, I discovered this legacy was still deeply woven into the culture. It was absolutely emancipating to be able to hike as a woman alone and find cultures that supported and protected that. This was very different from my experience of hiking in the USA, which I have never done alone.

### The Camino hikes

Walking the Camino (especially the Camino Francés and

Camino del Norte) really taught me about my capabilities and self-sufficiency, and emboldened me to set off on lesser-known tributary trails or smaller routes, be they for pilgrimages or simply hiking trails. I was in my mid-forties when I really began doing this—buying good topographical maps, studying local terrains, and setting off, talking to locals as I went, and forging more and more solo hikes in France and Spain.

The most memorable of the Camino hikes was when I made my home base in the Dordogne department in France and set off each day with maps, pack, water, and a sense of adventure to explore that inordinately ancient landscape with its limestone caves and river valleys that had been inhabited by humans for more than 400,000 years. To this day, the region is still protecting its natural landscapes, and so I found myself walking into dense native oak forests and seeing not a human all day but encountering all forms of wildlife.

Had I been with even one other person, those encounters would have been more timid or not at all. It was exhilarating to feel strong enough to go into such territory on my own, often far from settlements, and even those were accessible only by the power of my own legs and feet. I navigated with a compass and maps, read the land, learned about the plants, and even gathered edible foods (nuts, berries, herbs, and cautiously, mushrooms, which I took back with me to have a local pharmacy identify as edible and not poisonous!).

I think solo hiking is incredibly self-empowering, spiritual, and uplifting, but it also requires more preparation, especially knowledge about the place through which you are hiking. The biggest mistake solo hikers make is to hike into an area without learning about the culture and language in addition to the trails and terrain.

## I think Yogi Berra nails it

His comment, "Baseball is 90-percent mental. The other half is physical," applies to long-distance hiking too. Long-distance hiking is very physical but so much more overwhelmed by the mental, especially if you begin to listen to others about what you are about to undertake. It is key to separate any adrenalin-laced bravado coming from others from truly good information about the trek!

But the truly mental part is coupled with the physical; both hit you when you least expect it and make you feel like the mountain you are climbing is impossible to ascend. The mental does this even more than the physical because it begins to make you doubt you can do it or makes you wonder if you can sustain the long trek for the two, three, four, or five weeks or more set out before you.

As physical challenges arise—tight muscles, sore hips, foot issues—is it not often the mind that kicks in darkly about all the scenarios that will keep you from going on? It seems to even overtake the physical challenge and make it more complicated. I think a successful long-distance hiker trains well on both fronts, the physical and the mental, and keeps the training up once on the trail.

For the physical, this means taking good care of one's body and stopping to rest when tired, airing out your feet, re-lacing the shoes, and at the end of the day, stretching to nourish muscles and joints that have worked so hard. For the mental, it is preparing well, studying as much as you can about the trail, its people, culture, wildlife, terrain, etc., and also learning about these things from others who have hiked the trail.

And, returning to the first point about discerning between useful and factual information from ego-inspired information intending to impress: On the trail, the mental comes into play when one is swinging between exhilaration and doubt about making it. Those are times to stop and take a break, too, and refresh the mind as much as the body. Also, if one really realizes that all the best-laid plans will be altered once on the trail and that it is important to be flexible to let the best plan emerge, it not only helps a great deal but also allows for the unexpected (and often greater) gifts that come into play.

**When tired and I feel I can't go on...**
I have a few things that work, depending on the extent of

my circumstances and mood. Most involve visualizing the reward at the end: a hot shower, dry clothes, a good meal, and best, a frothy cold beer. Sometimes I just let myself stop (if it is not raining) and sit and contemplate the surroundings while resting, airing my feet, and re-centering my thoughts with a grounding mindfulness meditation (just focusing on my breathing). I also remind myself of the gifts, of why I wanted to do the trek in the first place, the sense of learning, being out in the wild world, having a potentially life-changing adventure, meeting interesting people, meeting myself in ways I'd never met before, feeling or discovering my strengths, and savoring the immense beauty that I get to see and experience by persisting.

## Challenges big and small

Beyond the mental aspects noted above, and beyond the basic physical aspects of training well and taking care of my body, a couple times I've gotten sick on the trail—food poisoning in both cases. I had to persist through it, either to get to help (a pharmacy) or to reach a place where I could rest and mend before continuing the trek. And once, my hamstrings got so tight after a brutal mountain descent in an ice storm that I could not walk and simply folded on the trail. As I lay there wondering what to do, many miles away from any settlement and in a spot with no cell-phone reception, two fellow trekkers I had not seen for two days arrived over the summit and came to me, immediately recognizing that I needed help. They were the only two people I saw that morning until they got me to the nearest village. As luck turned out, they were both emergency-room doctors from Buenos Aires and had a full medical kit with them in addition to their combined knowledge.

I could call that luck or I could call that trail magic. Either way, aid has come to help me out of my binds each time, always in the form of many kind and generous people with amazing timing!

## An exceptional encounter

I've had a handful of times when I encountered people I did not have a good feeling about or incurred an injury that required getting help and rethinking the day's plan, but luckily, I have had many, many more exceptional encounters, but the most stunning, unexpected, at first frightening, and then quickly sublime experience that rises above all these was an encounter with a wolf. I was walking on a tiny tributary footpath of the Camino del Norte, just after Luarca, and felt myself being watched. I turned to see a full-grown wolf twenty meters behind me. We stood that way for seconds, and I didn't know what to do except that I felt I was safe.

Soon, I felt a warm, amazing sense of communion, and then a feeling of being fully woven into the fabric of the universe—full connectedness between me, the wolf, and all that is—a state I think is actually our true state. And then, three dogs in the nearby village took up the scent and began to bark violently, and the wolf fled and was gone. I feel blessed to have had such an unexpected experience. It could not have happened were I not out hiking on a remote tributary trail by myself.

**Hikes changing over time**

The biggest change for me involves my ego. As a younger person, I was so full of physical bravado, knowing that if I pushed myself, I'd recover quickly. Now, at 57, I know better—I cannot forego stretching, resting, taking care of my feet, pruning my pack size, and letting others brag about how fast and far they walk each day without needing to participate. I just quietly go at my own jolly pace.

I find that I see more anyhow, and experience a more powerful pilgrimage, when I explore, experience, and allow the trek to positively transform me, not just cover distance and get somewhere before others.

**Advice women can use**

My advice is for women to do it and know they can do it spectacularly, especially if they learn everything they can, train every day even at home on neighborhood paths, network with other women trekkers, and learn about the language, culture, geography, history, and prehistory of the place they plan to trek through. I encourage them to do this because of how empowering it is and how it translates to other areas of one's life in fostering greater self-confidence and grounding.

I am finding that women less often underestimate their physical abilities these days, especially now that Title IX is a many-decades-long reality that has moved us toward establishing a more even playing field. But I still advise women to find out for themselves what their physical abilities are and to override any cultural or family conditioning that says anything other than the fact that they are strong, resilient, and incredibly capable. They must discover their capabilities and superpowers firsthand by trying things out that interest them and finding out what drives them.

## Not all advice is helpful

The worst advice I've heard concerns gear, especially shoes. Even experienced people have biases that they are unaware of, and shoes are a big area with the range from heavy hiking boots to lightweight trail runners that are hailed or critiqued. I think people need to take in all the information, but most importantly, study the trail and its contours and then try many types of shoes to see which one fits their feet best and will support them best for the terrain they will tackle. Some people need ankle support; others will have problems if they use such support. Some people get blisters like nothing; others seem immune to them (though most are in between). As with anything, learn and gather as much information as you can but then test it on your own with practice hikes in the gear you've selected while still at home. Fine-tune and revise as you go until you find your true answer to these matters.

The other bad advice is specifically on the Camino. A lot of people say a person doesn't need to prepare or even need a book to go. This is true because the trail is so well-marked and the support structures so plentiful, but so often I find that these same people do not bother to learn anything about the Camino—not its history, not its languages or cultures—and so they make many faux pas as they go, taxing the energy and efforts of the kind locals who live on and support the trail. I would love for even the minimalist hiker who does not want a guidebook or trail map to at least read up on the cultures and history and learn some Spanish— even some words in French—to show their respect for the places through which they walk.

### What works for one person may not work for others

I am passionate about my backpack and hiking shoes because I spend so much time testing them and making sure they are absolutely a perfect fit. Beyond these essentials, I love my navy-blue cashmere cardigan sweater, instead of a puffer or a fleece, as a layer over a T-shirt and under a rain jacket because is it light, soft, brings a splash of elegance, and goes to dinner as nicely as it works on the trail. It also doesn't get smelly and needs little washing, especially if I wear it over T-shirts.

### Looking forward to walking...

I want to walk more of the trails of the Camino de Santiago across Europe, which will feed my body, mind, and soul for the rest of my life! I am also excited, now that I have written a guidebook on the most historic route, the Camino Francés across northern Spain, that I get to return to it annually. It is an old friend and one like any other that changes, evolves, matures, grows, and deepens. I love reconnecting with it to see where it is, and by synchronistic extension, where I am. And for my next trip? I am heading back to the Chemin du Puy in south-central France of which I have walked a portion and which I hope to finish walking as soon as feasibly possible.

### And our world changed with COVID-19

[April 2020, East Coast] We are doing our best and so lucky to be in a good place and well. So lucky. My walks have been narrowed to short walks outside when I can—mostly around our neighborhood—and a lot of pacing in my office, which I have measured out. I now know how many hundreds of paces add up to one mile.

Our island is bursting with spring but also some second-home owners who decided to travel down here from New York and Pennsylvania as if it is a normal time. It makes us all cautious about outdoor walks, especially since two weeks ago when our mayor and governor closed beaches and boardwalks.

I am a mere 400 meters from the ocean but have not seen it for over two weeks! I do not dare to surf just yet or even go into the water. It is so odd to be landlocked on an island and see no water while being entirely surrounded by it.

At the same time, boy, the Camino has taught me so much about weathering the unknown and trusting it as well. As such, there is greater grace happening than all this icky stuff. For instance, I am writing like a dervish and working on a new travelogue that traces a medieval mystery on the Camino through three different pilgrimages in France and Spain. In fact, I am having a rollicking time with it and am so grateful to have this to take me away on deep travels.

*The Camino has also taught me that all will work out and in ways that we cannot even begin to imagine right now. Just one step at a time, and focusing on that, will help work the magic!*

**Susan:** On her blog, author Stephanie Elizondo Griest captured this quote from Beebe: "I have striven to make 'home' an interior place and to try not to cling to a physical place as home because it could change. I could instead spend my energy savoring what it is and where I am now." stephanieelizondogriest.com/interview-with-beebe-bahrami.

You can follow Beebe at beebebahrami.weebly.com. Check this book's Contributors' Books section for her excellent publications. Her blogs are Cafe Oc (France blog), cafeoc.blogspot.com and Pilgrim's Way Cafe (Camino blog), pilgrimswaycafe.blogspot.com.

Beebe's podcast with Dave Whitson and Sandy Brown, about writing Camino guidebooks, is episode 46 on Dave's podcast davewhitson.com/index.php/2019/03/24/the-camino-podcast/.

**Beebe Bahrami — near Commarque Castle in the Dordogne department, Southern France**

# Jan 'Pooh Bear' Barlow

**Susan:** Jan has a motto: "An Adventure a Day Keeps the Doctor Away." They are not empty words to her as she has hiked a staggering number of challenging trails.

**Jan Barlow:** I started hiking around five years old and absolutely hated it—it was buggy and hard and I just wanted to go home. Unfortunately, no one knew I was very sick at the time and I just could not physically hike. Fast-forward to when I was feeling better, and you could not pull me away from it. I enjoyed every minute. I loved the challenges, pine tree smells, fresh air, birds singing, and the views.

## Why hiking matters

Hiking plays a major role in my life. When I am not on the trail, I am constantly daydreaming of backpacking, and I am always trying to figure out my next hike. My bucket list of hiking trails is overflowing. My slogan is, "If there is a trail, I will hike it," so I will be happy to hike anywhere.

I love setting goals and working my way through them to get to certain places each day. Sunrise and sunset need no words. I never know ahead of time where I am going to set up my tent for the night; some tent sites are breathtaking. I like getting up early and starting to hike when the sun comes up.

I have met so many wonderful hikers that I am still in touch with. They are long-distance relationships, but it is great to hear about their hikes—Subman, Suds, Bright, Story, Two Hats, Moonwalker, Aussie Bill, and Moonshine...there are too many to list all of them. These are their trail names. I have wonderful memories of them on the trail.

I love to share my amazing pictures and stories with my family and friends; they so enjoy being a part of my hikes as they hike vicariously through me. I would definitely say hiking is a need for me to be able to function in this world—my escape and my form of freedom.

## Trails completed

All 67 of the 4,000-footers in New England. Maine has 14, New Hampshire has 48, Vermont has five. I have hiked them all. [A 4,000-footer is a mountain with an elevation of at least 4,000 feet and a minimum of 200 feet prominence. All criteria are determined by the Appalachian Mountain Club (outdoors.org)].

I have hiked most of the long-distance trails on the East Coast:

- Thru-hiked the Finger Lakes Trail (NY)—950 miles. And in one shot with my dog, Happy.
- Thru-hiked the Long Trail (VT)—273 miles.
- Thru-hiked the Midstate Trail (Midstate Massachusetts to the Wapack Trail, New Hampshire—92 miles (twice). Continued onto the Wapack for 22 more.
- Thru-hiked the Robert Frost Trail (MA)—47 miles.
- Thru-hiked the Allegheny Trail (WV)—330 miles. (This trail ended with a bang as it was the first day of hunting season!)
- Thru-hiked the Benton MacKaye Trail (GA, TN, NC)—300 miles.
- Thru-hiked the Metacomet-Monadnock Trail (M&M Trail)—114 miles. Then connected to the Monadnock Sunapee Greenway Trail in southern New Hampshire (stretching from Mt. Monadnock north to Mt. Sunapee) for an additional 50 miles for 164 miles total.
- Thru-hiked Northville-Placid Trail (NY)—138 miles.
- Appalachian Trail (GA-ME)—2,181 miles

Also, the following long distance trails of the western U.S.

- Thru-hiked Tahoe Rim Trail (CA, NV)—165 miles.

- Thru-hiked the John Muir Trail (CA)—211 miles.
- Pacific Crest Trail (Mexico-Canada through CA, OR, WA)—2,650 miles.
- Continental Divide Trail (Mexico-Canada through NM-MT)—1,400 of the 3,100 miles so far. (Trail distance changes year-to-year with reroutes. In 2019, I had to stop early due to snow.)

## My greatest accomplishment

Regarding my greatest hikes, I would have to say my goal of a Triple Crown. I have only 1,700 miles left to hike on the Continental Divide Trail—that with the Pacific Crest and Appalachian that I have already completed will earn me the Triple Crown. I grew so much on those trails, there is not enough time or paper to write it all down.

My Mum passed away in 2017; I dedicated my Pacific Crest Trail hike to her. I had quite a few meltdowns that year on the hike. She knew I wanted to hike that trail; she made me promise I would complete the trail in 2017. I was my Mum's caregiver for a long time. She had cancer—she knew I would need this time to get my life back in line. So the Pacific Crest Trail is most meaningful to me. Even though she was gone, I felt her there with me. My Mum understood my hiking; she got it, and not everyone did. There are so many other trails that I have hiked, but these are the ones that had a wonderful impact on me.

## Solo hiking

I like to hike solo. I can hike at the pace I choose and stop for views whenever I want to do that. There is no drama. I may hike a day or two with someone, but that is usually it. I did hike with Aussie Bill longer because I loved his Australian accent. I also did hike with my dog Happy—her trail name is Happy Tails. She is 15 (about 80 people-years) and unable to hike anymore, but she also loved it out there.

This is my selfish time—it is time for me—time to heal and move on. If people are critical of my hiking alone, I always point out the positive things about it and why I prefer it.

### Genuine challenges

Once when I was on the Pacific Crest Trail, I ran out of water for quite a long time, and it was well over 100 degrees. I also was missing my Mum—this was just after her passing. I carried her picture with me, and when I had my meltdown, I pulled out her picture then picked myself up, dusted myself off, and started hiking. I remembered my promise to my Mum; that is what kept me going. So, going with a purpose is a major motivator.

On the Continental Divide, it was in the middle of a major fire. I was way too close; it was completely dangerous to stop. I put my big-girl shorts on and continued to hike. I had no choice; if I hadn't, I would have been a burned marshmallow.... I could not turn around because the fire was now behind me and to the side of me, plus the Chinese Wall (a spectacular 1,000-ft. high cliff alongside the trail in Montana) was on the other side. Signs were posted to watch for grizzly bears because there were dead carcasses of horses nearby.

This had to be the scariest time on the trail for me. Plus, I did not have phone service, so I could not even call for help; I was miles and miles away from civilization. I did make it out safely, but I was never sure I would make it out alive.

Another time in New Mexico while on the Continental Divide, I was chased by a mountain lion. It was running at top speed. My heart nearly jumped out of my body, but at the last minute, the lion turned and ran up the mountain. I stood there with my mouth wide open for a minute before I moved.

More than once, I've gotten down to 75 pounds; I just couldn't keep any weight on. I had to stop in towns for a week and eat like crazy; I was so sick of eating. I left town with so much food in my backpack! I had to stop at every town and eat as much as I could. This is my biggest challenge on all of my long hikes. I still have not overcome it.

The other big challenge is that when I get off the trail after my long-distance backpacking hikes, I have to adjust to real life again. It sometimes takes me more than a month to adjust even a little.

## Hiking long-term

The only thing that has changed with getting older is that I hike slower and take in the beautiful views. It's not about the miles; it's about enjoying the views and the trail. But I can still out-hike some of the young hikers. I have been called a "bad-ass hiker." I will never quit hiking, but I am sure I will slow down even more. By slowing down, I will have to carry more food, and I will have a heavier backpack.

Do your research and take it slow—remember, it's not a race. Pack your backpack as light as you can. Hike with an experienced hiker, or join a hiking club to start and learn.

## Women on the trail

It is great to see more women on the trail now. When I started hiking more than 55 years ago, there were not many women. There were no women's-sized backpacks; packs were heavy and bulky. There were only external frames with things tied on them swinging around.

Now Zpacks makes a great backpack that fits small women. I really like the Arc Haul backpack. It's one of the lightest backpacks on the market—24 ounces. I will be honest the backpack is not cheap, but it's worth every penny and has a great warranty. The lighter the backpack, the more miles you can hike in a day. There are numerous sizes to choose from; I bought the kid's size because I'm small. I'm still a kid at heart. The company will send a new backpack right to you on the trail if you have any issues. Zpacks also has awesome tents. Check out their website; I guarantee you will not be disappointed with their products.

I do believe women underestimate their ability. But with that being said, you should not bite off more than you can chew because you can get yourself into trouble at the drop of a hat. There have been so many deaths on the trail because the victims thought they could do more than they could. I try not to think about it, but it is heavy on my heart that hikers I have met on the trail have passed. Most of the deaths and close calls were due to pushing too much.

**Advice, good and bad**

Determination! Never give up!! There is never a bad day on the trail. I usually don't ever want to stop; I would rather be on the trail. I am so blessed to be able to continue to hike. If times are getting tough, I will spend a day in town and regroup, regenerate, and head back to the trail. I sing and just put one foot in front of the other.

My home is on the trail. I need to rely on myself 100-percent out there while backpacking. I think of the great food I will eat when I get to the next trail town. The feeling of accomplishment, too. I can't wait to see what is around the next corner or mountain, or the next beautiful flower or animals I will see. I can't wait to see the unexpected.

*I've been told not to,* but when someone says don't worry about it—*worry about it!!!*

**Next up...**

My dreams of completing the Continental Divide Trail in 2020 and receiving my Triple Crown may be crushed because of the COVID-19 pandemic. But I am blessed to still have my health, and pray that it will be over soon and no one else loses their life due to this horrible virus.

I am looking forward to reaching my goal of completing the Triple Crown. I will be hiking through Colorado with magnificent views. I plan to slow down and enjoy the last section of my hike before completing it. I want to remember it and hold it close to my heart. I could never explain to anyone the peace that hiking gives me.

In conclusion, I would suggest to 'Hike your own hike'. Do your research before stepping onto the trail. Bring your maps and compass. Let your family and friends know where you will be. Pack your backpack as light as possible. Never drink untreated water. But most of all, have fun!!

**Then the hiking world takes a big hit**

[May 2020, New England] Unfortunately, I did have to cancel my hike for this year. It was a very sad thing, but I would never want to infect anyone or get infected with the COVID-19. I am devastated that I will not complete my goal this year; this has been a longtime goal to complete the Triple Crown. I am still wrestling with my decision, however, deep (very, very deep) in my heart I know I made the correct decision to put others in front of something I want to do. The trail will be there next year, but if I infect someone, they may not be here next year. I live in Massachusetts, one of the *big* hotspots for the virus. Everything is closed, and at this point, all state forests are closed as well but due to open soon.

I have been riding my bike and training my three-year-old horse. I also have a downstairs gym where I hop on my treadmill and watch hiking/backpacking/running on YouTube. I sometimes turn the fan on to get the full effect of the wind in my hair, ha-ha. No, I will not turn on the hose to get the full effect of the rain! Ha-ha-ha!

This helps me feel like I am out there backpacking. Yes, I do put on my full backpack, and most of the time this helps. Backpacking is a big part of my life. I do feel lost not backpacking this year.

I do have a 21.5-acre farm; I can walk around with about 3,000 acres behind me. I cannot see my neighbors from my farm. I am so lucky in that respect because I can just walk out my door and feel safe, not having to wear a mask or worry that the person next to me has COVID-19. It does take some of the stress off me.

My employer has not called me back to work yet, so I spend more time with my horse, Dreamer, and my dog, Happy. I also get lost in my backpacking pictures from past years; this has helped as well, but it is not the same as going.

The way I look at it, I am so blessed to have my health where others have not been so lucky. I will backpack next year, or if possible do part of the trail this year. It does not look promising, but thinking about it helps me get through all of this.

Ending on a good note, as I look back on my backpacking adventures, I am so blessed to have been able to hike/backpack so many different trails. Backpacking keeps me on an even keel. I am still friends with hikers and other people I have met along the way on the trails. I have seen so many beautiful views that are imprinted in my brain forever—my pictures never captured just how beautiful it really is to be out there. I have had experiences of a lifetime, memories that have made me who I am today. We will make it through this with a positive attitude.

**Susan:** Beyond the long list of hikes that Jan has completed, she has also thru-*biked* the C&O Canal Trail and the Great Allegheny Passage. She lives in Massachusetts when she is not traveling or hiking, and is on Facebook as Pooh Bear (for hiking) and Miles-To-Go (for cycling).

Her *POOH-BEAR's Big Adventure on the Appalachian Trail* first appeared in Trail Journals, Oct. 23, 2006, and is used here with Jan's permission. (Uncut version: trailjournals.com/journal/1481.)

## POOH-BEAR's Big Adventure on the Appalachian Trail
### ~Jan Barlow~

Most hikers who hike the Appalachian Trail either make up a name or are given one. Trust me, in most cases, you are better off making up your own name. This story is how I received my name.

While hiking in the peak of bug season, swarms of bugs attacked me, getting in my ears, eyes, and mouth. With the black cloud of bugs all around me, I was "poohing" them out of my mouth, so I earned the name 'Pooh.' Then, as I turned a corner around some bushes, I saw eight black furry legs. I stopped dead in my tracks because I thought it was bear cubs and I wondered where Mama Bear was. I did not want to come between them. As I moved slowly forward, my stomach was doing flip-flops. To my relief, out of the bushes came two big, black Newfoundland dogs. That's how my trail name of POOH-BEAR came about.

The Appalachian Trail, called simply 'the A.T.' by those who hike on it frequently, is the premier recreational hiking trail in the United States, a continental-scale wilderness pathway set aside by Congress and the National Park Service for foot travel only. The route of the A.T. closely follows the ridgeline of eastern America's

Appalachian mountain chain for 2,176 unbroken miles, beginning on the summit of Springer Mountain in northern Georgia and ending on the summit of Mt. Katahdin in north-central Maine. As it winds its way through the mountains, it passes through 14 states, eight national forests, six national parks, and numerous state and local parks.

About 99 percent of the route is on publicly-owned lands, and no fee is charged nor is special permission needed to hike anywhere on the footpath, though in some high-use areas registration is required for overnight stays and fees may be charged for use of shelters and other constructed facilities. The trail is marked with two-inch by four-inch white blazes (painted markings) that I dream about all the time.

Before I decided to challenge myself on this historic footpath, I had done some bike touring from home [Massachusetts] to Pennsylvania, and in Canada, along with many other places. I enjoyed the bike tours, but I found that the cars and their exhaust fumes, along with dodging cars, trucks, and dogs, were sometimes a bit much to take at times. I had also done quite a bit of hiking and loved being out in the woods, so I increased my hiking time. I joined the Pioneer Valley Hiking Club.

I did some more backpacking and decided that it doesn't get any better than this. I would have really liked to thru-hike the A.T. but my job held priority at this time in my life. After 20 years, I did not want to start a new one. I thought that it would take me 12 years to complete the A.T. hiking in sections and only during vacation time and long weekends. To my everlasting surprise, I completed my goal in just four years—July 3, 2002, to July 9, 2006.

*Back at home now, sitting at my computer as my fingers dance around the keyboard like a tap dancer in full motion, my mind drifts back to the A.T. and all the fun times I had hiking my way south. I saved the last 100 miles to hike north because I wanted to savor the grand finale of hiking Mt. Katahdin (the northern terminus) last.*

In Maine, I ran into the 'Naked Hiker', and that was a real eye-opener. I had heard of him, so you would think I could have done more than stutter, "Hi, nice weather, huh?" On more than one occasion, I hiked in the dark with my headlamp on. One night hike in Maine I almost landed in a lake, discovering in the morning that I was just two steps away from the lake—close call when at all cost I try to keep my feet dry. Dry feet are happy feet.

In New Hampshire, I saw a moose with magnificent antlers at Lonesome Lake. I was lucky coming over the White Mountains as I had the best weather ever. In Vermont, I loved the music at the Long Trail Inn (the trail goes right by the inn), a nice place to hang out after a long day's hike.

As I was sitting at Lion's Head in Connecticut, enjoying the beautiful view, two people showed up. A very nice lady sat down next to me and started chatting as though we were old friends. After talking with her for several minutes, I figured out that she was actress Kyra Sedgwick, and with her was husband Kevin Bacon. His laugh was a dead giveaway. I didn't let on that I knew who they were because I thought they wanted to just relax. The funny thing is, I almost asked them to take my picture with the beautiful view in the background. That would have been a switch for them.

In New Jersey, my feet were flying, and this is where I did my first 27-mile day. The views were gorgeous with water snaking all around. When I crossed the southbound bridge at dusk, the bridge was moving under my feet. I was on the sidewalk but not feeling really confident about it. Car headlights seemed to be heading right for me at incredible speeds. When tractor-trailers went by, I held on for dear life as not only did the bridge sink but the wind threatened to blow me right off the bridge. I came close to losing my Pooh hat but managed to keep it. Actually, I enjoyed crossing the bridge, a bit of a thrill.

After crossing the bridge into Pennsylvania, I saw a mama bear and two healthy cubs, my first sighting of bears. This is the land of rocks, or as I called it at the time, Blister City.

I blinked my eyes and was through Maryland. The cicadas (a bug that emerges every 17 years) were out in full force, and their singing was ear-piercing, to say the least. They were all over, hanging from trees, on the ground. For the most part, they quieted down at night so I could at least sleep.

In Virginia, I really had to hang on to my Pooh cap. These

were the most interesting states I had hiked when it came to weather. You could say that I had to fly by the seat on my pants! In the Shenandoah Valley, I encountered two hurricanes and one tornado. The wind was blowing so hard that it was hard to put my feet where I planned to, and the rain felt like pins and needles on my skin.

In Tennessee, after I had been on the trail for weeks, I developed two hollow legs; I just couldn't seem to fill myself up. (If you are hiking in Tennessee and see a sign that reads, "Please stop in and say Hi to Uncle Johnny," please do. It is a great place to stay and is right on the trail. They give you door-to-door service. I was dropped off at Pizza Plus and wolfed down 10 plates of pizza, plus a salad bar plateful and dessert.) I went to the grocery store *after* eating because I knew I would have bought so much food that my backpack would have weighed more than me.

The Smoky Mountains are beautiful, and the weather was pretty good as I hiked through. There were a lot of rules to follow in the Smokies, but I thoroughly enjoyed being there. I met a fellow on the trail who told me his name was Johnny Knoxville. Later, I saw previews of *The Dukes of Hazzard* and recognized he was the actor who played Luke Duke in the movie. He may have wondered why I was not awestruck and asking for his autograph.

Hiking in North Carolina, I saw and heard lots of bears, but seeing as my name is Pooh-Bear, I thought I would be fine. I saw one very big black bear with a shiny coat who took off like a bolt of lightning. Fortunately for me, he was going away, and I could hear him for quite a while galumphing down the trail, breaking branches on his way.

One night in Georgia, I had just put my tent up when the rain came down so hard there was water under my tent, and I was hoping there were no holes in the bottom of it. It felt like a waterbed. I sat in my 1.5-pound tent with my head touching the top of the tent, and it hurt. I looked out and saw hail the size of marbles piling up like snow.

I was so excited to be reaching the summit of Springer Mountain that my feet hardly hit the ground. I signed the journal and enjoyed the view, and spent the night in the shelter at the top. I headed down to Amicalola Falls feeling a little bit sad that my hike was almost over. When I got to the Stone Arch, I felt somewhat overwhelmed at being around so many people after being in the woods for so long. After a shower, I went to the train station where more people were crowding around me. I felt a bit like a sardine.

I left Georgia with a feeling of accomplishment; I was ahead of my schedule and looking forward to Maine and Mt. Katahdin. As I had hiked most of the A.T. southbound, it felt strange to be going northbound. I entered Maine's 100-Mile Wilderness for my last and final section of the A.T. with a full belly and a full pack with nine days' supply of food inside.

The trail was wet and muddy with slippery roots, and the next thing I knew, I was on my butt with a stinging pain. I ended up with a big tattoo on my butt of black, blue, and many other colors. I continued on and, *bam*, I went down again! After hiking more than 2,000 miles with no major problems, this was unbelievable!

I slowed my pace and was fine. I was determined to have fun on this last stretch. I enjoyed the few rock scrambles and did the 5.2 loop into Gulf Haggis (The Little Grand Canyon), which was gorgeous. I walked from waterfall to waterfall and enjoyed it immensely. A memorable day.

At one of my campsites, a cow moose and her two calves were only eight feet away from me—boy, was the cow moose big, and the two calves stayed right behind their mama. From the last section at Abol Bridge, I could see my destination and felt as though it was really real; I was going to finish!

I entered Baxter State Park, the last chapter of my journey. There were beautiful waterfalls for miles; I slowed down to only 10 or so miles per day so that I could savor the stretch. There was a feeling of relaxation and peace as I listened to the water babbling around rocks and washing its own course over the rocks, leaving grooves in the rocks from years of moving over the same rocks. As I refilled my water supply, the water was cold on my hands as it whizzed by, tugging at my container. Drinking nice cold water on the trail is a plus in the hot summer months. What a grand finale!

I continued on to Katahdin Springs Campground at the base of the mountain ready to start for the summit the next day. It was a beautiful day as I started up the next morning, passing a breathtaking waterfall. As I got above the tree line, it was unbelievable. I could see where I had hiked the day before. I continued on rock scrambling, which I love, until I came to a sign. I thought it was the end, but as I got closer, I saw that I still had another mile to go. I followed the sign until I came to the end of my trek of 2,176 miles.

My eyes watered as I tried to read the final sign; I got my picture taken hugging it. It was actually a dual celebration because, in climbing Mt. Katahdin, I also completed another of my goals that I had started out to complete four years before—to climb all 67 of the 4,000-footers in New Hampshire, Vermont, and Maine. I was so thrilled to have accomplished both of my goals.

There is so much to see on the trails that are impossible to see from a car. My footprints may have disappeared from the Appalachian Trail, but I will always hold the miles I hiked close to my heart and will cherish the memories.

**Jan Barlow**

# Jane Blanchard

**Susan:** In 1975, Jane and her husband Dennis lived in a tent in Winchendon, Massachusetts, for six months (until December) while they built a log cabin. After two years of living off-the-grid, they lived a self-sufficient lifestyle on a five-acre "gentleman's" farm. Nowadays, when she is not on the trail or busy writing one of her Woman on her Way books, you might be lucky enough to bump into her in Sarasota, Florida.

**Jane Blanchard:** Practical considerations: When it comes to hiking clothes, my choice is a Royal Robbins hiking skirt. These are lightweight (quick-drying) and wrinkle-resistant, which makes them practical when washing clothing on hikes. They also have a UPF 50+ factor to keep the harmful sun rays off and help keep me cool. I like these so much that they are a big part of my non-hiking wardrobe.

In my early years of hiking, I used no gear other than an external framed backpack. For my first long-distance hike at age 60, I purchased modern gear, my favorite being the Osprey Talon 33 backpack. It had many compartments and places to attach things to the outside of the pack. I also recommend this company for its service—after years of usage, the back support broke and the company replaced it without hassle even though that model had been discontinued.

In 2016, I realized I could no longer hike without poles. Since then, I have come to rely on my Leki trekking poles (Jannu model). These poles are designed for women and are light and compact. After learning to use the poles, I realized that I might have prevented the shin splints I'd had earlier had I been using them.

I treasure my Rite in the Rain weatherproof notebook. Without it, I would not be able to recall cherished hiking memories, names of other hikers, or the lessons learned on the trail. Nor would I ever have become a writer.

### Early years

Growing up in the Connecticut Valley capital offered little possibility to climb mountains or hike in the woods. Yet, I enjoyed walking into the center of Hartford, the various parks, and visiting friends. Even though at that time a long walk was only several miles, I enjoyed the outdoors and the freedom of traveling on foot.

My husband introduced me to hiking. My first ascent was Mt. Washington in May 1975. I was unprepared for the snowcapped mountain. Clad only in sneakers, I was stepping in Dennis's footsteps as we crossed a snowy incline—and then I fell through what was a snow bridge. To prevent my fall, I grabbed a twig that turned out to be the top of a 30-foot tree at the base of which was a gushing river of snowmelt. Had I not reacted quickly, I would have been swept away. Undaunted by the near-fatal incident, I continued to the summit and completed the seven-hour roundtrip hike.

During the following 35 years, my hikes were weekend events in New England. Of the 48 4,000-plus-foot peaks in the White Mountain range, I climbed 15, several multiple times. I celebrated turning 30 with a five-day adventure so I would not have to face anyone as I turned that dreadful age. Being in nature helped me transition without freaking out. That five-day pause in my life was like taking a deep breath, providing me with a new perspective: Life did not end at 30!

### A life altered

My first serious hike was 500 miles on the Camino de Santiago at age 60. This first pilgrimage (in 2011) was a turning point for me, connecting me to the present and essential to my health and happiness. Those 43 days completely altered my life. What had been important no longer was. What had been difficult was now easy. My love for my husband was reawakened. My wanderlust was roused and can no longer be appeased.

As I walked, I talked with women of all ages and cultures. From them, I learned that life is what one makes of it—at any age. Two New Zealand women, 10 and 15 years older than I was, were quicker and suffered less than younger ones. From a group of Vietnamese women, I learned that wisdom, as well as the burden of the pack, can be shared between various age groups.

**Hiking has many rewards**
There is so much to like about hiking: getting away from the humdrum life, being out with nature, being present in the now, exercising the body while relaxing the mind, discovering new places and experiences, and tasting new foods. Most importantly for me are creating new memories, sharing the experience with my husband, meeting new people, and practicing new languages.

On my first Camino, the camaraderie with other pilgrims was paramount. Though we did not create a 'Camino family'—a group of people who traveled and planned to stay together for meals and a bed—we did meet up repeatedly with people traveling at the same time as we were. Each time we saw each other, it was like a homecoming with hugs and kisses and sharing of experiences. This feeling of belonging taught me a lot about the kindness of others and the respect that is often missing from interactions during busy lives off the trail.

Surprisingly, many single women hiked alone. One taught me that life can go on after a relationship ends, finding the strength to continue within herself. She learned to handle grief, accept her loss, and find joy in the present. One middle-ager found a soul mate in another woman (not sexually), and they joined together as companions for the completion of the journey. Another solo woman showed courage in accepting her loneliness, missing her husband and children in Korea. Her desire to finish the task facing her provided the strength to persevere.

All these single female hikers displayed a curiosity for what was ahead, the courage to listen to the beckoning call of the unknown, an acceptance of their abilities, and a willingness to forge ahead alone. Most were not solitary women. They joined in (and often led) the merriment and enjoyed the company of others. I hope that if my husband predeceases me that I will have the strength to proceed on my journeys alone.

From the many couples I observed, I realized that sharing experiences is the glue to lasting love. Many couples our age and older were hiking the Camino. For them, it was a renewed commitment to each other, another memory to share. For the younger ones, it was a chance to test each other's compatibilities. One Korean woman stated that her hiking partner's positive outlook during the difficulties of the trail led her to believe that he could be a partner for life.

Most seniors, male or female, underestimate their physical abilities. When I was 50, I read Shirley MacLaine's *The Camino: A Journey of the Spirit* and thought that she was nuts to undertake such an adventure, alone and at such an age (60). Ten years later, when my husband asked me where I would like to go for my first long-distance hike, I told him about the Camino. I never once considered that I would not be able to complete the journey. I exercised, rode a bike, walked the dogs—nothing as challenging as walking 500 miles. But I was undaunted. This was my adventure!

## We all have challenges

On my first Camino, I developed shin splints. I had been walking too long, too quickly, and with too heavy a pack. To heal, I took three days off. It was sad seeing the other pilgrims continue on their journey, but I had to accept that for me to finish, I had to stay immobile, ice the leg, and mend. Once I was back on my feet, I only traveled a few miles the first day and then slowly increased the distance until I was fit. Within a week, I had caught up to those who had gone ahead.

While walking on the Hadrian's Wall Path, I came face to face with a bull. My only defense was an umbrella and a cool head. I stared into the beast's eyes and talked softly as I made my way out of the field. This was very unnerving.

I have acrophobia, a fear of heights. While hiking a particularly steep ascent on the Vermont Long Trail, it took all my courage to summit, one well-planned step at a time. Once at the top, I realized that there was a side trail to the peak. Though not cured of my fears, I learned to look for the least difficult way. Though it may not be easily spotted, there usually is more than one way of doing something.

### European hiking

Since my first pilgrimage on the Camino, I have trekked in Spain again, as well as Portugal, England, Ireland, Northern Ireland, Scotland, France, Amsterdam, Belgium, Luxembourg, the Netherlands, and Denmark.

To be a successful long-distance hiker, you need to enjoy the hike. Liking what you are doing, seeing, and experiencing will help you overcome the obstacles, pain, and mental negativity. Be present. Be aware. Have fun. Listen to your body and mind. If everything is telling you to stop, do so. Taking a day or two off renews you physically and mentally. If after the hiatus, the hike is still no longer fun, it might be time to stop.

### What other accomplishments stand out

My greatest physical accomplishment was hiking the Vermont Long Trail (VLT) at age 65. The trail is challenging: 273 miles of rugged terrain with steep peaks and swift rivers. That year, 2015, there were record-breaking rains, mud everywhere, and unusually cold temperatures. Because it took longer than expected and because I had a planned engagement, I only completed half of the trail. Even though I did not finish the VLT, it remains the most draining and challenging two weeks of my life.

Following my first long-distance adventure in 2011, I began to write about my experiences. Becoming an author is an unexpected and ongoing undertaking that would not have happened if I had not taken that first step on the Camino.

### Adjusting to aging

After attempting the Vermont Long Trail, I decided that I preferred hiking in Europe to wilderness hiking. As I approach 70 years old, trekking with 30 to 40 pounds on my back, fighting the cold, and sleeping on the ground or platforms is not appealing. I prefer light backpacks, retiring to a warm and cozy bed or cot, and ordering meals, possibly with a glass of wine.

When I was younger, I hiked without poles, did not mind the weight of the pack, and loved skipping from rock to rock on the descents. I was fast and enjoyed the rhythm of the pace. Now, I am more cautious, and I must double (or more) the expected time needed for the distance.

My next long-distance hike will be the Via Francigena from Switzerland to Rome. I am looking forward to hiking eight to ten miles a day, speaking with the locals (I am learning Italian), and having fun. If the distance proves too long, I will adjust to my abilities. For me, aging does not mean I can't, but I can with accommodations.

**Final thoughts**

I would advise anyone of any age new to hiking to:

- Invest in appropriate lightweight clothing (no jeans). Consider a broad-brimmed hat that has a tie to keep it on the head when it's windy.
- Get fitted with a backpack. If you are only doing day hikes, consider a fanny pack.
- Bring enough clothing (think layers), but do not overpack.
- Start and end with stretches. Flexible muscles help protect the joints and can prevent injury. Post-walk stretches can reduce pain, stiffness, and lactic-acid accumulation.
- Use hiking poles. They reduce the impact on the knees and leg muscles, can prevent falls, and can assist you on slopes, adding a break on the descent and providing a boost on the ascent.
- Start with simple climbs. As the body adjusts to the demands of hiking, increase the distance and difficulty of the climb.
- Make sure the footwear matches the trail. Why wear hiking boots if walking shoes will do?

- Be safe. If you are hiking alone, tell someone where you are going and when you expect to return. Carry an emergency pack with first-aid supplies, a lighter (to start a fire), and a whistle.
- Drink plenty of water.

If you are unsure about trying a new trail, research it by getting a guide book and/or trail map. See if you can find a hiking partner. Check out women's hiking organizations to see if one is perfect for you.

**Pay attention for prevention!**

It's a dangerous thing to overestimate your physical abilities. Self-awareness is crucial to hiking without accidents or hurting yourself. Accepting your limitations does not mean that you must stop hiking. It means that it might take a different strategy to accomplish what you used to do quite easily. Increase the time allotted or do it in the company of others rather than alone. For example, younger hikers might be able to climb over a fallen tree, but older hikers might have to find an alternate, safer way to get over the obstacle.

The worse advice is the 'no pain, no gain' mantra. So many people believe that unless you exercise until it is painful, you are not getting the full benefit of the workout. Overstressing one's muscles, tendons, and joints can lead to harm more than rewards.

I do believe in training and preparing for hiking, just not getting hurt doing so. I also believe that if you feel pain while on the trail, you should take time off to get better and/or see a doctor. Pursuing the trail can be detrimental.

Many injuries on the trail can be avoided by listening to your body and not pushing it to extremes. Instead of 'no pain, no gain,' make your mantra 'pay attention for prevention.' While hiking the Camino, I saw one woman with exercise-induced vasculitis, an irritation of the blood vessels that presents as a rash on the legs. It occurs mostly in those over 50 who exercise in warm weather and become dehydrated. Rest, drinking water, and wearing cooler clothing can alleviate the symptoms. This woman, though, continued to walk, and her leg swelled and needed medical care and time off from hiking. Pushing yourself to the extreme is not always the best thing to do.

Another woman was having cramping, fatigue, amenorrhea (loss of menstruation), and trouble continuing on her journey. Her low body weight and high energy expenditure while hiking was the cause. Not seeking medical attention because she did not want to leave her friends while she recovered resulted in a visit to the ER and extended time off to regain her weight and strength. Had she listened to her body early, she might have avoided having to take a week off to recuperate.

My advice is to enjoy your life, be aware of your limitations, and keep on hiking!

**Susan:** Jane V. Blanchard is the author of the Woman on Her Way series: *Women of the Way: Embracing the Camino* (translations in Spanish and Italia); *Hadrian's Wall Path: Walking into History*; *Camino Tips: How to get the most out of "The Way," A Peek at the Remarkable Camino de Santiago: A Photo Journey*, and *Camino Quotes and Poems: The Meaning of the Journey.* You can find her at janevblanchard.com.

**Jane Blanchard summits Baker Peak**

# Carolyn 'Ravensong' Burkhart

**Susan:** Carolyn is believed to be the first woman to solo thru-hike the Pacific Crest Trail. It was 1976; she was 20 years old. She was wearing the heavier gear of the time—including mountaineering boots and a 50-pound pack designed for men—and was one of only 12 hikers who signed the register that year.

She studied at the University of Washington and currently lives in Mazama, Washington, where she runs Ravensong's Roost/Hiker's Hut near Hart's Pass on the PCT.

On September 28, 2019, Ravensong's dedication to PCT hikers was recognized by ALDHA-West with the Martin Papendick Award for "Outstanding Trail Angel of the Year." Her tribute was accompanied by the comment, "For longstanding generosity and steadfast dedication to the long-distance hiking community."

Her story that follows is based on Facebook posts of the last few years, two phone interviews I did with her in February 2020, follow-up email correspondence, and newspaper accounts.

**Carolyn Burkhart:** 10/25/2016, "It's been 40 years since I solo hiked the Pacific Crest Trail from Mexico to Canada! Wow, how time flies. I started March 30, 1976, on the Mexican border and reached the Canadian border on September 30, 1976. Mom and Dad picked me up the next day in Manning Park [Canada]. Thank you, Mom, for being a mountaineer and bringing us kids in the wilderness you loved from the time I was 2 years old! "

12/01/2016, "[It's now] 40 years later...reaching the Canadian border on the PCT again. What a welcome from PCTers of 2016!!! " "[Mom] thank you for sending my many boxes of food to me along the trail. For my 21st birthday, I discovered a dulcimer from you in the post at Mammoth Lakes. You helped me follow my dreams and bring music to the trail!"

5/9/2019, "My mother passed away last week, the day before her 95th birthday. I was with her most of the time over her last month of life, and we shared many special moments together. Thank you, Mom for the life and joy you have given to me and our family. I'll always remember your last song, 'Valderi, Valdera, my knapsack on my back!!!' You were the one who got me on the PCT starting at two years old and cheered me on when I thru hiked the PCT by myself in 1976, when I was 20! Mom's love of the wilderness has inspired our family and community to truly love nature and to do our best to respect and honor mother earth."

Carolyn earned her trail name, 'Ravensong,' many years back when another hiker heard her calling to a nearby raven. So, it seemed entirely in character that when I first caught up with her to do an interview on February 18, 2020, she was outdoors watching goldeneye ducks. She had spotted the ducks while she was walking along a hidden estuary near her mother's former cabin on Puget Sound in northwest Washington. While the weather at Puget Sound was sunny and clear, at Carolyn's home in Washington's Northern Cascades, there was four feet of snow on the ground.

Carolyn is part of a "family of hikers," as she put it. Her great-aunt was a mountaineer in Washington's Olympic Mountains in the early 1900s. Carolyn started hiking when she was three years old, encouraged by her aunt and her mother. Her mother was an ardent hiker and mountaineer who still did some backpacking on the PCT when she was 86. She remembers from her early childhood that her mother would sing to her while they were hiking—which is what Carolyn did with her children when they were young and still does when hiking solo.

Those early happy years on the trail led to increasing interest and experience in the outdoors and hiking as Carolyn entered her teens. She wanted to take the Mountaineers Basic Climbing course when she was 12 years old, but found out she was too young to qualify, so she learned to climb from her older brother, Dick

Burkhart, who introduced her to roped climbs such as Mt. Fernow in the Northern Cascades within Glacier Peak Wilderness.

She had to wait until she was 14 years old and find someone to sponsor her in the climbing class. She prusiked up out of crevasses on Mt. Rainier when she was 14, and climbed Mt. St. Helens when the mountain was still shaped like Mt. Fuji. She took an Outward Bound course and gained greater confidence in her self-sufficiency and leadership skills. She learned map and compass skills through a Mountaineers Basic Climbing course and was very good at route-finding.

In her late teens, she looked into becoming a ranger but found out she was too young to qualify. Instead, she was hired as a seasonal interpretative ranger in Stehekin, where she gave talks on botany, issued permits, and otherwise assisted visitors to Northern Cascades National Park. That year, 1974, was the first summer the National Park Service hired any women as interpretive rangers; they had lost a federal lawsuit over a policy stating that the position was only for men. Carolyn and Maxine Franklin, the other female interpretive ranger, were not allowed to work in the backcountry. The National Park Service believed that the women would distract the men from doing their work!

On her days off, Carolyn explored most of the trails around Stehekin and Holden. She became known as the 'Wild Woman' of the valley. She saw PCT thru-hikers en route and wrote in her journal, "I want to hike the PCT next summer." Two years later, she found the opportunity to step outside the box of a college education and set foot on the southernmost point of the trail, next to a barbed-wire fence separating Mexico from the United States.

### Her solo hike of the PCT

When Burkhart hiked the PCT, she found lots to enjoy. The habitats through which the trail goes—the deserts and mountains of Southern California, the mountainous range of the Sierra Nevada, the Southern Cascades of Northern California into Southern Oregon, the volcanic landscapes of Oregon, and finally the wilderness areas and rugged miles through the Northern Cascades into Canada—offered an amazing diversity of plant life. She also found that the people she met—whether encountered on the trail or in the small trail towns along the way—were friendly and helpful.

It didn't go without problems, however. One morning in Southern California, she set out from her campsite near Highway 15 carrying three days' worth of water. The next place ahead where water was said to be available was a water tank. Unfortunately, when Carolyn reached the tank, it was empty. Seeing no other option, she decided to walk back to Angeles Highway and picked up a ride to the nearest town, Wrightwood. As a single woman, she was wary of the male drivers she saw when she tried hitching, but fortunately, it went well.

**Employing Strategies**

Although hitching remained a bit worrisome for Carolyn, she offered several suggestions to women hikers. Trust: Follow your instincts. Mutual Aid: If you are in a group, talk with other women about 'code words'—words you can use that would signal to others that you don't feel comfortable with something or someone. Women need to support one another. Plan: When hitching, look in the driver's window before you get in the car. If you don't like the look of things—drugs, alcohol, uncool behavior—don't get in the car. "Oops, I forgot my camera." Ask: Don't be shy. Ask for help when you need it.

**Accomplishments beyond the PCT hike**

While most think being the first woman to solo the PCT was a huge achievement—and Carolyn would agree—she thinks she's done even more difficult hikes. "Going solo with a young child is a heavy responsibility. The amount of planning involved in taking a child of five or seven years old on a month's backpacking trip [in the remote mountains of northern Washington] is much more difficult. Hypothermia and other risks…"

But when she started her own family, she took each of her children backpacking. Carolyn took along her oldest child, Tamara, on a hike to scramble up to Camp Muir at 10,000 feet on Mt. Rainier when she was only a few weeks old. She was so tiny that someone started spreading the rumor that a baby had been born on the mountain.

When Tamara was four or five, they backpacked from Canada to the North Cascades. To keep her daughter motivated, Carolyn would play 'elephant' with her; she would tie a tail made of rope on the back of her backpack and tell her daughter "baby elephant" as a signal to hang onto her 'tail' when the trail became narrow or rough.

Another time, when Carolyn was noticeably pregnant, she was asked when her baby was due. She replied "today," and indeed went into labor later that day.

With all of her children, she learned she could keep them motivated by giving frequent 10-minute breaks and goodies. Carolyn started out with her aunt and mother on a day hike along the Cascade Crest Trail (on the PCT) the summer she turned three. Now her four adult children carry on the tradition; they also began hiking when they were tots.

Of Carolyn's five children—Tamara, Keith Erick, Heather, Leanne Jordan, and Melody—all except for Melody (who is severely developmentally disabled) hiked the full length of Washington when they were between six and nine years old.

"Tamara, Keith Erick, and I, along with their two dogs hiked from Mexico to Cabazon [Southern California]. Tamara thru-hiked the PCT NOBO in 2018."

Daughter Heather has also continued the family hiking tradition. "She walked Yosemite to Mt. Whitney with me when she was ten. Some northbound men we ran into at the first pass tried to talk me out of taking her on my own the length of the John Muir Trail. They believed I had no idea what was in store for me and did not comprehend that I had thru-hiked the PCT from Mexico to Canada and that Heather had already hiked the full length of Washington with me. Then, when she was eleven, she walked with me from Tahoe to Yosemite; Leanne and Keith Erick joined us south of Mammoth Lakes."

Leanne had first hiked on the PCT when she was four years old. Later, she and Carolyn hiked on through to Oregon. She turned seven and had her birthday party with family at Diamond

Lake. When they reached Crater Lake, they went to a ranger's fireside chat. The ranger asked the visitors how they had gotten to the park. "We walked from Canada," said Leanne.

Even with her challenges, Melody can hike short distances. That she loves it is shown by the fact that the only words she can say are "Let's Go!"

## Ravensong's Roost and Hiker's Hut

Carolyn, with her lifelong love of hiking, also enjoys sharing her enthusiasm with others. In 2013, she sold her former house and moved to her current cabin near Mazama—near the intersection of Rainy Pass and Hart's Pass on the PCT. Then, "I had just purchased my cabin and needed to go to the ALDHA-West gathering. I saw a storm coming and near-freezing temperatures. I had opened my cabin for PCTers. I came home to a house full of hypothermic hikers full of stories of being caught in a snowstorm. I had one tiny corner in my cabin for myself and decided after being woken up by 'Otter' rummaging through my refrigerator at 4 a.m. that trail angelling would have to be done somewhere other than my tiny home."

She decided she would turn an old building out back, used for slaughtering pigs at one time, into a hikers' hut. Once that decision was made, she started making some changes, and volunteers from the hiking community got involved in the effort. A sleeping loft was created by putting a floor on the overheard rafters and adding insulation. Downstairs rooms were decorated by hikers—one follows a Mexican theme designed by 'Slim,' another has a Canadian theme complete with flag. Hiker 'PK' created a mosaic of the PCT emblem from salvaged tiles for a shower wall. Carolyn thinks it's so good that it deserves a more prominent location.

With the large increase in long-distance hikers on the PCT and the PNW (Pacific Northwest Trail) in recent years, the number of people needing shelter as they hike through the area has grown. Last year, 400 people signed the logbook at the store in town—and a high percentage of those came to her place for the night. Hiker's Hut is generally open July to October, but the prime season is September and October for the north-bounders. The place can hold 20 people if needed; the loft holds 10. Big tents can be set up outside. She wasn't able to host in July and August 2020 but hoped she could in September—it all depended on COVID-19.

Her current dilemma is how she can continue to do her own traveling but also be available to hikers. It's been suggested she do a GoFundMe campaign to raise money to improve the hut and that she approach the local hiking group to see if she can find more volunteers to relieve her so she can travel. "It all takes time," she said.

Initially, people found out about Hiker's Hut by word of mouth, but now Carolyn has a website to spread the word. It's a good thing because this is an area where severe storms can render the trails impassable.

**Her notice reads:**

"Pacific Crest Trail through-hikers, you are invited to come visit at the beginning of your southbound (SOBO) journey to Mexico or at the terminus of your northbound (NOBO) PCT adventure at Canada. Ravensong welcomes Pacific Northwest Trail trekkers to stop by and stay at the Hiker's Hut, too.

"Her Roost is just west of the halfway point of the PNT between Glacier National Park and Cape Alava on the Pacific Ocean. Mazama is the closest community to where the PCT and PNT share the same trail in the North Cascades.

"Drop by and camp out by the Hiker's Hut for the night. Come team up with others in rough weather and during wildfires to learn about alternate routes and strategies to help you safely complete your journey.

"Take a break at the Roost and go to Mazama Store for fresh-baked baguettes, scones with real fruit, and homemade soup. Next door, Goat's Beard Mountain Supply offers hiking and mountaineering gear. Resupply boxes can be sent there, too. The community of Mazama and Winthrop are excited to help PCT/PNTers; many having been through-hikers themselves.

"Ravensong is a volunteer Trail Angel for long-distance

through-hikers—open from July to October."

Carolyn and the townspeople believe it is very important to keep track of who is on the trail nearby—especially as hiking season dwindles and storms can threaten. Without a log to keep track of who comes through the area, people who could respond if someone is reported missing from the trail may not have good information on whether a hiker ever came through. This uncertainty puts hikers as well as Search and Rescue teams at increased risk.

### A quirk in the system

Because PCT thru-hikers like to end their trek in Canada, they need to have documentation—generally a permit to get in and a passport to reenter the U.S. Check the link for updates. pcta.org/discover-the-trail/permits/canada-pct-entry-permit/ If they don't, they can be arrested or turned back. Sometimes, hikers can't get permits because they have been arrested for some kind of misdemeanor such as illegal alcohol use, etc.

Those who don't choose to enter Canada or who get turned back face a 30-mile hike back to reenter the U.S.—and another opportunity to make their way through challenging, sometimes dangerous, wilderness back to Ravensong's Roost for a second overnight stay. Carolyn has come up with alternative routes back to Mazama for hikers so they can at least enjoy a new and different route for their return.

### Today's hikes

Carolyn's ancestry is Norwegian and so it followed that she would want to spend time there doing research on her ancestors—as well as hiking. When doing the research, she learned that some of the women, even when elderly, would go into Norway's wilderness, the far northern tundra, for four or five months at a time to herd goats and sheep.

She also learned that her great-great-grandmother, Sønnev, left Norway in 1880 on the ship Beta headed for Hawaii (the Sandwich Islands at the time). The Norwegians were used in slave labor for the sugar industry for three years to pay for their passage. Sønnev was never heard from again by her family back home; later it was learned that she had died in childbirth.

In 2019, Carolyn began hiking the E-1, a European long-distance path. The path through Norway was opened on June 4, 2013, after the Innovasjon Norge and Norwegian Trekking Association marked it. As Carolyn can attest, it is not an easy path to navigate.

Norway's portion stretches 1,200 miles/2,105 km, and though it has 60,000 waymarks on either cairns (stacks of stone) or trees, the markings (or lack thereof) differ in various places. Sometimes, there are E-1 markers at border crossings or intersections with other paths, and in between those crossings, the signs and markings of the local routes are used. In sections such as Børge-fjell National Park in Norway, and sometimes in other regions to the south, there are no markings at all and hikers must rely on devices—assuming there's reception—and a map and compass. (The length of the total route as envisioned—Norway, crossing from Sweden to Denmark by ferry and continuing on to finish in Italy—is 4,960 miles/7,980 km.)

On her trek, she found that the rivers could be a real challenge. She came to one that she could find no way across because the bridges were out. She ended up stripping down and wading across. That would have been alright, but just about the time she was bonking, pulling herself out of the water on the far side, a little boat came "putt-putting along."

Coming to one point where the trail came to what would have been a dangerous river crossing, she searched a couple of miles upstream to find a safer place. In the process, she found an old abandoned cabin of the sort that the women of earlier generations of her family would have stayed in when watching sheep. These *seters* were built for the sheep to live in the front and the people in the back. Nowadays, these cabins (as well as the *rorbuers* formerly used by fishermen) are very popular vacation rentals in Norway.

The 1,500 miles of it within Norway are of the most interest to Carolyn because of her heritage. She hopes to return to do an additional 750 to 1,000 miles of it.

**Susan:** Beyond opening the Hiker's Hut to provide a place for hikers to stay overnight, find information on the trails ahead, and learn where to get any needed supplies, Carolyn volunteers with outdoor organizations. She has been on the ALDHA-West board and has volunteered on such projects as the Canadian Reindeer Project in Inuvik (in Canada's Northwest Territory).

Hikers can find out more about Hiker's Hut at Ravensong's Roost at ravensongsroost.com. It's located on Highway 20 just east of the fire station in Mazama.

**Carolyn Burkhart — Harts Pass, October 2013 (credit PCTer Muk Muk)**

# Judy Chovan

**Susan:** After a stint with the Peace Corps in Tonga while in her twenties, Judy worked for the National Park Service for three years—in Cuyahoga Valley National Park (NP), Channel Islands NP, and Santa Monica Mountains National Recreation Area (NRA). She went on to graduate school at UCLA to pursue a degree in Marine Biology. She is now retired and continues to enjoy her lifelong love of the outdoors. She and her husband, Bob Stavers, live in the San Juan Islands, Washington, where they hike, bike, and kayak.

Her overseas trips often relate to volunteerism (2019 was sea turtle rescue/rehab in the Maldives). Her extensive list of foreign trips reflects her continuing interest in long-distance hiking and cycling as well as dive and snorkel trips.

**Judy Chovan:** I started multiday hiking seriously when I was around 45; I started doing long-distance hiking when I retired. When I am home, I typically hike solo or with my husband, my sister and brother-in-law, or friends. But even when I am with others on the trail, I often walk alone or at least silently.

### Hiking near home, hiking abroad

Bob and I do our multi-day hikes primarily overseas as we are at an age where we like sleeping on a bed staying in a hut/albergue/refugio/pension overnight and having a travel company schlep our bag from place to place so we just have to carry a daypack (a big one but a daypack).

We have hiked the Camino (twice for me), the Chemin across France from Le Puy to St. Jean Pied de Port, the Salkantay to

Machu Picchu, Peru; the Coast to Coast and the Cotswolds Way in England; the Pennine Way, Great Britain; the Routeburn and Milford (twice), New Zealand; the West Highland Way, Scotland; the Tour de Mont Blanc through parts of Switzerland, Italy, and France; as well as treks in Bhutan and Cinque Terre, Italy.

I am in the middle of solo walking the Thames Path (Gloucestershire to Greenwich). I've also done several one-day classic hikes—the Tongariro Pass in New Zealand, the *Fimmvorduhals* (*Fimmvörðuháls*) Trek in Iceland, and Croagh Patrick in Ireland.

I hiked part of the Kumano Kodo in Japan, which earned me the Dual Pilgrim Certificate—for walking both the Kumano Kodo and the Way of St. James (Camino de Santiago). I could not hike it all due to a broken hand.

## What hiking offers

The first thing is simply being in nature—seeing it in its grandeur but also at its smallest. We started hiking the Tour Du Mont Blanc (TMB) the last week of June 2019, before the season officially opened, specifically because I wanted to see the alpine wildflowers—those above treeline (where the snow had melted) are some of the tiniest, most fragile-looking flowers in the world—yet they survive in this harsh landscape with such a short growing season. My husband, on the other hand, was in awe of the majesty of the mountains.

Second, as a biologist, I love nature and identifying everything, and research has shown that being outdoors provides a much-needed psychological boost.

The third thing would be what we call the 'monastic' lifestyle. Your whole world revolves around getting up, getting dressed, eating, heading out to hike (after checking the weather), eating, more hiking, dinner, and sleep. Very simple and uncluttered.

The fourth thing would be the friends I have made. I just got a birthday wish from someone I met on the Camino twelve years ago. I have friends from all over the world—some we continue to meet up with or specifically to hike.

**Greatest accomplishments**

I think my biggest accomplishments would probably be the Tour du Mont Blanc (TMB), and doing my first Camino solo. The Tour du Mont Blanc circles the Mont Blanc massif. It goes through parts of Switzerland, Italy, and France. My training for the TMB took a hit when I broke my hand that March, a few months before we were to leave. I was free diving off a Japanese destroyer in Chuuk Lagoon [aka Truk Atoll—a major Japanese naval base during World War II]. Although my cast came off in May, I had to wear a splint until the week before we left for France and then again while hiking.

We live right next door to San Juan Island National Historic Park, WA, with its 20+ miles of trails. I train on the same trail for all my trips—Mt. Constitution on neighboring Orcas Island, which gives us a 2,800-foot elevation gain in less than four miles so that's a pretty good conditioning trek.

In the months before the TMB, I was not able to hold a trekking pole in my left hand, which pretty much limited our conditioning hikes up Mt. Constitution, so my aerobic/hill climbing training was nonexistent. That made the Mont Blanc trek an even bigger challenge—but even with worrying about my hand and weak left leg, I finished the TMB—110 miles with 32,000 feet of climbing in 12 days.

I am proudest of the fact that on one section of the TMB where you have a 2,000-foot elevation gain in 1.1 miles, I did not sit on the side of the trail and cry—but I cried as I kept hiking.

This trip was also where I had my most frightening hiking experience. We knew the highest pass, the Col de Bon Homme, was covered in snow. We were told by a local at the start that we would not need crampons, so we did not take them with us. The snow was very deep and starting to melt in the heatwave that was hitting Europe at that time—we slipped or postholed (sank) with every footfall.

At the top of the pass was a snow balcony that meant that a slip might end up with a fall of several hundred feet. The downslope was to my right, which meant I needed to use my left pole to secure myself—this required using the hand that I had recently broken, which was still weak. By the time we crossed the balcony, I was sweating profusely from both fear and straining.

I first hiked the Camino in 2008 when I was 55. I had realized I wanted to do something I had never done before to see what I could do both physically and mentally. Some friends had hiked it, and I had heard about it and decided that was the challenge I was looking for.

This was before the Martin Sheen movie about walking the Camino, *The Way*, opened in the United States. The walk was not as popular or well-known to Americans as it is today. For example, there were 278,490 pilgrims on the Camino in 2017 but fewer than 70,000 (according to what I learned in the pilgrim office in St Jean Pied de Port) when I hiked it.

I hiked it in April at the beginning of the season, and let me tell you, the rain in Spain does not stay mainly on the plain. It rained pretty much everywhere. During the 34-day hike, I had about 27 days of rain/snow. Because there were far fewer Americans on the trail there was a very international feel to it. When I hiked it, Americans ranked 11th or 12th among all the nationalities. Now we are third on the list of those coming from outside of the country. [Note: 347,578 people received their Compostela in Santiago in 2019.]

## There definitely have been challenges

I hike at two miles an hour! I am pretty much the slowest person on the trail. This is in part due to an old injury (broken pelvis when I was 24) that did not heal properly so my left leg does not work well. Sometimes it completely gives out—which impacts my balance as well. That being said, my slow pace allows me to really take it all in.

## Hiking changes

We actually hike more now (at 67 and 76, respectively) as we realize we have few years left to hike. Our hardest hike, the TMB, though not the longest, was the most recent—2019. I think with age, we realize we can do it and also have to do it—and just go for it. But yes, changes are definitely on the horizon.

Hiking plays a huge role in our life. When we retired, we moved to the San Juan Island specifically for the outdoor lifestyle—the hiking/kayaking/cycling opportunities the islands provide. Our vacations, long-distance hiking, cycling and/or snorkeling/diving, are active as we don't know how long we will be able to remain active.

## People face challenges in different ways

I love long-distance hiking, but I don't want people to think that I am strong or fast or without fear. I whine. I cry. Midway through the Coast to Coast (C to C) across England, I started the morning with "Let the Whining Begin." At the end of one day, I sat in the foyer of our Bed and Breakfast and wept because I was so exhausted. I threatened to not go on the next day. But after a good night's sleep and a hearty English breakfast—go on we did!

It's usually Bob who is a great motivator yet very patient. He is fast, and if I am not fast enough, he will walk ahead at his own pace and then wait for me to catch up. Some days, I will start before him so he does not have to walk as slowly. I find though, when I am walking alone I self-motivate, which is a plus. I am able to keep my morale up because I have no one to whine to and no one to blame but myself. So hiking solo is really rewarding.

Once in a snowstorm on Scotland's Pennine Way when we were walking into a north headwind sweeping across the moors (think no windbreaks, no shelter), I turned to my husband and told him that I wished he were dead. Not my finest moment.

I stormed ahead after he pointed out that turning around would have been a farther distance (but at least with the wind/snow at our backs). I did not speak to him until we got to our village—which was in the bright sun, of course. That was the last day of the hike portion—two days from the end of the Pennine Way.

We had made it across the border, but the last two days were at elevation on a high mountain with no shelter. It was early spring and the snow was deep. To get to a bed after day one, we'd have had to hike down the mountain to a road, arrange a taxi to pick us up, take us to a village, and in the morning, repeat the process except we'd have had to hike back up the mountain. Instead, we had a lovely time touring Sir Walter Scott's home. I was happy.

## What to do when you run out of steam

When I am tired or exhausted from the hike, it is usually because I am bonking. Both Bob and I know I need fuel. I really have to learn to eat earlier and more often. I am not strong or particularly fit, but for me, the challenge of hiking is mostly the mental aspect. My motto is: Worry early, worry often. I worry about whether is it going to be too hot or too cold. Also, where is the next source of water? Where is the next place to get food? Will I get lost? Will I make it to our destination? Yet I do it and love it (at least when the day is done and I have a beer in my hand).

Besides the mental condition of worrying over everything, my challenge continues to be my left leg. After finishing the challenging Tour du Mont Blanc, I fell walking down the small path to the beach at our house—the difference was I used my hiking poles while in the mountains.

## The appeal of hiking solo

I love hiking solo. I love being alone. I loved the Camino because it is unique in terms of a long-distance hike with the atmosphere of a collective pilgrimage. Later, Bob and I hiked the [LePuy] Chemin across France, and while it is the same distance, it felt more like a hike. It's almost an intangible feeling with the Camino. While I hiked the Camino, I was very clear that I would meet up with people in the albergues [hostels for hikers] for dinner, but I wanted to hike alone.

## For those new to hiking

I think there is a difference between walking and hiking. I view the Camino more as a walk than a hike—perhaps this is simply because, to me, a walk is flatter and a hike has more elevation gain and perhaps some technical ladders, bridges, stream crossings, and/or navigational challenges.

Just do it. Go with an organized group like REI. Join your local Sierra Club or hiking club and practice at home first. But hike/walk regularly and not just on weekends if you are attempting to hike. The only way to train for the Camino is to hike every day so your body gets used to the daily physical exertion and you don't have to worry about blisters.

Those who are unsure of their physical abilities should keep in mind that unless you are in a race, there is no prize for getting in early. Take your time. Rest.

### Looking forward to this next hike

I am looking forward to re-hiking the Tour du Mont Blanc and the Coast 2 Coast when things open up. As I have mentioned frequently, I worry about everything, so I have wanted to re-hike a hike I have done previously with the idea that I can relax and enjoy it as I know the terrain and I know I can make it to the end.

### Hiking gear matters

I consider my hiking gear as key to my success. I am obsessive about what I pack for a trip and pretty much take the same thing for every hike as we have been doing it long enough that I know what works.

My Icebreaker long-sleeved quarter-zip black sweater would be #1. I thought I was allergic to wool (even to the point of going to the doctor after being forced to wear formal wool uniform pants in the NPS). Twenty years ago, I was very cold and wet in a hut in New Zealand in the Whirinaki rainforest (we had waded through the Whirinaki River 86 times that day) and was cold in my polar fleece top and could not get warm. Some lovely Dutch man insisted I wear his Icebreaker sweater; I was hooked. I can wear Merino (only on my upper body) and it stays dry; you can wear it forever without washing it because it doesn't smell, and it's warm.

I believe in layering. My base layer is an Icebreaker short-sleeved t-shirt. For warmth, I wear the Icebreaker long-sleeved zip under an Icebreaker 320 sweater, a North Face down vest (I don't wear down jackets as I like the mobility of a vest for using my hiking poles and my arms don't get cold), and a lightweight Arc-teryx rain/wind shell.

I am also a big fan of Fjallraven capris for hiking in pretty much any weather. I take Sealskinz waterproof gloves for really cold-weather trekking. I have a new Sealskinz hat with earflaps for cold/snowy weather and a baseball cap for sunny days or rainy days as I wear glasses and it's better at rain protection than a soft, floppy, wide-brimmed sunhat.

After listening to a talk by Heather 'Anish' Anderson, I started wearing hiking skirts. As I age, I go to the bathroom more frequently (another motto is: 'The World in My Toilet'—but meant in a nice way). With the skirt, all I have to do is squat and pull my underwear to the side, and I can pee very, very quickly. I also carry a dog poop bag or two for used TP.

I have a pair of Mountain Hardware lightweight, winter long-underwear bottoms and a really good pair of Patagonia's breathable, lightweight Gore-Tex rain pants. A new item is a Buff to wear around my neck. It keeps my head/neck warm when it's cold, can be pressed into service as a handkerchief, and as a mask to help prevent COVID-19.

I also take Zensah compression sleeves; I have a hot-pink pair and a hot-turquoise pair. Again, it's an age thing, but my young doctor in Seattle recommended these over the tan hospital ones. I have rheumatoid arthritis in my left leg (the multi-broken leg I mentioned earlier), and the sleeves keep my ankle from swelling. They work as well as the compression socks, which I can't wear because they squish my toes together. I wear a pair of Injinji Toesocks paired with Smartwool socks to prevent blisters. Finally, I wear LaSportiva Ultra Raptor trail-running shoes or hiking boots.

To me, your clothes are not something ever to be skimped on. We typically hike during spring, fall, or slightly off-season, so the weather tends to be colder, rainier, or snowier than in the summer. What you wear is critical to your enjoyment and in some cases your survival.

### And other gear

Carabiners, tiny to big: The small ones hang off the chest strap of my daypack, and I attach my camera to them. Zip or cable ties are nice to use on my backpack when checking it into checked luggage on a plane. Lots of Ziplocks.

I also use a tiny waterproof pouch with a neck lanyard (the one I have is for kayaking). It's about 5x7 inches. I tear out the pages I need for a hike every day from my guidebook and stick them in the pouch to be referred to when trail markings (signs, cairns) and GPS fail.

Also: Light-weight Leki trekking poles, water bladders like Camelbaks for hydration, a trash bag to line my backpack when my pack liner fails in heavy rain (and it will), a good Petzl headlamp.

I also carry one or two metal Hydro Flask water bottles. Hiking in England in April was typically cold/wet/snowy. I filled the bottle with hot tea in the morning and it helped keep the chill off. In France, I filled it with cold water, and it helped cool us down. I also would grab handfuls of snow from the snowbanks along the trail and place them under my baseball cap and let them slowly melt—it was that hot. By using the Hydro Flasks for my rehydration/electrolyte solution I make with Nuun tablets, I keep my Camelback cleaner.

If I am hiking by myself, I take an old iPod Nano to listen to at night to lull me to sleep. For supported, multi-day treks, packing cubes are indispensable (whoever invented them should win a Nobel Prize).

## Importance of planning

We've been fortunate to not have had horrific, frightening, or unexpected experiences but have had enough small negative experiences to learn that preparation is key. As Roald Amundsen said, "Adventure is just bad planning." We have run out of food (en route to Pamplona), run out of water (TMB), not had enough warm clothing (Pennine Way), and been caught in a few rain/wind storms where my rain jacket failed and rain poured inside (C2C). We learned to carry extra energy/electrolytes: Shot Bloks (for glucose), Nuun tablets (electrolytes), and more water than we think we might need.

## When traveling goes on hold due to COVID-19

[April 2020, NW Washington] I am actually quite busy. So, in addition to the hiking five days a week (and I am hoping to add distance/elevation to that every week), I am sewing a Christmas stocking for a relative, making a photo album for my sister about her hike around Mt. Blanc last August, reading, doing school projects with the kids, volunteering as a monitor of bluebird nests in the neighborhood (we have a reintroduction program here on the island), and lots of Zoom cocktail parties and game nights (we love games!) with friends and family.

*My husband and I were talking about how there is a quality to this time that is similar to long-distance hiking—our days are reduced in terms of needs and what we do. It's actually quite nice. I'm not explaining it very well, but it's the same feeling that comes from the almost monastic aspects of long-distance hiking: You wake up, eat, walk, eat, go to bed. Repeat.*

[Summer 2020] We just canceled our trip around Mont Blanc for August of this year. While the trail and refugios are opening up, my doctor did not think it was a good idea to fly in the foreseeable future (especially long-haul, overnight flights in coach). Sadly, both age and medical conditions are a factor here.

To quote Dickens: "It was the best of times. It was the worst of times." On one hand, we live in a beautiful place—arguably one of the most beautiful in the world. And we live a half-mile away from a National Park Service unit with miles of hiking trails replete with coastal paths, classic Pacific Northwest evergreen forests, and the rare grassland prairie. The island has other swaths of protected land to provide a variety of hiking/scenery opportunities to prevent boredom.

Continuing on the good news side of the story, I am finally seeing improvements from the fall I took last July. My leg is better; I can walk more than a mile and do Pilates. I can't imagine how this period would have been had I not been able to exercise. I won our island's recreation district's walking challenge in July. I had 205 miles—40 more than the second place finisher.

Coming under the heading of the 'worst of times' is that the islands are smack-dab in the middle of what we affectionately call

'Junuary.' My hiking attire for mid-June has included a sweater, vest, rain/wind jacket, and yes, a stocking hat and gloves. Brrr.

Secondly, 'quarantine fatigue' is real and settling in—that and a genetic disposition to want to travel. I told Bob to basically not expect to see me in 2021. I am hoping to take trips that were canceled this year including Lebanon, Syria, Iraq, Afghanistan, Pakistan, Ethiopia, the Sudan, Eritrea, Djibouti, and Egypt. We plan to re-hike the Coast 2 Coast in England next April/May and the Mont Blanc circuit next July.

Supplies can be hard to come by on an island; the toilet paper scare was real. I had some Bay Area friends send me some imports from China. And I had to start getting my Peet's coffee through mail order. Fortunately, I did not start baking, so the shortages of flour, yeast, and sugar did not affect me. I write this knowing that we are lucky and blessed to live where we do with a stable economic foundation. There are others in the U.S. and worldwide for whom the pandemic and economic uncertainly are life-threatening problems.

**Susan:** Whether Judy is traveling to far-flung places or exploring the trails near home, her wide variety of interests and her ability to handle challenges serve her well.

**Judy Chovan — Pennine Way, UK**

# Emilie 'Dirty Emilie' Cortes

**Susan:** Emilie Cortes ran Call of the Wild Adventures for Women for several years. The company pioneered women's adventure travel in 1978, and I looked longingly at their trips for years. As you read Emilie's story, you'll get a sense of the range of their adventures—from cushier trips with comfy beds, hammocks, and whirlpools in Nha Trang, Vietnam to challenging backpacking trips to Annapurna in Nepal.

**Emilie Cortes:** I did not start hiking until I was 22. My little sister gave me a membership to the Sierra Club as a gift. I was a gym bunny and thought I was in pretty good shape. However, I started doing the weekly hikes and I got dropped by the female leader, who was over 70 years old. It was not cool to be left behind, but I was super-inspired by her speed and endurance, and I vowed to be like her someday.

I started seriously hiking when I was 29. I graduated from business school at Berkeley, and one of my girlfriends asked me to hike Half Dome in Yosemite National Park with her. It seemed quite daunting—17 miles and 4,800 feet of elevation gain. We actually trained for the hike. We researched all the tips from hiker forums: use trekking poles, bring your own gloves for the cables section, bring a water filtration system because you will certainly run out of water.

**Hikes have taken me...**
My introduction to hiking was primarily in California—the hills of both Southern and Northern California graduating to the mountains of Yosemite and the Sierra Nevada mountain range.

As my confidence grew, I spread my wings internationally. I have hiked on six of the seven continents ranging from luxurious trips in the Italian Cinque Terre to the super-rugged Makalu Barun trek into the Makalu Base Camp at 18,300 feet (followed by a failed attempt to climb the mountain, which is near Everest) to the Ugandan Rwenzori's trek to the glaciers that feed the source of the Nile.

I now make my home in Bend, Oregon, and benefit from the incredibly diverse geology here. I can do long, flat desert hikes one day and switch to steep hikes to the top of the Cascades volcanoes the next. When the pandemic hit in early 2020 and more popular trails were closed, I was forced to expand my horizons a bit farther from Bend, and as a result, my appreciation for the beauty and diversity of my region continued to grow.

### The importance of hiking

Where to start? Hiking and backpacking have so many aesthetic qualities—feasting on the beauty of mountains, forests, wildflowers; sensory delights like the warmth of the sun, tickles of breezes, and the refreshment of taking a dip in an alpine lake. This is what clears my mind.

Mixed in with that deliciousness is the challenge aspect—experiencing physical challenge seems to clear out the physical body, leaving me reenergized and decompressed to deal with my daily life. I'm quite short (5-foot-1) and not naturally athletic. It took a lot of training and learning how to be more efficient so that I literally don't get left behind when hiking with my long-legged friends. Mentally, I didn't really believe I belonged in the mountains until I got stronger and stronger, and then others began to look up to me for guidance.

Hiking is a critical part of my life. It is how I get my exercise, experience moving meditation that clears my mind, commune with nature, and really get to know people when I hike in a group.

I feel the difference when I am not hiking regularly—I have less energy and feel more stressed. I would say mountaineering is really my obsession, but it is hiking that I do consistently and keeps me in physical, mental, and spiritual shape.

## Meaningful accomplishments

At the ripening age of 46, I don't yet feel like my age is inhibiting my hiking options. When I was running Call of the Wild Adventures in my late 30s/early 40s, I would marvel at the strength and endurance of women nearly twice my age. Many had dedicated their lives to raising children, whether as stay-at-home moms or working in traditional fields of the time in nursing, education, or administration. Many started their outdoor adventures later in life, like at my age! Over and over again, I asked them what their secret was. Every single time, the answer was exactly the same: "Never stop."

There are many trips that I would consider great accomplishments—it's like picking between favorite children! However, just last year at 45, I joined an organized tour with Three Peaks Africa. My friend and travel industry colleague, Marie Cheng, was running a scouting trip to bag the three high peaks of Morocco.

I am always inspired by remote adventures in developing countries, and trekking for 10 days is a fantastic way to clear the mind! I had experienced acute stress in the year prior and put on some weight. I was not feeling particularly fit, and this trip was full of 20- and 30-year-olds. My girlfriend, Shonna, who was 52 at the time, joined us. The group called us "the elders," and we started calling them "the kids." Shonna and I struggled to keep up and decided to keep our own pace, a critical skill at altitude. We often rolled into camp feeling less tired with more spare energy than the "kids." I was able to bag two of the high peaks—Toubkal and M'Goun—the first and third highest in the country even though I was undertrained and an elder. I carry that sense of accomplishment through today.

## Thoughts about soloing

I love hiking solo, as well as backpacking and peak bagging. I feel I had the most personal growth when I was on the trail alone. Experiencing doubts and fears, and working through them, is incredibly powerful. I have often had people express surprise when I am on the trail. "Where is the rest of your group?" is what they most often say. I just smile and respond, "I am alone," and let my response hang in silence. I think the way that I deliver that answer tells them any follow-up questions are inappropriate.

## Being successful at long-distance hiking requires...

Body awareness, full stop. Being really in touch with your body is so critical. Noticing that little hot spot and catching it before it becomes a blister helps you keep going. Managing your thirst and hunger keeps you from 'bonking'—when your blood sugar drops and you feel like you simply cannot go on. Staying aware of your pace and heart rate so that you don't overextend early on. Knowing your body's tolerance for heat or cold helps you know your strengths and weaknesses, and when and how hard to hike so that your body does not get overtaxed.

Finally, being aware of what is going on in your mind is key. Are you ruminating on how much this section sucks, and you want to get into camp to eat? Or are you super-present and letting yourself feast on beautiful sights and sounds? To me, hiking is moving meditation—being in a physical rhythm helps me check out from an overly active mind.

## Your head and body beg you to stop—what to do?

It depends! If I need to get to my car with cold drinks waiting for me inside, that is much easier as there is a real end in sight. On longer treks, I need to play mind games with myself. I will repeat a Buddhist mantra or count to 1,000. I also set a goal in the distance and only focus on getting to that goal. Once there, I reset the next goal and only focus on that, keeping the ultimate destination out of my mind until it is in view.

## Scary things happen, leading to challenges...and learning

I have been caught out unexpectedly overnight twice after climbing a mountain. In each case, we were hiking off the descent and night fell, impeding our ability to navigate safely in the dark. Both times, we were unprepared for the night out—no tent, sleeping bag, cookware, etc. We found soft areas to lie on (rocks are cold and sap your body heat), spooned for maximum warmth, and shivered most of the night. It was terribly uncomfortable, but I learned the limits of what my body can handle. I would not recommend the experience to anyone, but getting through those two nights greatly increased my confidence and my body awareness.

## Words of wisdom

Going on guided hikes or trips is a great way to learn from experts and create your own community. Exploring in your own backyard is also great—expanding a little farther, a little longer, a little higher as your comfort level increases. Take a few basic courses on navigation and basic survival, and that will take you very far.

I have some favorite gear. Overall, I love the Arc-teryx brand—expensive but incredibly durable. However, I've recently fallen in love with their Taema skort. I have big muscular legs and normally don't even like shorts—they ride up and my thighs chafe. The Taema skort does not ride up, it has a better range of motion than shorts, and most importantly, it's cute!

## Women can underestimate their physical abilities

Absolutely, many women underestimate their abilities or they don't appreciate the different abilities they have. It is not always essential to be the strongest and fastest. I can't tell you how many times I have felt bad about being at the back of the pack with a group of men at altitude. However, when I roll into camp, they have terrible headaches and feel lethargic. I feel great, making me realize that one of my superpowers is the ability to pace appropriately at altitude. Your physical ability may be different than mine, but I guarantee you have one!

## The bad advice

Nearly all of the bad advice I've gotten was from men who convinced me to push past my limits even for a short time. "Can you wait another hour to stop for lunch?" "Can you just get to the top of this hill before dealing with that blister?" There is often a tension between making good time and taking good care of yourself. However, over and over again, I've learned that maintaining a reasonable pace (for yourself) and efficiently managing your self-care are critical for maintaining a solid pace overall.

It can be tempting to ignore your body's needs—failing to re- or de-layer to regulate your body temperature, ignoring your thirst or hunger, not stopping to treat that hot spot right away because you feel you would be a burden to your group.

However, ignoring those needs can actually cause you to become a burden to the group when you get overheated and de-hydrated, or develop hypothermia, or get a blister that cannot be treated in the field, or 'bonk' from low blood sugar. Not to mention that any of those things can put a serious damper on your fun quotient!

### Big plans ahead

As I have aged, I have become more adventurous as my confidence has increased. I enjoy doing things solo more, and I have become a lot more comfortable with exposure.

I am feeling the burden of the heavy pack starting to hurt my body more than in my 30s and early 40s, but I don't expect this to radically change my ability to spend my days on the trail.

I continue to enjoy trekking in remote areas of the world. I have two big trips planned. The first is to hike the Simien Highlands—a 10-day trek to Ethiopia's equivalent of the Grand Canyon and to do an easy scramble to its high peak, Ras Dashen at 14,900 feet.

Even as adventurous as I am, I do appreciate when someone else does the logistical planning for me and I get to relax a bit and meet some new fellow travelers. At this time, COVID travel restrictions are putting that trip on hold, but it will remain a high-priority goal for me.

Instead, I'm now planning a solo five- or six-day backpacking trip in Oregon's Wallowa mountain range, also referred to as the 'Alps of Oregon' and a rare instance of granite in the state. There are numerous peaks at around 9,000 feet with spectacular views.

I've been day hiking a lot for the last year, but I'm missing the peace that comes from settling into a campsite in the afternoon and relaxing in silence until the evening.

**Susan:** Moving from the SF Bay Area to Bend, Oregon, started a new chapter in Emilie's life. It's clear that she has embraced her new playground—the high desert of Central Oregon—that offers her everything from river rafting to mountain climbing, to caving in lava tubes.

When Emilie was operating the all-women's group, Call of the Wild, she wrote the following:

## Success in one area of your life leads to success in other areas.
~ Emilie Cortes

I'm a firm believer that success in the outdoors translates directly into success back home and at the office. In all cases, you tap into confidence, skills, communication, learning how to ask for help, contributing to a team, and finding power in your own mind and body.

So when I saw a good friend of mine, Gregg Swanson, the Warrior Mind Coach, write about seven enemies of success in his e-newsletter, I thought they were totally relevant to what we did on Call of the Wild trips. Gregg specializes in developing mental strength to help you achieve your dreams and objectives, and his blog is great if you want to check it out.

Here's my interpretation of his "Seven Enemies of Success" in terms of wilderness adventure:

**Ungratefulness:** Gratitude brings a mindset of success—it's the antithesis of negativity and cynicism. When I go on my own adventures, I'm immensely grateful for the perspective it brings me. Seeing how others live and often struggle in the rest of the world makes me grateful for my comfortable life. I feel grateful for the privilege to be able to walk, interact with others from around the world, and open my mind to endless possibilities. What are you grateful for?

**Apathy:** A lack of enthusiasm is the path to mediocrity. I rarely saw signs of apathy in Call of the Wilders though—it would be tough to be apathetic *and* have the initiative to register and prepare for an adventure. But be mindful of other areas of your life where apathy might encroach.

**Victimhood:** The belief that the world is acting upon you and you are powerless is a great enemy of success. It's also one of the biggest lessons we learned and reinforced on our trips. With all female participants and all female guides, we instantly became a team and a community. We learned that we cannot control the weather, injuries, even government intervention, and we figured out how to make a trip a success regardless of the obstacles that the natural (or civilized) world may present. Sometimes, the biggest obstacles can become the most cherished stories!

**Learned Helplessness:** Belief that you can't do something or learn to do it will "repel success away from you" in Gregg's words. Indeed! I have a friend who climbed Everest a couple of years ago despite missing most of his arm, and I met a gal in Bend who completed the Iditarod despite being legally blind. The experience does not have to be extreme, however. For many women, camping for the first time in their adult life is extremely empowering. I remember getting stranded in my car during a snowstorm and not being scared because I had learned how to snow-camp.

**No Vision:** You need vision, drive, and motivation to be successful. I have always been inspired by big goals. I could never get my booty out of bed to work out in order to look good in a bikini, but with a challenging goal like backpacking Mt. Whitney, I was motivated. I love the phrase 'ambitious realism' —set some goals that are ambitious but realistic for where you are now in terms of your experience, fitness, and comfort. What is your vision??

**Fear of Being Judged:** I think this is one of the biggest ways we women hold ourselves back. We are so afraid of failure and judgment, and often will not even try something new as a result. What was so great about Call of the Wild, and why I chose to focus my life on women only, is that much of this fear is reduced when you are in the company of women. Most participants worried about holding the group back, but when they realized that all of them were worried about the same things, they eventually just had to let go of their fears.

**Lack of Discipline:** Gregg likes to say: "To have what you want tomorrow, you have to forgo what it is you want today." All of our trips were active and ranged in difficulty, but all required that participants were regular hikers as a minimum and some required training for four to six months to be properly prepared. It's no good to sign up for a dream trip and then fail to do the preparation needed to be successful. Discipline will help ensure that your hard work maximizes your chances of being successful.

This is just some food for thought about how the "Seven Enemies of Success" might be holding you back, and how you can find your path to personal success!

**Emile Cortes — Summit of Acatenango, Guatemala**

# Lynne 'Sparkly Mañana' Davidson

**Susan:** Lynne is an excellent example of how one can evolve into a smart, brave world traveler and hiker one step at a time. Her hikes and other travel adventures have taken her to such far-flung countries as Nepal (where she volunteered at a children's school and camp as well as trekked), Georgia, Romania, and the Czech Republic.

**Lynne Davidson:** I did a few small hikes in my 20s, but I don't recall feeling very enthusiastic about them. Following a divorce in my 40s, I moved with my six children to the Pacific Northwest, where hiking opportunities abounded. Friends and relatives would invite me to join them on a day hike, and I'd bribe my younger kids to tag along, too, so I wouldn't have to beg a reluctant older sib to babysit them.

Later, as I grew to learn the trail system in the Columbia River Gorge, I would venture out with just my kids, minus the friend/relative. Whenever none of my kids could be bribed to join me, I went alone, with some amount of fear and uncertainty... and I typically returned with some tale of getting lost or injured on the trail. In fact, it became such a running joke at my workplace that colleagues would gather around my desk on Monday morning to hear the latest episode of 'Lynne Gets Lost in the Wilds.' It was all great fun, and I even adopted that moniker (lostinthewilds) as my Instagram name.

### Becoming a smarter and braver hiker

Eventually, becoming lost and fearful on the trail stopped being funny to me. I decided I wanted to become a smarter, braver hiker. I enrolled in a map/compass class at REI and later in an outdoor survival class. My daypack became permanently filled with the "Ten Hiking Essentials," in addition to three ways to start a fire [see Resources], I carried an emergency shelter, extra food, and spare socks, mittens, and hat.

Once in a while, I would join a group of other backpackers and spend a few days together on a trail, but usually it felt more enjoyable to me when I was planning the trek than when I actually executed it.

When I was 56, I finally won a slot in the Mt. Rainier permit system to backpack the 100-mile Wonderland Trail. I had been applying to hike this circuitous loop around Mt. Rainier for seven years, so I was ecstatic to finally win a coveted spot that summer. I invited two friends to join me, who both subsequently canceled at the last minute. My relatives and friends warned me against embarking solo on this trip, with my mother even chastising me: "Why must you be so stubborn? Just wait and go with friends another year!"

And yet, there was something about the yearning to test my mettle, to see if I really could do a solo backpacking trip. And I did! It was a memorable experience in so many ways—including the fact that my son accidentally dropped off my resupply food at the wrong ranger station. Because I had run out of food, I ended up pushing myself to finish the loop two days earlier than originally planned.

I grabbed some snacks from a 'hungry hiker' box [a box where hikers leave excess food and camping supplies for others] outside a ranger station on the route and condensed my eight-day hike into six, rationing the final calories.

That experience taught me so much about myself—mostly that I'm stronger and more capable than I ever knew! I'd previously often hiked with males and deferred to them for decision-making on the trip, guidance on where to ford streams, scheduling the day, etc. On the Wonderland Trail, I discovered that not only was I capable of making all those decisions myself, but I found an immense source of empowerment in doing so.

### Life changes

The Wonderland Trail was just the beginning for me. The following year, my employer was dealing with budget woes, and I was offered an incentive package to voluntarily resign. I was given five-months' salary as my severance pay. I could have been sensible, socked that money away, and immediately embarked on a new career. But I didn't.

Instead, I opted to hike some 1,200 miles of the PCT over three months. Because I had never done a thru-hike at all—much less by myself—I decided to begin with my home state of Oregon, where I felt safer knowing I could always bail if necessary.

At the beginning of June, I hopped a bus to southern Oregon and began walking north—460 miles home to Hood River. At first, I was nervous to be alone at night and sought to camp alongside other hikers whenever possible. But, gradually, I pushed myself to try camping alone and slowly grew more comfortable setting up camp away from other humans.

### On solo hiking

Now, my preference is to hike solo as I crave the solitude and peace that come from backpacking on my own. There is something indescribable about falling asleep to the rustling sounds of woodland creatures settling in for the night and nocturnal animals beginning their rounds. Some of my favorite moments on a trail have been the nights I was awakened by owls hooting above my tent, or listening to a glacier calve nearby, or the lonesome howl of a coyote in the distance. It's a magical experience for me, and instead of feeling sated at the end of each journey into the wilderness, I find myself aching for the next adventure. One of the ways I get through the necessity of earning a living at home is by beginning a plan for my next trail, my next adventure.

### Adapting to change

One of the things that has changed for me in recent years is a diagnosis of Raynaud's Syndrome, which has made me absolutely miserable (and physically sick to my stomach) when my extremities become cold. Even when backpacking through a desert landscape one spring break, the overnight lows were such that my fingers became frozen when I had to break camp the following morning. Unable to warm myself because I'd already packed up all my gear, the blood rushed from my head trying to warm my fingers/toes, causing me to feel vertigo. I had to lay down on the cold ground, shivering, to prevent myself from passing out while fighting feelings of nausea.

So, now I know that I can only backpack contentedly on trails where overnight lows don't dip below 40 degrees. (I can manage daytime hikes, snowshoeing, and cross-country skiing in below-freezing temps because I'm constantly moving and will eventually be back to a warm vehicle, a heated home, and a hot bath. Not so when out backpacking.)

I'm 62 now. I noticed after I turned 60 that my gait has slowed down a bit. If I am hiking with a companion, I notice that I have to push myself to walk faster in order to keep up, which really is not enjoyable for me. So, again, I feel drawn to solo hiking. Less experienced hikers want to take more frequent breaks or have less endurance than I do. Competent hikers might walk faster than I do. So, solo hiking again proves most enjoyable for me.

That said, when on a solo venture, I am notorious for stopping to talk to every single hiker who passes by. I'm an introvert, so this is curious behavior to those who know me! For some reason, I am eager to get to chat with every hiker I encounter, and whether it's a three-word exchange or a 30-minute conversation, I feel drawn to greet each one.

Hiking feeds my soul in a way nothing else quite can. There is something about becoming immersed in nature that simultaneously calms and elates me. Sometimes, a beautiful sunset or a mountain view will bring tears to my eyes, and my heart soars with gladness for the special moment.

I'm often asked whether I'm afraid to be alone in the wilderness, especially with bears. I inwardly roll my eyes as I explain that I'm so comfortable in nature, and the many times I've been fortunate to see a bear, I stop in awe and feel gratitude for that experience. I'm respectful of wildlife and try to be quiet so I don't startle an animal that may burn needed calories by running from me, the perceived threat. I go gently down the trail, stop when wildlife is spotted, speak or sing soft words of reassurance, and allow the animal to choose its own path of retreat before I move forward.

Because I love travel almost as much as I love backpacking, I save up my air miles and choose destinations where I can be exposed to new cultures, new languages, and new foods while spending time on a trail far from home.

### Learning about herself

One thing I've learned about myself on a thru-hike is that one month is about my limit. After a month of hiking, I start to miss my family, my friends, my home. So, I've begun planning my summer treks accordingly so that I might be away backpacking for a month, then home catching up with family and friends for a week, then off again for another month.

While I'm not fearful of bears, I am afraid of deep-water crossings, and I have a fear of heights so that walking a narrow ridge will cause my legs to tremble. At these times of fear, I acknowledge that my only choice is to quit and turn back, or to push forward. I hate the thought of being a quitter, so I tell myself that I can do this. I literally tell myself "You can do this, Lynne!" and I made up a melody that I sing to myself when I'm faced with a place on the trail that frightens me. I borrowed some of these words from a poster hanging in a classroom where I work: "I am stronger than I think; I am braver than I know. I can do this, yes I can." I sing that verse over and over to myself as I ford a turbulent creek or teeter atop a narrow precipice.

### Others can do this

I have women come up to me all the time, wanting advice and encouragement on how to get out on a trail. They are fearful of the unknown and lack the confidence in their abilities. I would love to see more women discover their inner tenacity in overcoming these fears that prevent them from strapping on a backpack and just going.

**It's a passion**
Today, hiking could accurately be described as my life passion. I switched jobs about four years ago and went from a more lucrative office management position to working as an instructional aide in the public schools. Not only did this career change bring about greater job satisfaction in knowing I'm making a difference in students' lives, but I now have longer holiday breaks and a 2.5-month summer vacation in which to plan travel and backpacking trips.

I find that getting on a trail at some point every weekend is absolutely necessary throughout the school year. Being surrounded by nature, soaking up the solitude, watching the seasons change on my favorite trails...this is what sustains me while my backpacking gear awaits summer break.

**And how we cope:**
[NE Oregon, May 2020] I've been doing a lot of biking these days, too, and am fortunate to have some lovely views of pear orchards and mountain views and farms. Otherwise, taking daily walks in the neighborhood with a friend has become a key part of my coping strategy. It's as important for me to get out into my neighborhood as it is for me to have face time (in person) with a friend (always from a safe distance).

**Susan:** After Lynne completed the Pacific Crest Trail through Oregon, she continued to hike sections of the PCT and more remote trails in Washington. One of her hikes, with the goal of following the Boundary Trail in the Pasayten Wilderness to the Canadian border, involved starting out for a climb over the West Fork Pass. It didn't go well...

"[I] started off counting the blowdowns, but three hours into my trek, I was at 482 blowdowns encountered and found it too depressing to continue counting. Instead, I started counting the number of steps I could take before hitting my next blowdown (62 was the max!). I'd guesstimate there were easily some 1,000 fallen trees that I had to contend with on that trail..." Read more of her adventures on her blog: lostinthewilds.blogspot.com.

Most of Lynne's hiking trips have not been as grueling. Her article below was first published in the *Hood River News*, December 4, 2019, and is used here with her permission.

## Hiking the other Georgia: Gracious people, living traditions, gorgeous vistas
~ Lynne Davidson

As an avid hiker, I recognize that there are beautiful trails throughout the U.S. But because I am also an ardent traveler, I love to explore distant lands, experience different cultures, try unique foods, and challenge my brain to learn a new monetary system and some rudimentary words in a foreign language. Whenever possible, then, I strive to combine my passion for hiking with this yearning for travel.

I'm often asked how I'm able to travel on a frugal budget. The answer: *free miles!* I find them (via special offers on credit cards), I accumulate them, I use them. Traveling within my meager means often translates into less appealing redeye flights with long layovers in airports. But I'm so excited for each new adventure that I have taught myself to sleep on planes, trains, and airport floors.

Last winter, I started researching new backpacking destinations and plugged various countries into the Skyscanner search engine in order to receive weekly fare alerts. Many months passed before a flight popped up that fit within my free-miles budget. And that is how I found myself on a plane to Tbilisi, Georgia, in June [2019].

I did some online research of Georgia in addition to borrowing *Lonely Planet* travel guides from the library, so I knew that I wanted to end up along the border of Russia and backpack the upper Caucasus Mountains between the Caspian and Black Seas.

Because I'm not a fan of big cities, I was ready to escape Tbilisi after the first days spent exploring some historical sites. English is not widely spoken in Georgia, but with the use of my handy Google Translate app, along with some amusing pantomiming and hand gestures, I was able to procure a ticket on the night train headed north (sharing a mixed-gender sleeping berth of four bunks).

## Inexpensive splendor

Arriving in Mestia, I was blown away by the many stone towers that remain standing throughout the Svaneti region of northern Georgia. Built in the 11th century, these five-story towers were once used as protection against invaders and feuding neighbors. Given that my experience with the Georgian population was one of warmth and welcome, it was puzzling to imagine their past was once riddled with distrust and fear.

In many ways, the views in the Caucasus Mountains paralleled what I'd seen in the Alps—but at a much more affordable rate. My 12-hour train ride to the Caucasus only cost about $7 U.S., my meals were never more than $3-$4 apiece, and guesthouses where I slept when not in my tent ran about $5-$7 a night—and included both dinner and breakfast. (Switzerland cannot begin to compare to these prices!)

Backpacking these mountains at the end of June, I hit the magic window when the snow had melted and the wildflowers were abundant, but the oppressive heat and pesky summer bugs were still at bay.

Bread is a staple throughout Georgia, and as a carb-lover, I was in heaven! Each day, I enjoyed delicious homemade breads filled with cheeses, vegetables, or diced potatoes. (I'm vegetarian, so I avoided the meat options.) There was a bakery in one rural hamlet where I bought a huge slab of Barbari (Persian flatbread), hot from a clay oven, for the equivalent of about 25 cents U.S. Yum!

The trail I backpacked meandered through small villages each day. I didn't need to carry much food as there were daily opportunities to pick up a loaf of freshly-made bread, a variety of cheeses, and fresh fruits. Each night, I found a secluded spot off the trail in which to pitch my tent, enjoying the dehydrated soups I had brought from home, cooked atop my backpacking stove. One of my favorite nights was spent falling asleep to the rumble of a nearby glacier as it heaved and calved under a dazzling starlit night.

I had camped beside this glacier as to cross its frigid river first thing in the morning when it would be less treacherous to ford. At first light then, I packed up my tent, ate some leftover bread with cheese then slipped on my trail runners to cross the thigh-high turbulent water.

The river was biting cold, rendering my feet numb within seconds. After reaching the far bank, I clomped clumsily down the trail, my feet feeling heavy as wooden bricks. When I glanced up, my suffering was quickly alleviated though by a jaw-dropping view of dawn breaking behind the glacier.

Most households in Georgia seemed to contain extended families living under one roof. In the guesthouse where I stayed in Ushguli, I watched the family matriarch arise at 5 a.m. to milk their cow. Her weathered face seemed to hold a thousand stories, and I was sorry that my inability to communicate with her prevented me from hearing any of them.

Despite the language barrier, I was greeted warmly as I passed through each village, with locals calling out and waving me over for a visit. Because backpacking foreigners are still a rarity in Georgia, I was treated as a novelty and often invited to join a family for a cup of chai (tea) on their front porch.

With the pristine beauty found on these hiking trails in the Caucasus, I worry that the tranquility, affordability, and congeniality of this region may soon be replaced with a crowded, expensive, Switzerland-type experience. While journeying to the Caucasus Mountains, I witnessed several primitive roads being bulldozed to enable tourist buses to one day carry visitors to view fragile alpine lakes and glaciers, previously reached only by foot or horseback.

I'm grateful that my available air miles enabled me to have this unique experience in Georgia, to enjoy its intriguing culture, delicious breads, and gracious people—before these traditions and natural beauty succumb to tourism.

**Lynne Davidson — Mt Hood, Oregon**

# Marion 'llamalady' Davison

**Susan:** I first heard of Marion about 15 years or so ago when Ralph and I did a bit of llama-packing with Grace Lohr, the 'Llama Mama' of Bishop, California. While going on three trips with Grace, I learned a great deal about the care given, and affection felt, by llama owners and their pets.

Llamas certainly can reduce the amount of weight their owners have to carry, but their care does require time. Anyone considering obtaining their own llamas, or renting them, should thoroughly research the pros and cons.

**Marion Davison:** My favorite gear item is the llama that carries my stuff for me. We have been llama packers since 1997. For many years prior to that, we were recreational backpackers. We would do trips of a week to ten days, and our packs were heavy. In 1996, when I was 40, we did a backpack trip from Johnsondale, California, to Yosemite. That was 300 miles, 35 days, and included the John Muir Trail. We loved everything about it except carrying those heavy packs!

On that trip, we met a man who was hiking with a donkey, and that started our llama-packing odyssey. By the next summer, we had a string of llamas and we were learning how to do it. We have had a total of 15 llamas since 1997. They live in our backyard so I interact with them at least twice a day. At present we have six llamas—two retired and four active packers. They are lovely pets.

### Where I began
I started hiking and camping in the Girl Scouts at age 10 or

so and took my first backpack trip at age 15. I did my first week-long Sierra Nevada trip that year, and that was the start of my obsession. I found my true home in the Sierras at about 10,000 feet. All year, I follow Sierra social media groups and email lists, watch the mountain webcams to check snow conditions, and read hiker memoirs and blogs. I get my big trip permit on the first day it is available in February. I find my mind straying to the mountains most every day.

Our backpacking is largely confined to California—the local San Bernardino and Angeles Mountains and the Sierra Nevada, generally on the east side of the range. Our favorite area to hike is the Ansel Adams Wilderness. We have made 17 trips to that area. We have also hiked extensively in Yosemite and Sequoia National Parks. We have done a few backpack trips in Utah. When we take road trips around the U.S., we do a lot of day hikes.

I love the *freedom* of backpacking—being able to travel where you wish, camp where you wish, and flex your trip to fit conditions, physical condition, and whims. I also appreciate the minimal cost involved while hiking. As long as I follow the rules, which are minimal, I feel utterly free in the backcountry. I love the isolation and the days upon days that go by that you don't see another person. By contrast, I pretty much hate car camping, where you are stuck in your little dirt cubicle and just have to endure the conditions around you such as smoky fires and sometimes noisy, rude, drunken neighbors.

## Accomplishments

It is not easy to choose the hikes that I consider the biggest accomplishments, but below are some highlights. For this 10-year period, we had a very solid llama team, and we were in optimum health. My husband is 20 years older than me, so consider that he went from age 60 to 70 during this period.

## Age, Days, Distance, Area
40  35  300  JMT plus northbound (backpacking)
43  28  300  Sonora Pass to Cottonwood Pass (llamas)
44  24  230  Sequoia loop, 14 passes

45  24  250  No. JMT loop with cross-country travel
47  25  217  Sequoia loop
48  24  200  PCT between Mammoth and Tahoe
49  21  153  Mammoth loops
50  24  242  Mammoth triple loop

I am proud of the fact that at ages 63 and 83, we are still llama packing every year, although our trips are shorter in duration and distance. The above shows our 'golden age,' if you will. I am most proud of our consistency and longevity.

### On solo hiking

I have never hiked solo, and I consider it to be extremely dangerous. I would never do it, but people have the right to do it. New technology such as the Delorme inReach and SPOT [satellite trackers] mitigate some of the hazards. I just feel bad that so many solo hikers have died. Believe me, I follow the stories. The death of Gerry Largay on the A.T. is a particularly egregious example of an utterly unnecessary death on the trail.

### Words of wisdom

First, you need to have the skills to live outdoors for weeks at a time. For example, knowing about choosing a good campsite, finding water, cooking, and keeping yourself and your gear safe and dry.

There is knowhow involved. You need to be a person who likes planning and organizing because route planning, and food and gear, are paramount to your success.

You also need to be flexible and not hung up on executing the exact plan you created. Once you are in the field, plans are only guidelines.

You have to be content with leaving most of the comforts of civilization out of your life for the duration of the trip.

### A variety of challenges

Hiking is great for my spiritual life; I spend a lot of time in prayer. If I am afraid, I sing praise songs, loudly. The backcountry makes me realize how small I am and how dependent I am on God's love and protection. If the weather is sucky, the llama is sick, you need a rest—pitch your tent and hunker. There is no shame in that.

I incurred a cross-country skiing injury at age 24 and ruptured three ligaments in my left knee requiring surgery. My knee has never been the same and has slowly deteriorated. I have hiked with a knee brace all these years. I have hiked out with injuries on several occasions. The only fix for this condition is knee replacement, but it won't happen until I become unable to walk. I can still hike a 10-mile day at this point.

The worst experiences we have had in the backcountry involved sick or injured llamas or dogs. At that point, I become overwhelmed with the sense of responsibility I have for getting my beloved animal safely back home. All plans go out the window, and all priorities change.

I am a retired elementary school teacher. So I am a stickler for following rules that are imposed by the bureaucratic agency that controls the particular wilderness I want to visit. My husband has a much more casual approach to rules. Our biggest conflicts in the backcountry have been power struggles over the following of rules.

Our family has battled cancer several times, but treatment for the Big C keeps getting better. My husband had surgery and radiation in 1994—and he's still hiking at age 82. I had surgery in 2017—and I'm still doing drug therapy, still hiking at age 63. My brother had proton therapy in 2015 for one cancer, immunotherapy this year for a different cancer, and is still hiking at age 77. My advice to others: "Hang in there, do the most conservative treatment possible, eat well, and keep moving."

### Aging gracefully

As we have both aged, the number of miles we do in a day has become shorter. We now consider a day of five to eight miles to be quite acceptable. In our 'golden age,' we typically hiked 11 to 15 miles a day. After menopause (age 50), I found myself much more susceptible to joint injuries, such as sciatic pain, and

I found myself falling much more often on the trail. I hike with two poles, wear my knee brace, and do regular exercise at home all year to maintain a fitness level that allows me to still enjoy hiking. We have owned inReach for the last 10 years or so for emergencies, but thankfully have not had to use it.

I think that women do underestimate their physical abilities; women are actually well built for endurance activities. Start with neighborhood walks, then day hikes, lengthen them, then overnights starting with short trips that gradually become trips of greater length. Go out with a group. The Sierra Club is great if you have no hiking friends or family.

Break in your body and your gear, and gather experiences that can prepare you for a longer trip. Strength training is also important as I believe it helps you avoid injury.

Be realistic about your current fitness and abilities and knowledge, and don't take on a trip that exceeds them. We aren't out there to be miserable.

### Looking to the future

Every year, we aim to spend 30 days in the Sierras, and every year, something happens that shortens the trip in duration. Our longest recent trip was in 2016—17 days. Some of the challenges that get in the way are smoke from forest fires (I have asthma and can't take a lot of smoke), rookie llamas that aren't up to the trip, high snow years that shorten the season, and injuries and illnesses in the backcountry.

### COVID-19 is a game-changer

[April 2020, S. California] I am going pretty stir crazy here. We really enjoy traveling, and we had four short road trips to distant car shows planned for March, April, and May. All were postponed or canceled. We go out about every 10 days to buy groceries, and that's it. San Bernardino County put heavy closures and strict rules into place on March 13, so there is no place to go.

When we realized we would be homebound for 10 weeks, we decided to throw ourselves into a big project to stay busy. So we are restoring a car that we have had for 30 years—a '76 Mercury station wagon. Because it is a 44-year-old car, absolutely everything has to be cleaned and refurbished and repainted or replaced. Because very few parts are available, we have to get very creative with repairs and refurbishment.

We can walk in the neighborhood, but the trails nearby are all in the national forest and officially closed. There is a PCT trailhead just 10 minutes away. We have several hundred acres of empty desert at the end of our block where we usually walk the llamas.

**Susan:** July 2020 brought Marion the happy news that she and her husband Ray had secured a wilderness permit to take the llamas trekking later that month.

On a less happy note, the death Marion referred to was in July 2013. Gerry 'Inchworm' Largay was backpacking the A.T. and left the trail to relieve herself. She became lost. She was supposed to meet up with her husband a day later. When she did not show up, he reported her missing. Over the next month, Gerry sent many texts asking for help that were never received because of the poor cell coverage. Search and rescue teams were not able to find her in the dense Maine woods. Two years later, a forester discovered her campsite and remains. She had survived for almost a month. nytimes.com/2016/05/27/us/missing-hiker-geraldine-largay-appalachian-trail-maine.

**Marion Davison with llamas**

# Mary E. 'Pastor Mary' Davison

**Susan:** Mary, sometimes known as 'Pastor Mary,' is a former volunteer with the Peace Corps, retired physical therapist with a specialty in pediatrics, and army wife. When home, she enjoys preaching (she has been a church pastor for 16 years), gardening, her two children and ten grandchildren—and playing the cornet.

**Mary E. Davison:** I have hiked and camped most of my life. In about the fourth grade, I went to Girl Scout Camp and adored it and hiking. I was in the Mountaineers [Seattle-based adventurers' organization focusing on the Pacific Northwest] for two years in my first job out of college and climbed Mt. Rainier, Mt. Baker, Mt. St. Helens (before it erupted again in 2008), Mt. Shasta, and Mt. Hood.

When I started backpacking/hiking, it was because I *fit* into the scene when I did not fit well as a teenager elsewhere, plus I loved the beauty of the mountains. There are many other reasons. I am toying with the idea of writing a short book about why hikers hike—not for hikers but for the people in their lives who do not understand why hikers hike. At this age, one of the reasons I hike is simply because I still can. Who knows how long that will last?

I always did a minor bit of hiking and backpacking, but the year I turned 60, I told my daughter we should really do the Wonderland Trail [around Mt. Rainier] before I got too old to go. That was the start of my long-distance hiking.

**What makes a successful hiker**
I think all long-distance hikers are a bit obsessed, or at least

goal-directed, to finish long trails. I am a long-section hiker, hiking two long trails a year, a spring hike and a late summer/fall hike—300 to 500 miles each (once 600 miles). It has become a lifestyle to do so each year.

Someone has to *want* to long-distance hike. That is at least half of it, perhaps 90 percent. I know many hikers my age who are better and stronger hikers than I am. They did not *want* to complete long-distance trails; I did. It helps to be in reasonable physical shape and to have a bit of creativity in problem-solving. But nothing replaces the *want* factor. Knowing what you can and cannot do and what you should and should not do help, too.

## Hiking accomplishments

Besides the Wonderland Trail, my long-distance hikes have included the Triple Crown (Appalachian Trail, Pacific Crest Trail, and Continental Divide Trail). I walked the Francés route of the Camino de Santiago in Spain and the Le Puy en Velay Chemin in France.

I've hiked some of the American Discovery Trail [which crosses the United States from Cape Henlopen State Park, Delaware, to Point Reyes National Seashore, California]. I've hiked from the Atlantic to Nebraska, half of Colorado, a bit of Utah, and 140 miles of Nevada. The ADT, especially east of Denver, is very different from National Scenic Trails. It is waymarked for foot or bicycle. And if you look at a map of the U.S., you will notice there is very little wilderness between the Atlantic Ocean and Denver. It is not a wilderness trail. The ADT is made up of many trails, country roads, even highways.

The American Discovery is not often traveled by hikers; the people I meet on that trail are the locals along the way. And one cannot just look for a bit of flat ground to camp on as most of that land is not public space but private property. I ask people if I can camp on their yards, have water, have a place to go to the bathroom. Because it is that kind of trail, I have met locals all along the way, and that has turned out to be the charm of that trail. I have written a new book, *Aren't You Afraid?*, about my experiences on that trail.

**Greatest accomplishments**

The most notable accomplishment was that I completed the Triple Crown at age 76—as far as I can tell, the oldest person to have done so, although I have not kept track the last couple years. All records are made to be broken, and that one surely will be as older hikers are on the trails. I completed these trails in section hikes, not thru-hikes.

One unique thing is that I did A.T. and PCT at the same time—each year I'd hike a section of one and then the other. I ran into some of the same people on those trails, just in different years. That was fun.

At age 79, I often think that my most notable accomplishment now is that I am still backpacking, so any hike at all is a great accomplishment.

My day hikes are primarily in Washington—Mt. Rainier National Park, the I-90 corridor, and a few other places locally.

**Overcoming challenges**

Well, it is always a challenge to figure out the logistics and plan the hike, but my major challenges have been recovering from surgeries, in particular from replacements of both knees and both shoulders, which involved four different surgeries. So I have four joint replacements—but hiking did not cause them. Hiking has helped me greatly in general health and as carrots to spur me to work in rehab after surgeries.

I am very intentional about slow and steady work to recover to be able to hike. (I said a lot about that in my book, *Old Lady on the Trail*.) I follow the instructions from my physical therapist. Having been a PT as my first profession, I know how important that is from the point of view of a PT as well as the patient. I add in walking in my neighborhood and build up my endurance. I add short hikes with elevation gain and loss, and longer hikes. As an older hiker, all that preparation and conditioning is more and more necessary.

There have been a few times I have stopped. Unexpected events have taught me when to get off the trail. Once because of very bad weather on Blue Mountain on the Appalachian Trail, another time when there was very wet and cold crummy weather in Wyoming on the CDT. Bailing is not a sin, and sometimes it is the best choice. In the Mountaineers many, many years ago, I was taught that the mountain will be there for you for another day. (Always true until Mt. St. Helens blew, though part of it is still there.)

I have learned that I can do even more than I think I can do if I have to and that I have problem-solving skills when needed. That was not only when I got off Blue Mountain in bad weather on the Appalachian but also twice while on the Continental Divide.

One time on the CDT a lightning storm blasted into the desert, and another time an unexpected cold front hit me in New Mexico. Problem-solving is deciding what is the safest course of action under the circumstances.

In lightning storms, supposedly the safest stance is a crouch in a gully. There were no gullies, and I am an old lady and I can't crouch all that long anyway. And there was nothing but me in that desert. I decided the safest thing was to lie down on my pad using the tent as a bivy pulled around me. I lived to tell the tale.

The incident involving unexpected cold was when I found the temperature dropped to 23 degrees, and I had snow all afternoon at 9,000 feet. I just kept going. Just at dark, I finally dropped to 8,000 feet. Speed at getting into my bag and food inside my body to make calories inside me was what was needed—otherwise, it would have been too cold to stop without getting hypothermia.

Neither one of these incidents made me get off-trail, though I consider both of them to have been potentially quite dangerous. Lightning on James Peak (13,294 feet) in Colorado, considerably above timberline, on the CDT was also dangerous.

## Staying safe

As a concession to old age and modern technology, I now carry an inReach, and my son likes to check up and see where I am. My children know I have hiked and backpacked for years. They have never expressed fear for me, although my son was once a little concerned as he could not figure out where I was on the A.T. one year as I was doing something unplanned and hadn't informed him (before I had the inReach). I do stay pretty much on my plan, unlike most long-distance hikers.

The one safety precaution I take when I solo is not to post my online journal on Trailjournals.com until at least four days later so casual readers do not know exactly where I am but can still follow my journal. My children and my cousin in San Diego get my journal entries promptly as long as I have cell reception to send them (not possible in some areas and at some times).

But I usually complete what I have planned to complete. Part of that is mindset. I have a couple of friends who sometimes come with me. One, before we start, plans where she could bail if she wants to. The other succumbs to temptation to bail if there is an opportunity. I never start out thinking about bailing. My mindset is that I will complete what I plan, and if I run into problems, I will deal with them when they happen. As a section hiker, I usually have transportation arranged at both ends, which also encourages me to finish what I have planned, especially if I have a reserved flight to catch.

### Changes in hikes

I don't think I have become less adventurous, but my adventures have changed. Age does make a difference. It is not just a number, at least not for me. I am slower, and replacement parts aren't as good as the original equipment. I cannot do what I once could. But that does not mean I have to quit. It does mean I have to take my changing abilities into account when planning. I used to plan 15-mile days in any kind of terrain. Now, I plan 13-mile days on level terrain and 10-mile days with elevation gain and loss.

I have also found that some things that were not attractive to me as adventures earlier in my life are now. I have found I actually like long level walking, meeting new people, even urban hiking. I scoffed at those in earlier years. I am not as capable of rugged hiking as I was in my youth. But there are many ways to have an adventure and many places to hike of varying terrain and difficulty. They are all good.

# Going solo

Backpacking has changed over the years, and my knowledge and skill levels have changed, sometimes for the better, sometimes for the worse. I try to reject bad advice, but evaluating that advice is related to what I have learned and how backpacking has changed. Certainly, going solo was something frowned upon by most in years past. That is not bad advice, but I have made a different choice many times.

I have met many people hiking, but have solo hiked about two-thirds of the time including when doing the long-distance trails. I love to hike with friends; I also love to go solo. They are different things. Going solo, I love to start a long-distance hike with a feeling that the world is all there in front of me, mine to go and see, waiting for me—almost like my private possession.

I simply have not found people who hike at my speed who want to do long trails. I tell those who question my solo hiking that I was trained by the Girl Scouts and the Mountaineers, and I know that three is the ideal number to hike so that if one is injured, one person can stay with the injured hiker while the other goes to get help.

But I have two fairly warped points of view: First, I have organized and led group hikes. I like that, too, but it is also very nice to only be responsible for yourself instead of everyone in the group. And second, I plan my hikes in some detail and send my hike plan to my hiking friends. If anyone wants to come for some or all of them, great—if not, I'm going anyway. I am too old to wait for some imaginary person to show up in my life to hike with me. I need to make the most of the time I have left to hike.

There are also many things I will not risk that others will. I am more concerned about falling as I age and have taken a couple of falls. There are things I will risk that others will not. I often knocked on people's doors while on the American Discovery Trail to ask for water, or directions, or other help, and I am rarely afraid of much of anything.

I suppose the outcome determines whether it was a bad decision. And sometimes the outcome is just luck. All of life involves risk. Risks, advice, and choices are rarely all good or all bad.

**To new women hikers**

My advice to new women hikers is to *do it!* Sure, there are ways to help in that effort. Increase your challenges gradually. Find like-minded friends to encourage each other. Learn the skills you need for new and different adventures. But the primary skill is to start. It has taken me many years to realize that I am a self-starter, and not too many people have that gift. Groups and classes certainly help.

Be accountable to someone. If I tell someone I am going to do something, I am more likely to actually do so. If I tell someone I am writing my next book, I really have to do so. That helps me to be accountable; I suspect it helps others, too. There certainly are many ways to find encouragement these days online, especially on Facebook with its multiple sites for hikers.

**As far as gear...**

I have lots of gear that is important and necessary. I'm not sure I have a favorite. This last year, I bought down pants because, with aging, I sleep colder. Currently, because they are new and keep me warm, I suppose they are my favorite. I even wear them at home.

**Perhaps everyone underestimates their physical abilities**

It's not just women who may underestimate their abilities. Maybe everyone does. I think everyone is capable of much more than we ever do. From my training as a physical therapist, I remember a fact from embryology. I cannot put numbers to it anymore, but I can remember the gist of it: Before we are born, we have a gazillion more neurons than we can possibly use. We start losing some even before birth. We only keep neurons that make connections with other neurons when we learn to do something—physical or mental.

Think about that. *We are gifted with far more than we need, and we are capable of far more than we ever think we are.* Try. Learn. Do. You will make new neuronal connections, and you will be surprised at what you can accomplish.

There may be generational changes, too. Now I am really

going to sound old. When I grew up, people weren't as careful or concerned about safety at every step. And life was not always as easy physically as it is today. I did any number of things that parents today would not allow their children to do, some definitely not entirely safe.

My parents played a big role in my outlook on life. My parents encouraged me to go and do things and be whoever I wanted to be. My parents were educated and had a worldview that was broad. I was expected to go to college. My mother's best friend was the daughter of a missionary to Congo. My mother and brother traveled to other countries. My dad had a desk job but bought a mountain property and carved roads with an old tractor, and built a house that required sawing down trees, constructing his own sawmill, and learning to dynamite rock for the foundation. I had good role models.

On the other hand, Title IX has helped generations of women after me to know they can excel in sports from which I was barred. Perhaps generational factors are mixed in effects.

## Looking forward

I like a long walk in the spring and a long walk at higher altitude or rougher terrain in the late summer or fall. I try not to compare hikes. I walk to go and see what I will find, and what experiences and beauty will be there.

At this age, many things can happen to derail my plans, but I still have them. I look forward to being on trail. At the rate I hike, it will take me another three to four years to complete the ADT. It could happen; it might not. But I am still walking now. At this point, the only records I set are related to being old, but the enjoyment is all mine, regardless of my age.

## And now we deal with a new challenge

[May 2020, Washington state] I have gone on two five- to six-mile hikes in the last couple weeks. My friend and I found a not-too-popular hike on a forest road. We drove separate cars and hiked on the road on opposite sides, maintaining six feet of distance. I don't know too many of those, but this one was wonderful western Washington deep-forest woods.

Mainly, I have been working in my yard. I have been enjoying all my flowers, pruning shrubs, and planting and pulling weeds in my garden. Yes, I had to cancel my spring hike and anticipate I must cancel my fall one as well.

But my home is lovely. I have a large yard that has suffered lack of upkeep for years as I have been gone each spring and late summer on long-distance hikes. It is hard to think staying home is a penalty. I am blessed with things I like to do here. I also have things to do to regarding my new book. I never lack things to do.

The more serious disappointments are not being able to hug my grandchildren. My daughter and her family, on a two-year trip in an RV after my son-in-law's retirement, are stuck in Corpus Christi, Texas. They were supposed to get here in August. Who knows when it might be or if I can hug them? My more local family—my son, his wife, and two other grandkids—are nearer, and I have seen them but only from six feet apart.

But life goes on. I wear a mask in public with one handy for passing hikers on a trail, though I have not yet ventured on real *trail* trails. I get my groceries once a month. Church and a couple of meetings are by Zoom. I have things to do and contacts.

But life is different. At this age, who knows if I will be a long-distance hiker again? Time will tell. Perhaps, God willing and if a vaccine happens. I do take this pandemic seriously.

**Susan:** Mary had planned to walk more of the American Discovery Trail in the spring and a chunk of Utah in the fall of 2020, but those had to be postponed or canceled as the coronavirus arrived.

Mary E. Davison's newest book is *Aren't You Afraid: American Discovery Trail from the Atlantic Ocean to Nebraska*. She is also the author of *Old Lady on the Trail: Triple Crown at 76*.

Her blog is maryedavison.com/blog. One series of posts that I found of particular interest was "Fear Not." One gem: "Twice I have knocked on doors [to ask for water or similar while on the ADT] where the guy who answered was on house arrest and was afraid he would get in trouble with his parole officer."

**Mary E. Davison (credit Kathy O'Toole)**

# Laurie Ferris

**Susan:** Laurie is the co-coordinator of the Northern California chapter of American Pilgrims on the Camino. Besides all that she does for the chapter (detailed below), she is a certified yoga teacher. Through her Laurie Ferris Yoga & Wellness website, lferris.com, she shares information about both the gentle yoga flow practice session she offers and upcoming events of interest to the yoga and meditation community. She also works at International House on the U.C. Berkeley campus. She and her husband Mitch live in Oakland, California.

**Laurie Ferris:** I was in my early twenties when I hiked Yosemite's Half Dome with college friends [Half Dome is Yosemite's most iconic attraction in the valley. It's a serious endurance hike where hikers gain 4,800 feet of elevation on the 14.8-mile out-and-back trail from Yosemite Valley.] I didn't know what I was getting into. I wore Converse high-tops and got the worst blisters. But we spent the night on top of the rock, which isn't possible now from what I hear.

I went into my first REI in Renton, Washington, in 1993, became a member, and bought a proper pair of hiking boots. These were Nike's 'Lady Half Dome' hiking shoes. I was and still am a sucker for a good name. I put them through the rigors until they had holes and worn soles.

Over the decades, I did a few day hikes here and there: Kauai, the San Francisco Bay Area where I live, and more in Yosemite. I got back into hiking seriously in 2015 when training for the Camino de Santiago in Spain.

## Hiking is a way of life

It's a way of life that helps keep me balanced and sane. I am at my best when I am hiking regularly. When I started my job at U.C. Berkeley 15 years ago, I discovered these great trails nearby where I could hike a 45-minute loop during lunch. I rallied some coworkers to join me and formed an informal hiking club. Whenever I did these hikes, I didn't feel sluggish in the afternoon. I gladly sacrificed my lunch hour to hike even though it meant eating leftovers at my desk. I actually saved a lot of money, time, and ate much healthier this way.

Some might say that it became an obsession when I was training for the Camino. I was hardcore and tracked every hike. I even wore ankle weights! Now I go less frequently because I do yoga and sometimes teach yoga to staff at lunch. Yes, hiking filled social needs when our workplace hiking group was more active. Over the last few years, my local Camino chapter has become a great outlet for weekend hikes with other pilgrim friends.

## Surrounded by nature

I enjoy getting away from it all and feeling nature surrounding me on the trail. Sometimes at [work or around home], I enjoy going alone to clear my head and think. In the past, I would listen to audiobooks during lunchtime hikes, but while on the Camino, I prefer listening to nature.

If you give yourself time to really listen, there's a whole orchestra of different sounds on the Camino: birdsong, woodpeckers, the crunch of footsteps on gravel, water rushing in rivers and creeks, cowbells, horses, dogs barking, locals yelling, pilgrims chatting in different languages, kids' laughter, and the rhythm of your trekking poles tapping in sync with each step.

## Savoring accomplishments

Besides that epic hike to Half Dome in my 20s, I would have to say walking my first Camino de Santiago when I was 47 years old was my greatest accomplishment. It opened the doors for a new lifestyle and kept me wanting to go back for more.

I've gone on four different Camino routes so far—the Inglés, the Portuguése, the Primitivo, and the Invierno. All four Caminos have been humbling and challenging, and each one was a little tougher than the last in both the physical and mental realm. It's not so much about an accomplishment or getting the Compostela certificate. More significant for me were the opportunities for personal growth, overcoming fears, letting go, and trusting in God. I am still processing the many after-effects of these trips. I have more confidence in other aspects of life now as a result of doing the Camino and living a simpler lifestyle. I turned 52 in February, and feel that I am in better shape than when I was in my 30s.

I have always had a rather fast walking pace, and I can hustle if I need to cover a lot of ground, but in the last few years, I much prefer taking my time. I am more in the mindset of 'slow strollers on the Camino' and will happily split a stage in order to have more energy to enjoy town when I arrive.

**Thoughts on hiking solo**

I understand that the thought of walking alone in a foreign country might scare some people. We are conditioned to be cautious, not talk to strangers, and not trust anyone. I actually feel safe walking alone on the Camino de Santiago. I have walked it three times solo and once with a group of 13. I feel like I have more freedom and control when I'm walking alone.

At first, my family was worried about me hiking alone and thought I was crazy. But I did a lot of research, interviewed pilgrims, and launched a blog that documents all of my findings of this Camino phenomenon. If anything, my writing helped my family understand it more and helped them all worry less about me walking alone. I prefer to write about my Caminos when I return home so that I don't miss out on the experience while I'm there. Many women have written to me about how my route reports and blog posts helped them let go of fear about walking it alone.

**When the Camino calls**

If the Camino calls, you must answer. Give yourself the time to make it happen. You might not know the reason why you have to do it until you get home or years later. They say the Camino doesn't end when you reach Santiago. For me, it was a lifestyle intervention. I returned from my first Camino with a strong desire to purge my closets and drawers. One of the lessons is that we don't need that much stuff.

### To fare well on the Camino...

You must be a little courageous, adventurous, and curious. You don't have to be extroverted, but it helps if you can get along with different people. Try giving up a bad habit and picking up a good one along the way. And please, take the time to smell the roses, talk to the locals, and revel in nature.

I listen to my body if it is telling me to stop, slow down, split or skip stages, or stretch my sore muscles. I always pack snacks so that I can maintain my energy. As I always tell my yoga students, listen to your body, and only stretch to the point of your own ability.

### It can be a challenge

My biggest challenge is not having enough time to walk a long Camino. I have overcome this by walking one- to two-week routes, usually after I've been on a trip elsewhere in Europe.

### Advice for women new to hiking regularly

I would suggest that anyone who is afraid of going solo might go with a partner or friends, but to try a few hours of walking alone each day so that they can really have their own inner experience. If one is social all day, it is hard to hear the orchestra of sounds I mentioned earlier.

Train with the gear and clothing that you will wear as much as you can beforehand.

Perhaps some women underestimate their physical abilities, but some might overestimate it. We are stronger than we know, but every woman is different, and there are so many factors such as age, weight, illness, previous injuries, etc. I suggest to not analyze it too much as that might make you not want to proceed. Ever heard of analysis paralysis? It can prevent you from doing something wonderful. I say give it a try and see how you do, but listen to your body and adjust as needed.

When you are on your long hike, study the trail a day ahead to know what you are in for.

I personally haven't received any bad or risky advice, but I have heard a lot of pilgrims with strong opinions. I have a pretty good sense of discernment, so I can filter out what makes sense for me.

### Favorite gear

I have too many favorites to list, but I love my zip-front Fabletics jacket with thumb holes. The long sleeves protect the top of my hands from the sun and also provide a thin layer of protection for my palms. This seems to help prevent blisters from daily trekking pole use. I love pockets, and this has four zipper pockets on the outside plus two inside pockets. It is stretchy and can be tied around the waist when I get hot. It washes up nicely and doesn't wrinkle. I love the mulberry-pink color. I actually lost this jacket before starting my fourth Camino and had to make do without it. The company no longer sells this, but luckily, I found the same exact jacket on Poshmark in great condition for $25.

### On the next long-distance walk

I'll be working on balance in everything—from accommodations to food, time hiking, and rejuvenating. I'll be wanting to do another solo Camino and would like to write a little every day, and do some spiritual readings and yoga and meditation practices. But that doesn't mean I am going to be antisocial; I love meeting other pilgrims. I would like to strike a balance between inner contemplation and social fun because the Camino provides both.

### And then we had to cope with the coronavirus

[Summer 2020, San Francisco Bay Area] I have been doing okay, but the first few months were really tough. I had fatigue and brain fog and had no energy to walk more than 30-minute dog walks each morning. Working from home has its challenges, and I've had more screen time and Zoom meetings than I'd like to admit. My husband and I have been enjoying hunkering down, cooking, gardening, enjoying the backyard, and our doggie. But I was starting to feel like a sloth. When I noticed my legs were losing muscle, I realized that atrophy has set in. If you don't use it, you'll lose it!

What a difference a pandemic makes. Before March, I was on a roll with a 10-plus mile hike every month and four to five miles every day. I have been gradually working my way back up to longer hikes. I added a second dog walk in the afternoon. I have started to take longer walks on the weekends. Little by little, I'm getting my Camino mojo back!

There are a few silver linings. I recently finished a certificate program through UC Extension and took two journalism courses.

Our NorCal chapter has been hosting virtual meetups, presentations, and a book club. We've had guest speakers and great discussions through Zoom meetings. People seem to enjoy it. This is my social diversion and my stay-at-home Camino for now.

**Susan:** As a coordinator for the local pilgrim group, Laurie helps plan the chapter's frequent outings and other activities. She posts the calendar on the national pilgrim group's website (americanpilgrims.org) and on social media. She has given several talks on Camino-related topics including a current 'how-to' series (how to pack, stay healthy, etc.). She frequently posts on her blog, thecaminoprovides.com, about such topics as hiking snacks and wellness along the way. She says, "There is much more I would love to share on this hot topic."

Below is a portion of Laurie's "Favorite Snacks" blog post, which is oriented to those hiking the Camino de Santiago routes but could be helpful to hikers of any trail, whether long or short.

## Favorite Snacks for Hiking the Camino de Santiago
~ Laurie Ferris

We've all been there. You find yourself overreacting to something that normally wouldn't bother you. Your hiking buddies suddenly become annoying. The day's walk seems like it will never end. Your stomach is growling, and so are you. You've reached the state of being both hungry and angry, or 'hangry.'

*HANGRY (noun): A state of anger caused by a lack of food. May evoke negative change in emotional state.*

This unfortunate state can happen anytime, but having low blood sugar can make or break your Camino hiking experience. Take control of the situation by always having snacks with you. Below are my favorites that are both easy to obtain and eat along the Camino de Santiago routes in Spain.

Apples, bananas, cherries, peaches, and tangerines are my favorites for a few reasons. Not only is fruit packed with vitamins, minerals, and fiber, but the natural sugar gives you an instant boost of energy. The high water content of fruit helps to quench your thirst while making you feel full. In addition, fresh fruit has its own packaging, so there is less trash to carry out and dispose of. What's not to love?

I recommend buying whatever fruit is in season (such as fresh cherries in the spring). Buy whatever is a specialty of the region from farmers' market stands or *fruterias* (tiny shops that only sell fruit and vegetables). You'll be supporting the local farmers and getting a real taste of the land.

Fresh fruit can be heavy, so only buy what you can consume for the day or share the bounty with your Camino family. Fresh fruit is the best antidote for all the bread and potatoes that are offered in the hearty pilgrim meals; dried fruit is also good because of its portability.

A handful of peanuts, cashews, pistachios, or almonds can stave off hunger until your next café stop, but my favorite snack is the shelled sunflower seeds that you can buy for cheap at any of Spain's wonderful little *supermercados* such as Froiz or Dia.

Other options I like: almond butter in a packet and hempseed bars. Just make sure you dispose of the wrappers so you don't add litter to the Camino.

I am a huge fan of gazpacho, the chilled soup that is popular throughout the southern region of Spain. Gazpacho is a savory blend of tomatoes, cucumbers, garlic, bread, olive oil, and vinegar. It is especially refreshing when it's hot and you're exhausted.

If you don't find it in restaurants, look for it in the refrigerated produce section of markets.

Cheese and yogurt are great sources of protein that can instantly banish the 'hangries.' Both are widely available. I find the yogurt more flavorful than back home—they don't remove the fat or add artificial ingredients. On top of that, it helps with digestion.

Last but certainly not least, chocolate! Spain is known for its delicious chocolate in all forms, from thick hot chocolate to chocolate-filled pastry. For hikers, the snack of choice is dark-chocolate bars with almonds. Dark chocolate doesn't melt as fast as milk chocolate, and it contains more antioxidants.

*Why should the hike be grueling when you can be refueling? The more you can take care of your own hunger, the more comfortable your days on the Camino will be.* thecaminoprovides.com/2020/01/20/favorite-snacks-for-hiking.

**Laurie Ferris 'Victory Pose' — Santiago de Compostella**

# Lorie 'Veggie' Florence

**Susan:** Lorie, like Laurie Ferris profiled previously, is involved in the Camino community. After her walk of the Camino Francés in 2018, she became actively involved in helping others learn about pilgrimages.

In 2019, a small group of hiking enthusiasts began to envision and establish the Camino de Sonoma, a 72-mile pilgrimage trail in California that extends from Mission Solano in Sonoma to the Holy Trinity Chapel in Fort Ross State Historic Park. Lorie was excited to be included in the steering group, helping to add insights about the pilgrimage and pilgrim community as well as learning the way and sharing it by leading walks along the newly established route.

Sections below in quotation marks were written by Lorie and first appeared in a blog on Laurie Ferris's website, *Camino Provides*.

**Lorie Florence:** My first backpacking trip was in ninth grade. Then I took a long break to raise kids and then started again at age 44 by section hiking with my husband, Mark 'Snickers' Florence.

### Hiking in the U.S.

I am in Annadel State Park in Sonoma County every week as a volunteer park steward. I take friends to other county parks.

Mark and I have section-hiked the Pacific Crest Trail for our vacation every summer except two between 2002 and 2017. When Mark and I went on my first section hike, I dropped my kids off with a friend and headed out with him in all the gear he had picked out. We ate the food he chose and the route he chose, and I even wore the shoes he recommended. It was really his hike, and I was along for the ride. He hiked so much faster, waited impatiently for me to catch up, and hardly ever spoke.

I was miserable. I missed my kids and felt incompetent. It was really hard and hot, and the trail was rocky and high and dangerous. "All we did all day was walk—up hills, up mountains, across sketchy, loose, scree-covered narrow trails. Mark just kept walking, and I just kept trailing along." I sat down and had a good cry, which helped.

By the time the week was up, though, I didn't want it to end. "The stars were beautiful at night, I was met by a dazzling sunrise each morning, and we had long hours of just being together without interruptions, which was priceless."

The next year, I helped in all the planning and picked out my own gear. Making it my hike, too, has made a world of difference for me. After that, "I followed my husband, walked alongside him, and even sometimes led him as we hiked a section of the Pacific Crest Trail each summer.

I became more and more accustomed to it and even got to the point where I looked forward to our trips into the wilderness. I came to cherish the quiet days we walked together through pure nature—flowing streams, towering trees, pure blue skies, and solitude."

"I got to know my husband better with every trip, and we learned each other's strengths (and weaknesses) and relied on each other for companionship, navigation, food preparation, and as lookouts for each other when we answered those important calls of nature that require a little privacy.

We completed all 2,650 miles of the Pacific Crest Trail in 2017 and were not ready to settle down."

## Hiking in Spain

We did the Camino de Santiago in 2018 because I wanted a trail we could do all of in one year; I wanted to see Spain; tickets were cheaper to Spain than to the East Coast to do the A.T.; I liked the idea of devotion being a big part of the pilgrimage and the type of community that fostered.

And it all proved to be true. The easier walking and frequent showers, beds, and restaurant food made the Camino de Santiago feel like a real holiday! I kept a trail journal of our trip. trailjournals.com/journal/22608

The Camino in early spring did not disappoint, but by August, I was longing for some wilderness trail.

### And on the Continental Divide Trail

Once we had experienced the Camino, we were ready for a wilderness trail again, and the CDT seemed like the next logical choice. I had heard it is a tougher trail, and I found that to be true for many reasons. It is much more isolated, the trail is not as well-defined, getting to and from the trail for resupplies and beginning/ending sections seems a little trickier, and water sources were often iffy (plus I was dealing with some nasty intestinal issues).

We hiked in April/May southbound from Lordsburg to Silver City, New Mexico. One of my favorite memories from that trip is an unexpected layover in the small town of Reserve. The people were just lovely and welcoming, and our waiter at the diner/bakery was 11-year-old Elias in a bowtie and European cap.

I loved the Gila River section, too. Something about the way the light filters down into the canyon is just beautiful. I enjoyed being on the water for so many days (and out of the desert and long stretches of farm roads) and especially enjoyed the hot springs.

The diversity of both plant and animal life kept me amazed. We never got to see the javelina [also known as peccary], but saw signs of them as well as deer, bear, elk, and so many hummingbirds.

I really had the sense we were walking in the footsteps of the ancient ones, especially as we neared the areas with cliff dwellings. [CDT hikers sometimes can choose alternative routes from the official one. The Gila Alternate takes hikers through the Gila National Forest, basically following the Gila River and crossing it countless times while allowing a slight detour to the Gila Cliff Dwellings.]

## Hiking is important

I get nervous and antsy when I haven't been to the woods in a while. I try to get out at least once a week, but of course, sometimes that just doesn't work out. At the least, I do a two-and-a-half-mile trail twice a week with my best friend. Hiking keeps me sane, centered, healthy, and fit. It is also a good way to spend time with loved ones and friends—talking and catching up.

I like the open sky and trees, and the smell of freedom. Also, the cadence of walking—the sound of my feet on the trail and the feel of my arms swinging (or poling), and the rhythm that starts to happen in my head. I also enjoy the time to think or sometimes to just talk to others. Taking my kids and grandkids out is a special joy—sharing what I love with the people I love.

## Sense of greatest accomplishment

The Washington section of the PCT in 2017, when I was 60, was my best hiking. Absolutely stunning scenery, I met some great people, and even though I had some bad blisters, I never gave up. I felt strong and capable, and there was never a monotonous moment of trail—each bend and rise opened up a new, different, and beautiful view. I also spent a lot of time preparing our food, and I really enjoyed our meals.

## What about hiking solo

I don't hike solo much. I've got this great built-in hiking partner. Our styles differ somewhat—and he is much more about the destination and I am more about the journey—but all in all, we strengthen each other's weaknesses and are good company for one another.

## The attributes that success requires

To be successful at hiking—especially on a long trail—requires perseverance, for sure. But a sense of curiosity and wonder are important, too. If it's not interesting and you're not filled with awe, I don't know how you'd keep going.

Because we only go out for a few weeks at a time, only once have I wanted to quit. When that happened, we made camp for the day, had a good meal, and things looked much better in the morning.

### Challenges and lessons to share

My advice to new hikers is to start easy. Find a hiking partner or group, and have fun with it. Sing. Rent some equipment or borrow from friends, and get to know what you like before you buy. Learn to breathe.

I definitely think women have doubts about their abilities. Learn to trust yourself. Wander out often so you know what you are capable of, and what does and does not work for you. Get to know yourself, and find another hiker that you trust who stretches you out of your comfort zone—but not too far at once.

My biggest challenge is stupid blisters. My toes usually blister when we go out, and usually, I lose a few toenails. But I had no blisters on the CDT, thanks to great coaching from my friend Jill Duncan.

If you develop shin splints, make sure you are getting plenty of water and electrolytes. My favorite is Vitalyte because of the ingredients (we know the inventor). It's available online and at REI. KT tape can offer some relief, and I also highly recommend a regimen of stretches. Also, on a practical level, I recommend a pee rag and a little bidet bottle.

### Well-meaning but risky advice

'Billy Goat' [a well-known hiker of the PCT who has hiked all or most of it a dozen times] told us we shouldn't have any trouble getting through "that bit" of snow. We were not prepared for the snow at all, and Mark slid and was injured.

I think if you listen to someone much more experienced, you tend to believe them because they know so much more than you. But they know what they can do—not what you can do. My greatest advice is to listen to your gut. If you don't think it's safe, don't go.

### Looking to the future

I want to do the CDT portion of the Colorado Trail

next—beautiful scenic views and challenging terrain. We got a glimpse in 2019 when we met a good buddy in Twin Lakes, Colorado, to resupply him and walk a bit. The high passes are breathtaking—in more ways than one after having come from sea level!

I don't expect we will do the entire CDT, but we do plan to cherry-pick the nicer sections over the next few years. I am very much looking forward to Wyoming's Wind River Range.

We hike fewer miles in a day now, and I carry a cushier sleeping pad. I think when I can no longer hike, I will pick up a paddle and start kayaking. We may do more inn-to-inn hikes in the future on flatter ground. I hear the Dingle of Ireland is lovely...

**Staying close to home in Spring 2020**
[April 2020, Northern SF Bay Area] Our walking has been quite limited as we have both been working extra hours to help our companies meet new demands caused by the pandemic. My company, Junior Achievement, has been producing a lot of extra lessons and activities that parents and teachers can access online. It's good but exhausting. I have been trying to get out in the morning and evening even if just for a mile or two through the neighborhood.

At the March National Pilgrim Gathering at Lake Tahoe's Zephyr Cove in Nevada, we met a lot of new hikers and made new friends. One of the ladies, Kathy Kehe from Colorado, has formed some Zoom groups to help us retain hiking community during this seclusion. That has been a great source of comfort.

We still hope to return to the CDT this summer to do the CDT portion of the Colorado Trail.

**Susan:** Lorie does a great deal of food preparation for hikes—both because she likes to avoid processed and strange-sounding additives and because she is vegetarian (hence her trail name, 'Veggie'. Mark's favorite trail snack is Snickers, which gave him his trail name.)

When they head out, Mark carries his supply of candy bars, and Lorie packs a bag of cut carrots. Opposites attract? She generously provided us several of her favorite recipes.

## Recipes for Dayhikers and Backpackers

### Peanut Butter Protein Balls
- 1 cup rolled oats
- 2/3 c shredded coconut
- 1/2 c creamy PB (I usually use almond butter or Tahini)
  1/2 c dark chocolate chips
- 1/3 c ground flaxseed
- 1/4 c brewer's yeast (or use a protein powder you like)
  1/3 c honey
- 2 T hemp seed or sesame seed
- 1 tsp vanilla extract or rum
- dash salt
- dash cinnamon.

Blend, press into golf-ball-sized balls, and chill. If it seems dry, add a little cold water or almond milk, a tablespoon at a time. High in protein, completely adaptable to additions and substitutions.

My grandkids like them best rolled in cocoa powder or coconut, which keeps them from being sticky, too.

### Sweet and Sour
- 2 T coconut oil

Chop or dice fairly fine:
- 1/2 lb carrots
- 1 onion
- 3-4 stalks celery or bok choy
- some spinach or other dark leafy green like kale
- 1 red or green pepper

*Drain, saving the juice:*
- 1 can crushed pineapple

*Sauce:*
- 1 cup broth
- 1/4 cup soy sauce
- 2 T vinegar,
- juice from the canned pineapple
- 2 T corn starch

Sauté the veggies in 2 T coconut oil.

For sauce, combine 1 cup broth, 1/4 cup soy sauce or Bragg Liquid Aminos (gluten-free and vegan), 2 T vinegar (your choice—I like rice vinegar in this dish, but apple cider works well, too), juice from canned pineapple, 2 T corn starch. Stir until all is dissolved, then pour into pan and simmer. Add 1 can crushed pineapple.

Simmer until fairly thick, then spread on silicone mats into the dehydrator and leave until nearly crispy. Break into small pieces and bag. To rehydrate, add 2 cups boiling water and stir; let sit until ready (about 5-10 minutes).

We often put 1 cup of water into the mix an hour or so before we stop for dinner, then add the second cup of water (boiling) just before we eat. This takes less energy and helps the food reconstitute better. If you'd like, carry a box of firm Mori-Nu Silken Tofu, which you can cut and add in just before eating.

## American Chop Suey

*Chop fine* and sauté:
- 1 onion
- 3-4 stalks of celery
- 2-3 small garlic cloves
- 1 red pepper
- 3 leaves kale or cabbage

*Add*:
- 1 can black or kidney beans
- 1 can diced tomatoes with juice (or use 3-4 fresh tomatoes, peeled, seeded and chopped fine)
- Diced black olives (1 small can or about 1/2 large can olives, cut small)
- 1 tsp chili powder
- 1 tsp salt and some pepper

Simmer until the mixture is thick. Spread fairly thin on silicone mats onto dehydrator trays and dry for 12-14 hours at 135o.

When dry and crunchy, break into small pieces and pack with vacuum sealer. To rehydrate, add 1 cup boiling water and simmer for 10 minutes (add more water as necessary).

## Ratatouille

*Chop fine* and sauté in 2 T olive oil
- 1/2 cup diced onion
- 1/2 cup diced red bell pepper
- 2 cups cubed (small pieces work best) eggplant
- 1 small zucchini
- 1 small squash (I like delicata squash the best)

When onions are transparent, add the following:
- 1/4 cup dry white wine or vegetable stock
- 1 can diced tomatoes (or 3-4 small fresh, diced, and seeded)
- 1/2 tsp basil
- 1/2 tsp tarragon (or herbs de Provence)
- 1/4 tsp garlic salt
- pepper to taste

Bring to boiling, cover and simmer about 20 minutes or till tender. Cook uncovered about 10 more minutes or until thickened. Spread on silicone mats on dehydrator trays and dry for 12-14 hours at 1350. Pack into sealed bags. To rehydrate, add 2 cups boiling water and simmer 10-15 minutes.

## Cashew Chicken

- 2 T ghee or oil

Chop or dice fairly fine:
- 1/2 lb carrots
- 1 onion
- 3-4 stalks celery or bok choy
- some spinach or other dark leafy green like kale
- 1 red or green bell pepper

*Blend together:*
- 1 cup broth
- 1/4 soy sauce
- 1 T corn starch

Sauté the veggies in 2 T ghee or oil. For sauce, combine 1 cup broth, 1/4 cup soy sauce, or Bragg Aminos, 1 T corn starch. Stir until all is dissolved; pour into pan with vegetables. Simmer until fairly thick, then spread on silicone mats into the dehydrator and leave until nearly crispy. Break into small pieces and bag. Add up to 1 cup minute rice or homemade dehydrated rice, 1 cup cashews, and if desired, 1 can chicken, dehydrated. Or you can add a pouch of chicken when ready to serve on trail

To rehydrate, add 12 oz boiling water and stir; let sit until ready (about 5-10 minutes). We often put 1 cup of water into the mix an hour or so before we stop for dinner, then add the other 4 oz of boiling water just before we eat. This takes less energy and helps the food reconstitute better.

If you'd like, carry a box of firm Mori Nu Silken Tofu. Cut and add in just before eating. Another nice addition is 1-2 T of ghee and some more cashews to serve.

**Burritos**

In a vacuum or Ziploc bag, place:
- 1/2 cup minute rice
- 1/2 cup dried refried beans
- 1/4 cup dried bell peppers, red or green
- 1/4 cup freeze-dried onions
- Any other dehydrated or freeze-dried veggies you like, especially corn
- 1 to 2 oz dehydrated salsa (or use small packs of taco sauce)

Rehydrate this mix with 8 oz water (I cold soak) and spread onto tortillas. You can add pouch chicken and freeze-dried or fresh cheese, which makes it even tastier. The addition of the dried salsa really makes this a tasty meal.

### Why I walk
~Lorie Florence

It's mostly about the connection to the earth—the rhythms, the constancy, the knowledge that the earth continues its cycles, and I am a part of it all.

There is a joy in starting out my day walking in the fresh air. There's a sense of expectation and hope.

There is a world of possibilities awaiting my discovery, and

I am at the beginning of it, fresh every day. I walk to find my true self, to center myself, to align myself with my purpose and with the created world. I can greet each new bit of nature, each experience and view, or tune it all out and just be.

There is a reverence in walking at the end of the day—a deep sense of gratitude in knowing that I am here, present, in the Presence of the Source of Life. I connect myself to the earth's cycle in seeing the sun slip below the horizon, the sky change color, the shadows and silhouettes appear, the light fade. I feel once again the cool breeze on my face, the wind in my hair, fresh air in my lungs.

I have come full circle, connecting morning and evening in the ritual of walking. My breathing takes on a purposeful rhythm, my brain quiets, and my soul awakens. I walk to find everything and to find nothing.

I walk because it is the Way.

**Lorie Florence — PCT 2018**

# Laurel (Ibbotson) 'Happy Feet' Foot

**Susan:** Laurel is unique among the contributors to this book because I first interviewed her and included her story in 2001 in my *We're in the Mountains* book. From her comments made 20 years ago: "We were in Georgia [on the Appalachian Trail] toward the end of March. Although the snow was an inch deep, Bill assured me there was nothing to worry about."

They set out. A blizzard hit, and before they were three miles into their trip, the snow was five inches deep. A snowplow came along, so they hitched a ride into town to outwait the blizzard. After a day's layover, they were again anxious to be on their way. They were the first to break the trail.

"It was absolutely beautiful—the snow cushioning the sound—pristine, wilderness... The snow was three and four feet deep. To continue on, we had to crawl through and over drifts. It was challenging, and at the end, a real accomplishment," said Laurel.

As you'll read, lots of changes have happened in her life since that earlier conversation, but her love of the outdoors has not diminished.

**Laurel Foot:** I started hiking in my mid to late twenties but didn't start hiking seriously until I was 39. That's when I took my first long backpacking trip—a thru-hike of the Appalachian Trail with my husband Bill in 1987.

Ten years later, in 1997, we were the first people to complete a combination 'bike-pack' and backpack across the country on the American Discovery Trail (ADT) following the southern route in the middle of the country. (As I recall, it was about 4,300 miles by mountain bike and about 700 miles of backpacking.) We basically biked where we could and backpacked where bikes were not allowed—wilderness areas or places impractical due to trail conditions for bikes with panniers. The following year, we bikepacked the northern route of the ADT in its midsection from Denver to Cincinnati.

Later, after my husband Bill died and I remarried, my husband Gary and I enjoyed a number of hiking-related vacations. Our honeymoon included hiking the 'W' route in Torres del Paine National Park in Patagonia and hiking across Easter Island. We have hiked the Coast to Coast Trail across England. We did what we called our 'Little Countries' trip, hiking across the five smallest countries (other than island nations) in the world—Andorra, Liechtenstein, San Marino, Monaco, and the Vatican (which we had to circumnavigate because we weren't allowed to cross certain parts of it). We have also hiked on the Dingle Peninsula in Ireland, including Wicklow Way.

I'm 72, and hiking is still an important part of my lifestyle and has become part of my identity. People often refer to me as a hiker when meeting or introducing me. Most of our hiking now is either in the Blue Ridge Mountains near where we live, with our local trail club, or on day hikes while visiting other countries.

**Why I hike**

I enjoy being outside, experiencing nature and challenging my body to keep moving. I like to say that one of my skill sets is being able to put one foot in front of the other. I like being with someone to talk to and enjoy the experience.

As I mentioned earlier, I rather 'cut my teeth' on serious hiking by thru-hiking the A.T. when I was 39. That gave me the confidence to do the American Discovery Trail hike/bike at age 49. It was quite a challenge for me because I wasn't sure what I was getting into. Although a scouting team worked to lay out the trail, there was little in the way of signage and printed material to follow. This was before the days of available and accurate GPS mapping. We created our own turn-by-turn notes based on maps from the ADT office and the scouting team.

## What makes for a successful long-distance hiker

You have to be able to put up with a certain amount of discomfort. You need to be able to persevere when the weather is not good and the trail is difficult. It's not all sunny days. Bill and I used to play a little mind game when conditions got bad. It involved coming up with scenarios of how things could be worse than what we were experiencing at the moment.

## There are daily challenges and sometimes big ones

One I can think of is how to balance home life and jobs with the ability to get out for long hikes. Bill and I were once hiking in a wilderness area of Nevada, far from any towns and roads, when the trail just dwindled away. We had a topo map of the area, but the trail marked on it didn't exist on the ground. We needed to use compass and mapping skills (well, Bill's really) to bushwhack until we could connect back onto a trail on the ground. It made me realize how important it is to be able to read maps and use compasses well.

## Time changes a few things…

Gary and I are more likely to take advantage of some creature comforts now. In Patagonia, we stayed in *refugios* rather than camping out. On the Coast to Coast Trail, we had our duffel bags shuttled to B&Bs so we would only be carrying daypacks on the trail. We're more likely to do day hiking now.

We have expanded to more bicycle trips. A few years ago, we biked about 400 miles along the Danube River between Germany and Hungary, staying at *pensions* along the way. In the Spring of 2019 we took a bike-and-barge trip with about 200 miles of biking in the Netherlands while sleeping on a barge.

## Sage advice

A practical tip: I love Smartwool socks and tops. They don't itch, they're good in both warm and cold weather, they look good, and they never stink.

More broadly, my advice for women is to go with a friend or a group. We can learn so much from each other. I have found many women hikers who are confident and strong. I think being out in nature helps you to build confidence in your abilities. For those who are nervous, I would suggest that they start with small trips and expand the distance as their confidence and knowledge grows.

I can't think of any bad advice I was given by experienced people. But, I have found that non-hikers are poor judges of distances and have unnecessary fears, such as recommending that you need to carry a gun.

## Facing the virus challenge

[April 2020, East Coast] Gary and I are doing fine while under stay-at-home orders in Virginia. We have been taking lots of walks around nearby neighborhoods, usually about five miles a day, and doing plenty of needed yard and home projects.

Luckily, spring in Virginia is beautiful, and getting outdoors is a real mental and spiritual pick-me-up for me. My extended family has set up an online group, Marco Polo. (If you're not familiar with it, it's like leaving little video messages instead of text messages that others can access at their convenience.) It's fun to see how everyone across the country is coping and to get little snippets from their lives.

**Susan:** When I wrote that I was dealing with shin splints, Laurel sent the following information: "I had difficulty with shin splints while on the ADT 20+ years ago. What helped me then was doing some slackpacking rather than carrying a backpack, or when we switched off to a section of the trail and bicycled… I also found that cycling helped with a knee issue I was having then, probably because it built up my quads to provide additional knee support."

Laurel and her husband, Gary Nero, not only enjoy bicycling and hiking on trails near their home in Lynchburg, Virginia, and worldwide, they also support many trail organizations. They volunteer with the Appalachian Trail Conservancy and American Discovery Trail Society, and do trail work in their community. Laurel currently serves on the board of directors for the ADT

Society and is the newsletter editor for its quarterly publication, *Discover America*.

The following excerpts are from an article, written by Laurel, which was first published in *Along the Towpath* in March 2018, by the Chesapeake & Ohio Canal Association, an independent, nonprofit, all-volunteer citizens association supporting the conservation of the natural and historical environment of the C&O Canal and the Potomac River Basin. It appears here with her permission.

## Discovering America under Your Own Power: The American Discovery Trail
~ Laurel Ibbotson Foot

Have you ever taken a walk or bicycle ride on the Chesapeake & Ohio Canal towpath and wondered, What would happen if I just kept going? What is around the next bend, and how far can it take me? The American Discovery Trail (ADT) discoverytrail.org was developed to allow people to do just that. In 1997, my husband Bill and I bicycled and backpacked the ADT. We dipped our toes in the Atlantic Ocean at its eastern terminus, Cape Henlopen, Delaware, on a brisk March day, and started heading west on the conglomeration of trails and back roads that would eventually lead us to its western endpoint, Limantour Beach in Point Reyes National Seashore, California.

Because it is a big country, our goal was to bicycle as much of the trail as we could and backpack the remaining parts where bicycles were either impractical or not allowed (such as wilderness areas). I was not sure what I was getting myself into. My main expertise was in backpacking, having hiked the Appalachian Trail 10 years earlier, and I had never done any long-distance bicycling before this trip. Here we were on mountain bikes with all of our gear, heading into what was to me something of a great unknown. But isn't that what makes it an adventure?

The ADT is a unique long-distance trail. Co-aligning with and linking together a multitude of existing national, state, and regional trails, such as the C&O Canal, by mostly little-used roads, it is able to showcase the diversity in scenery, ecosystems, culture, and history that comprise our nation. Within its 6,800+ mile length, it traverses 15 states, 14 national parks, and 16 national forests; links five national scenic trails and 12 national historic trails; and passes countless local historic, cultural, and natural treasures that lead to a true discovery of the spirit of America.

In the midsection of the country, it splits into northern and southern route options between Cincinnati, Ohio and Denver, Colorado. Purposely traversing urban greenways as well as wilderness, the intent is to bring trails to the people to encourage everyone to get outdoors and enjoy non-motorized transportation such as hiking, bicycling, or horseback riding. Although there are parts of the trail where bicycling or horses are not allowed, there are alternative routes in some states for these activities.

By acting as an east-west 'backbone' of the national trail system, it connects some of the iconic north-south long-distance trails such as the Appalachian National Scenic Trail and the Pacific Crest National Scenic Trail with the rest of the country. It includes challenging climbs over mountain ranges such as the Rockies, converted rail-trails through bucolic farmland, pathways in remote desert canyons, and rural roads through small towns.

Besides the breathtaking scenery, along its route are more than 10,000 sites that reveal our country's values, accomplishments, and interests. For example, one can visit the NASA-Goddard Visitors Center in Maryland, the Jefferson National Expansion Memorial (Gateway Arch) in St. Louis, the U.S. Air Force Academy in Colorado, and the Golden Gate Bridge in San Francisco.

History comes alive whether one traces the steps of commerce on the C&O Canal towpath or the migration of early pioneer settlers along the Oregon National Historic Trail. So, where would the trail lead you once you got off the C&O Canal towpath? If you headed east on its path, you would get off at Georgetown, with nearby access to the National Mall and its memorials and museums. Continuing on the ADT, you would join the Rock Creek Park trail system, passing the National Zoo, before hopping on the Western Ridge Trail. From there, the trail passes a restored, operating grist mill, picks up the Anacostia

Tributary Trail System, and heads toward Greenbelt Park and eventually the Atlantic Ocean at Cape Henlopen, Delaware. Heading west from Oldtown, Maryland (the ADT does not use the last 17.9 miles of the C&O Canal towpath), the ADT crosses a privately-owned toll bridge into West Virginia.

Then, it's on to the East Coast's high-altitude plateau of Dolly Sods Wilderness followed by the North Bend Rail Trail, passing through 13 tunnels and alongside a marble factory before entering Ohio and points west to the Pacific Ocean.

You might want to know what long-distance travelers say they liked best about the ADT. You may be thinking of dramatic vistas such as Lake Tahoe in California and Nevada or historic places like Bent's Old Fort in Colorado. However, the majority of users actually say it was the American people they met along the way.

When Bill and I were bicycling in Colorado on a hot July day, we decided to splurge on a motel room in a small town. It was Independence Day, and the elderly couple who owned the motel (which was partly functioning as a senior living facility) invited us to their Fourth of July cookout with the other residents. We dined on hot dogs, potato salad, and baked beans and topped it off with a red-white-and-blue iced cake complete with 'cannonball' doughnut holes surrounding it.

We talked to the residents, who described the red, rocky canyons that surrounded them as "the most beautiful place in the world," and revealed their pride in their land and this country. Our trip on the ADT reinforced and educated us to all that was good about this nation while challenging us physically and mentally. It lived up to its goal of encouraging connections—of people as well as trails. candocanal.org/atp/2018-03.pdf

**Laurel Foot**

# Nancy 'Why Not?' Huber

**Susan:** In one of her posts, Nancy quotes John Muir, "I wish I knew where I was going. Doomed to be carried of the spirit into the wilderness, I suppose. I wish I could be more moderate in my desires, but I cannot, and so there is no rest."

You'll see Nancy's name mentioned in other stories in this book, and if you follow various trail association events, you'll see her name pop up frequently too—because she shares her enthusiasm and knowledge with others and gives back to the hiking community.

**Nancy Huber:** When I was young, my family went on outings almost every weekend. Many were hikes. We almost always had fun, but we always complained that we had to go. I am the third of eight siblings spread out over 18 years. The outings had to be dumbed down to the youngest, so we didn't hike that far.

When I was about 13, we (parents and seven children, youngest three years old) went backpacking in Lassen National Park in California. We hiked in only a few miles and had a wonderful, memorable time. We had several lakes to ourselves and could make all the noise we wanted.

Looking back now, it makes my head swim to think about the amount of preparation it took to make it happen. My father and older brother's packs were heavy. My mother carried the youngest when he didn't want to walk anymore. We cowboy camped so no one had to carry tents. We cooked over a fire, so no stove.

### And later...

I stood on the top of Pyramid Peak and looked down on

Lake Aloha and Desolation Wilderness in California. I was in awe. I was stunned by the beauty and the fact that I was only 70 miles from home. Why hadn't I been here before? I needed to experience more of this.

I was 50 years old, and it was 2003. Most of my athletic pursuits for the previous 15 years had been centered on running, biking, and swimming. I was in fairly good shape but wasn't hiking. Some friends had recently asked me if I wanted to join them to hike up Mt. Whitney. I said sure, but let's do a practice hike first. This was it. A few weeks later, I stood on top of the highest peak in the lower 48 states and had a similar emotional reaction.

I had known there was a John Muir Trail and a Pacific Crest Trail, but I didn't know the difference between them. I didn't know anyone who had hiked either one. I had done some backpacking before but not much. The idea of it always seemed better than actually doing it. My pack was always too heavy.

### After her success on Whitney

I was more motivated now. There had to be a better way. I went to REI and bought Ray Jardine's book, *Beyond Backpacking*. On the internet, I found backpackinglight.com and started reading articles and following the forums. There was a way to go lighter! I was going to do it.

I met a man, Dave, at my gym who had hiked the JMT. I was impressed and started dating him. I sewed a Ray Jardine tarp. I bought a quilt. I went to REI to hear Andrew Skurka talk and won a GoLite backpack. [Skurka was the first person to hike the 6,875-mile Great Western Loop and the 7,778-mile Sea-to-Sea Route.] Dave and I went backpacking together a few times. The light pack made all the difference.

The longest trip was five days; most were shorter. I always had to return to work. I started reading hiker journals on postholer. com and trailjournals.com. These people were out for four to six months! I wished I could do that. I couldn't see how. I had my own dental practice, and I couldn't take off more than one to two weeks at a time. So I just read about others and dreamt. I wasn't dating Dave anymore. I went backpacking with friends on some short trips. The thought of going by myself never occurred to me!

## And then, 'Why Not?'

I have hiked the long trails of America using the moniker 'Why Not?' Here is the genesis of that name…

In November 2007, I read one more book about someone else's adventure. This time it was *Rowing to Latitude* by Jill Fredston. She lived in Alaska and explored that state and more in a kayak converted to a rowing shell. As I was reading, the conversation in my head went something like this:

*This should be my life. Why don't I get to live it? Why someone else? Why not me?*

*If that is your life, what is stopping you?*

*Well, first, owning my own dental practice. I can't take off more than one or two weeks at a time.*

*Then get rid of it!*

And with that, I saw a path to freedom, adventure, and the life I wanted.

I was a dentist for 27 years and had my own practice for most of that time. I liked it and was good at it. I had great patients, and many had become friends. I had the best staff ever, which made my life so much better and easier. I found a wonderful dentist to take over, and on January 1, 2009, I was done.

## Reinventing a life

A little less than four months later, I set off to hike the entire 2,650 miles of the Pacific Crest Trail. This 159-day experience was the best adventure of my life. I met so many incredible people, was the recipient of so much generosity and goodness, and witnessed some amazing scenery, plus I had time to just think. I've continued to hike since then and have loved almost every minute of it. Meeting the physical and mental challenges has been good for body and soul. It has brought me a joy and a peace that is hard to explain.

Hiking the PCT the first time in 2009 (age 56) was life-changing for me. No other hike has changed me so profoundly. I'm proud of myself for actually making a dream turn into reality.

Before I started, I had talked to two people who had hiked it. One I met because he gave a talk at REI and the PCTA [Pacific Crest Trail Association] after his 2006 hike. The other I crossed paths with in the Wind River Range in Wyoming when she was hiking the CDT in 2007.

Fortunately, I had read so many journals that I had a clear idea of the 'hike, eat, sleep, repeat' routine required to make it to Canada before the season ended. I just didn't know if I could do it. During all the years I had my own dental practice, I had taken two three-week vacations, plus lots of shorter ones. After three weeks on the PCT, I often marveled at the fact that I didn't have to go home yet.

### Achievements

Since 2009, I have hiked the PCT twice, CDT, A.T., Arizona Trail, Te Araroa in New Zealand, Tahoe Rim Trail, Sierra High Route, Wind River High Route, Canada's Great Divide Trail, Pacific Northwest Trail, and a couple of trails in Patagonia and Europe. If I'm at home, I hike near Lake Tahoe when there isn't too much snow. In the winter, I hike in the SF Bay Area—Mt. Diablo, the Dipsea Trail on Mt. Tamalpais, and Point Reyes.

### The importance of hiking

Hiking plays a huge role in my life. Most of my friends are hikers. Many are backpackers. Hiking gets me outside to gorgeous places. It's where I feel the happiest. There's so much to love—the air, the scenery, the exertion, the people, the stillness, the simplicity.

It's walking. We have all been doing that since about age one. And humankind has been doing it forever.

### The pluses and minuses of going solo

I've hiked more miles with others than solo. I've planned trips with hiking partners, and I've started out solo and then acquired hiking partners because pace, routine, and personalities work.

For a long time, I was intimidated about going solo. Not anymore. "Are you going alone?" is usually the first question I get asked. I agree with the saying, "If you wait until you have someone to go with you, you will probably wait a long time and maybe never go." Life is too short for that. Hiking with a great hiking partner can be wonderful, but hiking with the wrong one makes solo hiking seem like heaven.

Solo hiking allows more spontaneity and inner growth. All the planning and route-finding falls on you. Except in the case of some emergencies, I don't think it's necessarily safer to hike with a partner. I am way more conservative with risk-taking when I go solo. I have made decisions with others I would never have made if I was by myself. Hiking one's own pace also helps with internal temperature regulation. However, being lost with others is way less scary!

### My advice for being successful

Plan and know what you are getting into. Every trail is different. Plans change, but it's easier to change if you know what your options are. If you are in good physical condition for hiking long miles day after day then it probably is more mental.

Build up miles slowly so you don't get injured and have to take time off. Take the time to find shoes that fit. Everyone's feet are different, but usually wearing a larger size eliminates many problems.

There is so much info out there. Help is everywhere. When I started hiking long trails, there was much less info, but I found what I needed. Now, almost everyone seems to know someone who has hiked the PCT or A.T. Hikers like to talk about hiking. Talk to one if you can. Join a Meetup hiking group. There are lots of guided options. Look at Facebook hiking groups. If you live close to an ALDHA-West Ruck, you should attend.

### On questionable advice

On many trails, I have heard fear-mongering about weather, snow, and water crossings. They have been important to listen to, but often the 'go see for yourself' option reveals a completely different situation—usually for the better.

**Women *and* men underestimate…**

[their physical abilities.] Most people, male and female, can do more than they think they can. If you want to do it, you can do it. You need to find out what works for you. If you don't try, you will never know. It is empowering, fun, and rewarding.

**Challenges for me**

My biggest challenge was finding the time to hike the long trails. I fixed that problem by selling my dental practice and retiring. For many dentists, the money they make enables them to have the life they want. For me, I was unable to both have a dental practice and do long adventures. While hiking, I don't think I've ever felt that everything in my head (or body) was begging me to stop. And, though I wish I could think of something, I think I have either pushed any scary or risky experiences out of my consciousness or I haven't pushed myself hard enough to encounter any.

**Age and its impact**

I can't and don't want to carry as much weight as I once could. My longest hiking day was 36 miles on the PCT in Washington in 2014. I'm sure I can't do that again. But I don't want or need to either.

I hiked every step of the PCT, CDT, and A.T. However, last year I didn't finish the Pacific Northwest Trail. I packed resupply boxes for the whole trail, but from the beginning, I was pretty sure I would only hike to Port Townsend 260 miles from the end. When I got there, I was done. I'll go back and finish another year.

I also don't want to do another five-month hike. As I've gotten older, I've needed to make sure I start my hikes in better shape. I've been pretty fortunate with a lack of injuries; I haven't had to quit a trail or even take one extra day off due to an injury. I'm sure that maintaining decent physical shape year-round has lots to do with that.

However, I do have hip and knee arthritis and will have to address that at some point. I've been skipping road walks when that's possible the last few years. Especially pavement. If I can see it from a car window, I don't really feel I'm missing anything. And it's much kinder to my joints. In the last few years, I have loved exploring by road-tripping and day hiking. I see much more of that in my future.

### Good hiking gear helps!

My favorite gear is having a light pack! That means my favorite thing is to not bring too much—to leave things at home.

But actually, my wind shirt is my favorite item of clothing. For just a few ounces, it adds an amazing amount of warmth. I can take it off without fully removing my backpack and it's so collapsible that I can just stuff it anywhere. Plus, it's wonderful as bug protection and allows me to seldom use insect repellent (which I hate).

The one piece of gear that I never think of replacing is my Zpacks sleeping bag. I actually have two of them: a 5-degree and a 30-degree. My only decision before a hike is which one to bring. They have zippers, but I rarely zip them up. I drape my bag over me like a quilt and tuck the edges in around me. I roll around all night long and have perfected the tuck and roll without completely waking up. They are light, well-made, and it feels awesome to wrap myself up in them. Plus, they are handsewn in the USA.

### And now, at 67, what are you looking for in your next long hiking or backpacking trip?

Something different!

### When the virus hit

[May 18, Sacramento] With no end in sight, quarantine fatigue is setting in. At first, it was a nice change of pace and I looked forward to something different. I got different alright, but this definitely was not what I was thinking of. Before the virus hit, I had talked to several different friends about hiking trips for this summer. I hadn't settled on anything, so I didn't have any plans to cancel. Hopefully, it will be possible to venture out this summer. In the eleven years since I retired, I haven't spent a summer at home. As it gets nicer out everywhere and gets hotter in Sacramento, I will have a much harder time accepting staying at home.

I live alone, and being an introvert has made things much easier. But I do need people. In the beginning, it was easy for me to accept that I needed to stay home. This virus is super-contagious, and so much is still not known about it. I have enjoyed watching the learning curve of how to treat it and how to prevent contagion. I have reconnected with friends on walks and phone calls.

I've gotten some long-overdue organizing projects done at my house. I've spent more time working in my backyard than in all 30 years combined that I have lived here. I have a vegetable garden for the first time since I retired. It seems likely that I will be around enough to reap some of its bounty.

I started making sourdough bread at the start of the year, so I got a small jump on the sourdough craze.

Last November, I started attending an exercise class at a physical therapy office. It's been great for core, balance, strength, and cardio. During the shutdown, they switched to Zoom classes—it's been the best thing I've done for my body in a long time. I don't want to lose the improvements in my body.

As much as I am ready for this to be behind us, it doesn't take much inspection of history and comparison to other pandemics to realize how relatively easy this is. I no longer own a small business. I have enough money, enough food, a nice home, and wonderful family and friends. And so far, good health. I can (but don't always) go out my front door and take a nice walk along the American River. Sometimes, I have to remind myself of this to get back into the gratitude groove.

But... I do worry about wasting what precious time I have left to backpack. I know that a hip replacement is in my future, so I've been contemplating having it done as soon as possible. I could be well down the recovery road when things get back to some kind of normal.

**Susan:** In one of Nancy's blogs, a guest asked, "What does she do 'off-season' to stay in shape?" Another guest, 'Beekeeper,' responded, "Check out [her] blogs. [She] hikes, hikes, and hikes some more. For her, there is no off-season." You can find Nancy Huber and her blog at nancyhikes.com.

When not adventuring elsewhere in the world, Nancy lives and hikes near Sacramento.

**Nancy Huber — Canada's Great Divide Trail 2018 (credit Christy 'Rockin' Rosander)**

# Naomi 'The Punisher' Hudetz

**Susan:** Naomi is the treasurer of the American Long Distance Hiking Association-West. She has received the Triple Crown award for hiking the Appalachian Trail, Pacific Crest, and Continental Divide Trail.

I first heard about her from a friend who mentioned that Naomi had cofounded a company called Treeline Review, treelinereview.com, with Liz Thomas (accomplished hiker, award-winning writer, and now editor-in-chief). When I looked further into it, I was impressed by both their review process and Naomi's hiking cred. The stated mission of Treeline Review is, "Everything we do is around this goal: buy less stuff."

Treeline Review is a wonderful resource for hikers. Their reviews are made by experts in the field and not driven by manufacturers' advertising budgets. Currently, Naomi leads revenue operations and business strategy for Treeline Review and is director of analytics and digital innovation.

**Naomi Hudetz:** I was 23 when I took my first backpacking trip. All of my hiking trips between ages 22 and 40 were either day hikes or weeklong backpacking trips. All of my hiking has been in the U.S. and Canada.

My first thru-hike was the Pacific Crest Trail; I turned 40 on trail. Since then, I've done numerous other long trails: Continental Divide, Appalachian, John Muir, Tahoe Rim, Great Divide, Lowest to Highest [135-mile route from Death Valley to the summit of Mt. Whitney], Pacific Northwest, Grand Enchantment, Idaho Centennial, and the Arizona and Ouachita Trails.

It was on the Appalachian Trail thru-hike in 2014 that I got my trail name, 'The Punisher.' My husband Mike and I started a little early in the year—March 10. We had one really cold night—I think it got down to twelve degrees—and in the morning, the trail was a sheet of ice. Mike slipped on the ice and went down hard. The fall broke his thumb and gave him a black eye. So... people joked that I was 'The Punisher,' breaking thumbs and giving people black eyes!

## Lifestyle choices and changes

Hiking has become my way of life. After finishing my first long hike, the Pacific Crest Trail, I remember sitting in my hotel room in Canada thinking, *I am not ready for this to be over.* Since then, I have arranged my entire life to maximize my hiking time.

After living for five months out of a backpack, I realized I didn't need a big giant house and everything inside it. My husband and I downsized to a 540-square-foot house in White Salmon, Washington, to reduce our monthly expenses as much as possible. We sold most of our belongings, and I honestly couldn't tell you what was in all of those bags of stuff we took to Goodwill. I've never missed any of it. And while it was painful to go through that process at the time, it was truly liberating in the end. Today, we spend less time working and more time hiking.

## The importance of hiking

It took me ten years to figure out why hiking matters so much to me. But while hiking alone in the Sierra, it finally came to me—nature is where I belong and is where I am accepted.

That moment was probably the first time in my adult life that I felt like I truly belonged somewhere and had a place in the world. Nature doesn't care what my gender is, how skinny/fat I am, how clean my house is, whether I know how to chop an onion properly. It feels silly even to write these things down, but these are all examples of ways my fellow humans have judged me.

Nature accepts everyone for who they are right at that moment in time. On the other hand, nature doesn't care how prepared I am, if I'm scared, how much experience I have, or whether I have the proper gear. That's all on me. There is no judgment from nature—there is no good, there is no bad.

Imagine if everyone in the world felt like they belonged and were accepted for who they are?

## The accomplishments

Making it through the snow and creek fords in the Sierra in June on the PCT is by far the hardest hiking I've ever done in comparison to my skill set at the time. It pushed me far out of my comfort zone in so many ways. Hiking in the snow over mountain passes with a heavy pack at elevations I'd never been to before, with scary creek fords and bad weather, I still think back and wonder, *How did I do that?*

When we finally got to the town of Mammoth Lakes, California, I was mentally and physically wholly spent. However, the feeling of accomplishment was overwhelming—something I'd never experienced before or since.

## Solo—to go or not to go

I'm a huge proponent of hiking solo. There's so much good that comes from hiking solo:

- The freedom to set your own hiking pace and mileage schedule.
- The challenge that comes from having to do everything yourself: planning, navigating, and decision-making.
- The unity with nature that can happen in a different way than happens with hiking with other people.

However, it took me a long time to get comfortable hiking solo. I still remember the first time I went on a solo day hike; I actually felt panic. It felt like there would be a bear around every corner, so I hiked faster and faster to get back to my car. When I finally got up the courage to backpack solo, I thought I might have the same sense of panic when the sun went down. To my surprise, I fell asleep quickly.

To the critics: I understand that there are dangers associated with hiking solo. But in my opinion, a life without risk isn't living—it's merely existing. But I don't take crazy risks, and I do what I can to mitigate the risk.

- Get comfortable sleeping outside with other people first.
- Do a lot of solo day hiking.
- Work your way up to solo overnight trips.
- Carry a personal locator beacon (PLB). The device I carry is also a satellite messenger (Garmin inReach), but if you want to be totally off the grid then bring a true rescue beacon. The OceanSignal RescueMe, for example, is small and light, and the battery lasts five years.
- Tell people about your plans. Someone needs to know when you're overdue.
- Spend as much time as you can outside and in the backcountry. I found that the more time I spent outside, the less fearful I became.
- Carry mace if it makes you feel safer. Some women feel better knowing that they have some way to defend themselves if necessary.

**Why hike the long trails**

To be a successful long-distance hiker, I think you have to really, really want to do it for you. It can't be for your partner, Instagram, fame, or your blog. Long-distance hiking is hard, and there will be moments that will tax every aspect of your being—physical, emotional, and spiritual. And if you aren't internally motivated, those moments will probably end your hike. If you really, really want it, then you'll figure out a way to be successful—however you define success.

**And what about when you are wiped out?**

I try hard not to get to that point. I'm a believer in keeping it to 80 percent. For example, during a climb, I try to keep my heart rate under 80 percent of my maximum heart rate. I don't wear a heart-rate monitor, but in general, it's easy to tell when I'm reaching that point of overexertion. I find that if I keep it under 80 percent then I can hike farther and take fewer breaks.

However, there still are times when I get to a point and

think to myself, *I am never doing this again*. I just let myself have that moment, which always passes. If it's a prolonged period of horribleness (like bushwhacking in the rain through alder for miles) then I resort to singing songs out loud or find other ways to distract myself. This is when it's nice to have a hiking partner!

## There will be challenges

The biggest challenge I've had to overcome is my own self-doubt. Growing up, I was the last kid picked for the team in gym class. I was scrawny, small, and uncoordinated. Consequently, I grew up believing that sports and exercise were not for me. It became who I was.

Looking back now, I realize that I stopped trying. I unconsciously took on the role of the slowest, weakest person in every situation. On a hike or a backpacking trip, I insisted on being the last person in the group because I 'knew' I'd be the slowest. But being the last person in line was demoralizing…it became a negative feedback loop.

I didn't know it at the time, but all of that had to change with my first long-distance hike, the Pacific Crest Trail. There's no way I could have finished otherwise. It may sound like an exaggeration, but I truly think that thru-hiking rewired my brain. Those old, deep brain patterns had to be replaced. Things I thought to be impossible became possible—in all aspects of my life.

## A frightening experience brought trail wisdom

In the Bob Marshall Wilderness on the Continental Divide Trail, my husband and I lost the trail. We spread out to find it (but within voice range of each other) and finally did. We started back up the trail, climbing out of a valley. Almost immediately, we saw a grizzly bear with her cub coming down the trail towards us.

I pulled out my bear spray and took off the safety. My husband struck his poles together (and broke one), hoping to scare them off. That was not the right reaction—she lowered her head, huffed, and scratched the ground. We started talking gently to her, backed up, and did not make eye contact. We did not turn our backs to her. As we backed up, the trail curved and we could no longer see each other. I'm not sure where mother and cub went after that, but that was the last we saw of them. Bonus! We backtracked far enough to figure out where we lost the trail.

My biggest lesson from this was that bears don't want a confrontation any more than we do. It also taught me how vital a proper response is in these situations. I try to visualize this (and other) bad scenarios in my mind and how to respond so that if the situation arises, I will hopefully react appropriately instead of running, which would have been a natural impulse.

### Thru-hiking as the fountain of youth

There's a joke in the long-distance hiking community that thru-hiking is the fountain of youth. Obviously, that's an exaggeration, but I do think that long-distance hiking is a sport that people don't age out of. My husband met an 82-year-old man solo backpacking in the Sierra. I met a 75-year-old man thru-hiking the Arizona Trail, and I honestly thought he was in his 50s.

I'm hoping that I will be strong and healthy, and continue to hike into my 70s and 80s as these people are doing. So for now, I try to push myself to do more challenging hikes. And while there will undoubtedly be changes ahead, I'll do my best to push them out for as long as possible.

Also, the availability of lightweight gear is a game-changer for older hikers. Keeping my pack weight down reduces the wear and tear on my body and will hopefully allow me to hike relatively comfortably for many more years.

[And on a practical note] my favorite piece of hiking gear is the Six Moon Designs Silver Shadow Carbon trekking sun umbrella (aka 'chrome dome'). I struggle hiking in the heat, and the reflective properties of the chrome dome are a game-changer for me. I use a hands-free system to attach it to my pack so I can still use my trekking poles. It keeps me cool in two ways: it blocks direct sunlight and I don't have to wear a sunhat while I'm using the umbrella. It's also a part of my rain system. In all but the heaviest rain, I don't have to use my rain jacket because the umbrella keeps the rain off my head and torso. During lunch breaks in the rain, I can set it up in a tree to provide a little shelter. It's truly multipurpose!

### Advice for other hikers

Go to an ALDHA-West event! Their Rucks are 'all things long-distance hiking' for newbies to seasoned hikers, and they're also a fantastic way to find hiking partners. The friendships I've made through ALDHA-West are priceless!

Start slowly. Don't plan a thru-hike of the PCT if you've never gone hiking before. While I have met people who finished a thru-hike as their first hiking experience, I don't recommend it. Instead, go day hiking if you've never hiked before. Or if you're an experienced hiker, go backpacking for the first time. Master the current level before moving up to the next level.

Seek out experienced hiking or backpacking partners. Be honest about your skill level and nervousness. Don't pretend to have skills that you don't. If they're not comfortable hiking with you, they'll tell you.

If I take someone out on their first backpacking trip, I have a golden rule: It *must* be a great experience. Don't go if it's going to rain. Don't make it a 'death march' over steep and challenging terrain. Choose a beautiful destination so there's a reward for the work. Bring good food. Keep their pack weight down. Above all else, don't make them feel bad if they're slow. It's demoralizing for them to be at the back of the line knowing that the faster people are waiting for them.

As you gain more experience, take out less experienced hikers or backpackers. When you're the experienced hiker who's expected to keep it together, you will rise to the occasion. Your self-confidence will also get a boost.

### On women underestimating their abilities

Yes, yes, *yes!* There's no doubt about it—women underestimate their physical abilities, as I have my entire life. It took me a long time to figure out that I'm not a weak, fragile human; the things we learn as children are not easily unlearned as adults. We're not born thinking this way; we're 'taught' to think this way. It's really, really unfortunate.

My best advice is to use it as motivation. If people have ever been skeptical of your plans—or flat-out said, "You're never gonna make it" (both of which have happened to me)—prove them wrong. Nothing motivates me more than people telling me I can't do something.

I also strive to be a force for good. I try to encourage and support other female hikers in any way I can. By lifting up and encouraging others, we'll all rise together. This is one reason I started the website Treeline Review with my business partner (and friend) Liz Thomas. Because we couldn't find what we were looking for, we built it ourselves! We wanted a place where everyone felt comfortable and encouraged to find their place in nature.

## How to handle bad or risky advice

My favorite example of bad advice is that the trail will be your training. In other words, there's no need to train for a long hike—just show up off the couch, and you'll get in shape along the way. This might work for 20-somethings but not me.

While it is true that the best way to be ready to hike 25 miles a day is to hike 25 miles a day, there are other ways to prepare. In the off-season, I keep in shape by walking every day, lifting weights three times a week, yoga, high-intensity interval training (HIIT), and day hiking. Before a thru-hike, I'll increase my daily mileage and increase the length and intensity of my day hikes (carrying a pack with more weight). Hiking on actual trail is essential to keeping your ankles strong. I also try to focus on the mechanics of hiking properly uphill and downhill, as shown in this video: youtube.com/watch?v=cDIeu_QL51U

My second favorite example of bad advice is that it doesn't matter what you eat on a long-distance hike—doughnuts, candy, chips…just eat. I couldn't disagree more. Again, this may work for 20-somethings but not me at age 50. I need a lot of protein and fat; I don't need sugar.

## What the future might bring

I look for hikes in places I've never been to before—hopefully, some more international hiking. I also like incomplete trails or 'routes' with cross-country and bushwhacking sections. I love the extra challenge with [unmarked] routes—you can't be on autopilot. You have to know where you are at all times; you have to be comfortable with being uncomfortable. In other words, I look for hikes that get me to the point of saying, "I'm never doing this again!"

**Facing COVID-19:**

Somewhat unintentionally, I am following the sentiment of the saying, "Everyone needs someone to love, something to do, and something to look forward to".

**Someone to love:**

We got a foster cat! Our friends found a stray cat on their property. The cat needed to have his eye removed and needed a place to recuperate after his surgery. We thought we'd have him for two weeks until his antibiotics were finished. But, it's four months later and I think he's our cat now! It turns out we needed each other.

**Something to do:**

Hiking trails in the Columbia River Gorge were closed during the initial phase of the quarantine. So I compensated in two ways: hiking forest service roads—the rutted out roads with little traffic. I just thought of them as really wide trails. All I really cared about was being in the forest!

And, I bought a bikepacking bike. I've wanted to try long-distance bikepacking since 2012 when I met a bikepacker riding the Great Divide Route as I was hiking the Continental Divide Trail. I took my new bike out on the same rutted out Forest Service roads for some overnight trips. I'm still planning my first long-distance ride.

**Something to look forward to:**

I spent time planning hikes that I hoped would come to fruition as the country opened back up. So, in April I was planning for the hikes I could do starting in May, June, July, etc. And as the quarantine continued, I would drop the hikes that were no longer feasible.

**Susan:** In cofounder Liz Thomas's book, *Backpacker Long Trails: Mastering the Art of the Thru-Hike*, she refers to Hudetz taking time off "in the middle of her career as an actuary. She came back refreshed, focused, and rejuvenated." Hudetz added, "Employers see value in someone who can plan and follow through on a project such as this."

Naomi Hudetz

# Sandy 'Frodo' Mann

**Susan:** In 2008, I moderated a panel discussion entitled "Women on the PCT" for the PCTA Trailfest in Sacramento. Sandy, who with her husband Barney 'Scout' Mann had thru-hiked the trail the previous year, was one of our panelists.

Sandy has a Ph.D. in Molecular Biology and began her working career with the University of California, San Diego. She switched careers in the 1990s and began teaching high school students advanced and AP Biology—as well as coaching Academic League and Science Olympiad students. Now retired, Sandy participates in "Hike the Hill" each February. She accompanies a group of high school students to Washington, DC, as part of the PCTA contingent that advocates for the PCT and other National Trails.

**Sandra (or Sandy) Mann:** I grew up in Southern California and started hiking when I was 10. My family rented a cabin for a week in Mammoth Lakes, California, and my two older brothers and I would hike between some of the lakes. When we went to Devil's Postpile, I was the only child who chose to hike with my dad to Rainbow Falls, and I was pretty proud of myself. When I was 11, my two older brothers, then 13 and 15, got to go backpacking with the Boy Scouts. I was really jealous but couldn't convince anyone to take me on a backpack trip. I tried to join the Sierra Club at the age of 11 but was told I would have to wait until I was 12, even though I wrote them a pleading heartfelt letter.

So for a few years, I went on day hikes with my family and in some groups, and finally went on my first backpack trip with a church youth group when I was 15. I loved it! We hiked in the

Sierra from Florence Lake (no boat trip) to just inside Kings Canyon, then back out. It was a six-day trip, and I didn't sleep well because I had an old kapok [an organic filling] sleeping bag and I was cold all night, but I was hooked.

I met Barney a year later while working at a camp for disadvantaged youth (he was the director; I was a counselor), and we have backpacked together ever since.

I first learned of the PCT in the mid-'70s while we were backpacking in Oregon, where I attended the University of Oregon and Barney was in law school. There was a symbol or sign at a trail junction, and Barney told me about this trail that went from Mexico to Canada. That got us both thinking.

## Hiking the world

Mostly I have hiked in the Sierra Nevada, the mountains of Southern California, and the Cascades. Until after I thru-hiked the PCT in 2007, I had really only hiked in California, Oregon, and Washington. We switched to ultralight and hiked the John Muir Trail in 2003 to see if we could do this long-distance hiking thing. In the last 12 years, I've also hiked 600 miles at various locations on the Continental Divide Trail, about 100 miles on a couple of sections of the Wales Coast Path, a 20-day trek in the Himalayan Everest region, and a six-day trek in the French Alps. I am really enjoying exploring big mountains all over the world and working on my bucket list.

## What hiking offers

Personally, I feel a bit addicted to hiking. Nowadays, I generally go on a couple of backpacks each summer. As the months since my last hike go by, the hole in my life that is filled by backpacking gets larger, and I need to start actively planning my summer treks. It's not really an obsession, but I have a definite need to be in the mountains.

I really enjoy the planning aspect of trips, so I made up a really cool and detailed spreadsheet for when we were doing the PCT and showed it off along the trail.

Seeing photos of a mountain trail that rounds a turn or crests a pass brings back that urge to get out there and hike over that pass to see what my new view will be. On our hikes, we often exclaim "New stuff!" any time we get a new view. I love mountain scenery, the more craggy and spectacular the better. The best way I can explain it is that it feeds my soul.

But there's another reason we like long-distance hiking: I thought long-distance hiking would be about the scenery and the feeling of accomplishment, but the most important thing about it is always the community. We are still very close with many folks we hiked long trails with. My husband likes to say, "This is the community I always wanted to belong to and never knew existed." I feel the same way.

### Trail angels in Southern California

A less direct role that hiking plays in my life is that Barney and I host aspiring PCT hikers in our home in San Diego each spring. We began in 2006. We pick them up at the airport or train station, put them up overnight, feed them home-cooked meals, and take them to the southern terminus of the PCT early in the morning.

We host American hikers for one night but hikers from overseas for up to three nights. We do this for eight or more weeks. In 2018, we hosted more than 1,250 hikers—often 30 to 40 hikers each night. Obviously, we can't do this alone; we work with many local volunteers and also experienced hikers who come live with us for a week or two to help out.

It is our goal to relieve the stress that comes with arriving in an unfamiliar place and trying to figure out how to get to the trail, help hikers take care of last-minute preparations, and allow them to start the trail with other hikers they've gotten to know at our house so they already feel part of a community. We also give a talk each evening after dinner about Leave No Trace, being good trail ambassadors, taking care of each other, and making wise decisions. We like to feel we're sending a wave of kindness up the trail.

## A significant accomplishment

I thru-hiked the Pacific Crest Trail with my husband in 2007 when I was 48. It was five months and 2,650 miles of adventure and challenge and joy and pain and beauty and friendship. It is such a different life than we normally live; it is distilled down to the essence of what we need to stay alive and to travel. We still turn to each other at least once a week and say with wonder, "We hiked the PCT!"

## Thoughts about solo hiking

I have done very little solo hiking. I met Barney when I was 17, and we were both already enthusiastic backpackers. When we hike together, as on the PCT, we usually end up hiking apart for an hour or two each day. I enjoy that time alone but often find myself thinking, "Oh, I wish Barney were here so I could point out (these cool mushrooms, this interesting flower…) to him!" I admire women who backpack solo.

## Long-distance hiking requires toughness

So much of backpacking is about mental toughness. You have to be willing to put up with pain on a daily basis and to know that you can hike through that pain. You have to put up with heat and cold and rain and snow and all kinds of obstacles and know that you can overcome them. In other words, you need resilience—the ability to bounce back from adversity and not let it beat you down.

You have to have enough joyful time doing this tough thing—appreciating the scenery, spending rewarding time with other hikers—for the cost/benefit ratio to make sense. So, having the right attitude, to really grab and hold onto that joy, is important, and so is being able to ignore or tamp down your pain or discomfort. Of course, you have to know what kinds of pain are okay to ignore, and you have to be able to put that in the back of your mind and focus on what you love about the trail and your hiker community.

**Challenges to face**

Since my PCT thru-hike, I have had chronic and constant foot pain. Most long-distance hikers have their foot pain resolve within a couple of months after they finish hiking. Unfortunately, that hasn't been the case for me. On the PCT, I routinely hiked 20 to 25 miles per day, five to six days per week.

Now at 61, I try to limit my mileage to 10 to 12 miles per day, and I'm not sure I could do that for more than a few weeks. So, a second thru-hike of any long trail is just not in the cards for me. I never intended to do another thru-hike, so that's okay. I just want to ensure that I can hike and backpack with my grandkids. Right now, I have a two-year-old grandson and a new grandchild.

**Learning from frightening experiences**

When I was 18, I went on a hike in the Sierra with an older brother and a younger brother. Much of the 50-mile loop was on unmaintained trail. Everything went fine until our last couple of days. We were camped at Dragon Lake, above the Rae Lakes Basin, intending to climb cross-country over Dragon Pass the next day and then down to the Onion Valley trailhead. We woke to heavy rain and decided to wait it out. The rain continued, so we just dozed in our tent. The one watch we had among the three of us had stopped working, so we had no idea of the time.

We finally packed up in the rain and headed toward what we thought was the pass. It soon got dark, and we found ourselves trying to work our way down a very steep rocky face using ropes to pass our packs down. We finally got wise and scrambled back up, and camped near the crest. Our sleeping bags were damp, so we zipped the two driest ones together, and the three of us climbed inside, trying to get warm. We woke to snow all around us. We hiked out on the trail over Glen Pass and Kearsarge Pass, about 16 miles in drenching rain, the farthest I had ever hiked in a day up to that point. We came to realize that we had lost our camera and my older brother's wallet with most of our cash, probably while passing down our packs with ropes. We later realized that we had weathered the California version of Hurricane Kathleen.

I learned many things from that experience: 1) Know how

to read your maps and trust them. We should have realized that Dragon Pass was far south of the crest we hiked up to. 2) Carry a functional watch and have backup. 3) Don't do stupid things like trying to negotiate a cliff face at night in the rain. Jesus!

## Hiking plans evolve

For decades, we were old-school backpackers with heavy packs, hiking eight to 10 miles per day. Less when we hiked with our three kids—Sean, Jordie, and Nicky—which we did for many years.

We became ultralight backpackers before we hiked the John Muir Trail to see if we could handle long-distance ultralight hiking. After that amazing time, we had set our caps to hike the PCT. But there's no way I could have hiked the daily miles needed for a thru-hike had I been carrying the 35- to 40-pound pack I did when I was in my teens, 20s, and 30s.

Because of my foot issue, I not only limit my miles, I'm also a bit more conservative nowadays. And though I love cowboy camping under the stars, I did love the hut-to-hut hiking we did in the French Alps where we had little we needed to carry. It was rather nice being fed hearty meals that someone else had cooked and being able to share a bottle of wine. I expect I'll do more of that as I get older, but I am still planning a couple of 100-mile hikes in the Sierra for next summer. I have to admit, though, that I am very aware when I return to favorite spots along the JMT or PCT that this may be my last time to visit them, which does make me a bit sad.

## Gear changes

When we became interested in long-distance hiking, we realized we would need to have lighter packs, and we discovered Ray Jardine's books, Henry Shires's Tarptents, Gossamer Gear packs (then GVP Gear), Feathered Friends sleeping bags, etc.

I love my Western Mountaineering Flight down jacket. It keeps me so warm, and I hate being cold. It's compressible and very light, and I take it on every mountain backpack trip even if it does make me look like the Michelin Man. I hate being cold!

### When women doubt their abilities

It's always good to challenge and stretch yourself, but you also want to maximize your chance of success. Go hiking and get in shape. Make sure you have good gear and know how to use it. Do your research, and be prepared.

I think some women underestimate their physical abilities. I would tell these women that they're tougher and more capable than they think. They could set themselves a goal—run a half-marathon, go for a weeklong backpack—and then work toward it in a stepwise fashion. Don't try too much too fast. Listen to your body, and learn what pain comes with the territory and can be ignored and what pain must be addressed.

### Avoiding risk

I can't recall ever being given bad advice by an experienced backpacker. One of the things we talk about with aspiring PCT thru-hikers who stay at our home is the danger of crossing a high stream alone. It's always a good idea to start into a dangerous area, such as the High Sierra when there is still a lot of snow and dangerous stream crossings, as part of a group that will look out for each other. My best advice is, "Make wise decisions."

### The next adventure

Next, we plan to hike in Patagonia and then some other sections of the Alps. I am looking forward to beautiful rugged mountains with views of craggy peaks and rocky ridges. They give me joy to look upon and hike amongst. They lift my spirits and make me want to sing and shout with elation!

**Susan:** Sandy's husband, Barney 'Scout' Mann, has written *Journeys North: The Pacific Crest Trail*, an engaging book about their 2007 thru-hike of the challenging and rewarding trail.

In spring 2020 as the COVID-19 pandemic began, Barney referred to a *Washington Post* article that appeared on 3/16/20 with the headline, "Scout and Frodo closing for the season." He commented: "Never imagined us in the *Washington Post* this way: 'Last week, one couple known for hosting Pacific Crest

Trail hikers in their San Diego home announced that given the potential risks, they had made the "gut-wrenching" decision not to do so this year."'

"'We know you have been planning your PCT hike for months or years and have spent hundreds of hours planning for it,'" Barney and Sandy Mann, who are known in the hiking community as 'Scout and Frodo,' wrote on their website." 'Many of you have been thrown into utter turmoil by the U.S. travel ban. We understand your confusion, pain, disappointment, and anger.'"

Though that was going to be the couple's last year hosting hikers, in July 2020, they announced that they will host hikers for the spring of 2021, if it is safe to do so.

**Sandy Mann — Continental Divide Trail**

# Jan 'Jaunting Jan' McEwen

**Susan:** Jan has a motto: 'An Adventure a Day Keeps the Doctor Away.' It fits her perfectly. Jan lives much of the time in her car. "Wherever I park it," she says, "although my house lives in Redding, California and I visit it occasionally." You'll soon understand why!

**Jan McEwen:** I started hiking when I was in my early fifties and started hiking seriously at 55 when I quit working. I was introduced to this great sport in the wilds of far Northern California—carving out memories in the Trinity Alps, Mt. Shasta/Trinity Divide area, Lassen Volcanic National Park and Whiskeytown National Recreation Area. I've hiked primarily west of the Continental Divide—California, Oregon, Washington, Idaho, Montana, Wyoming, Colorado, Utah, Nevada—as well as a bit in western Canada.

Variety is the spice of life! I love exploring, hiking new trails, and learning about areas. Although I've hiked long distances on the famous trails (i.e. about 1,500 on the Pacific Crest, a few hundred on both the Continental Divide and the Arizona National Scenic Trail), my preference is loops and multi-day backpack trips of seven to ten days. My favorite jaunt thus far was the six weeks I spent exploring the Wind River Wilderness in Wyoming.

## The role hiking plays

Hiking is my life! For the past five+ years I've been traveling to hiking destinations six to nine months annually. I typically go out for about three months at a time, returning home for a month or two to regroup before setting out again.

Flexibility is key to my formula. I try to have several options for nearby hikes in a particular area. Though I prefer loop hikes, I will do out and backs to avoid shuttles. If I find I love one hike in the area, I'll seek out more.

Because I'm living on a very frugal budget, I sleep in my car while traveling when I'm not backpacking. I slept in my car on public lands 123 nights and my tent 42 nights in 2019. I also like sleeping in my car between trailheads so I'm not wasting time trying to get to a town and instead can begin another adventure. This is especially convenient when I'm doing a lot of day hikes. My philosophy is hike more, drive less.

## Joys of backpacking

I like the physical challenges, the views and fresh air, nature's sounds, the wonder of what's around the next corner or over the next hill. It's my happy spot! I prefer backpacking as I'm rarely ready to turn around after a day hike. I like finding special places to experience sunrise and sunset. I like walking until I'm tired and knowing I can just set up camp versus rushing back to my car. I like the feeling of my life on my back and continue to be in awe of where my feet take me.

I consider my greatest accomplishment to be my first solo backpack trip just before my 55th birthday. It gave me the confidence and courage to adopt a wanderlust lifestyle. I had planned to hike the Goat Rocks section of the Pacific Crest with four friends. One by one, they dropped out. Because it was peak PCT hiker season, I knew there would be others on the trail should anything happen.

With a year of planning, I was mentally and physically ready for this multiday trip. I met incredible hikers, several I'm still in contact with, including a couple engaged on Old Snowy with me as their photographer.

With the confidence gained during this solo experience, I immediately obtained a walkup permit for the Wonderland Trail around Mt. Rainier. It was great to add another solo multiday trek to my resume.

**More on solo hiking**

Having spent the bulk of my life single, I am comfortable being with myself, which I believe makes solo adventuring a natural progression. I've mentored several women who wanted the solo experience, but they had never spent a night at home alone nor participated in other activities without friends or family. For these individuals, it's important to test limits in advance. Some have too much noise in their heads, which makes for a miserable solo as they are dependent on chatter to keep those thoughts at bay. For a first solo, I don't recommend trails at campgrounds or near a road; instead, my advice is to hike into the backcountry with a friend then camp far enough away that you can't see or hear them.

My career included strategic planning and execution. I think this helps turn dreams and plans into reality. One phrase I use frequently is, "Are you a 'stewer' or doer?" I've always been self-motivated, independent, and a bit of a loner. I believe these traits help with solo adventures. It's frustrating to engage with 'stewers,' dreamers, and planners who just can't find the courage to become doers. These tend to be the individuals who get you excited and committed only to back out as it gets nearer to the date, which then leads to either disappointment or a solo adventure.

Finding compatible and available companions has been a challenge. As a result, I'd say I hike and backpack 95 percent of the time solo. My philosophy on this is that I can sit at home waiting for an invite or for someone to be available, hike with someone who pisses me off, or just do my own thing. I've also become a bit of an anti-planner and rarely want to commit to others' plans or permits too far in advance, which reduces my opportunities for group hiking.

I find myself much more aware of my surroundings when hiking solo. I stop more frequently to look around and take photos. Decisions are mine and mine alone. When I reach a trail junction, it's up to me. Do I want to go left, right, straight, or backward? When I'm with others, I spend my time chatting, trying to keep up, and compromising—more often than not encouraging others to be the decision-makers.

I've taken advantage of opportunities to find compatible partners because I enjoy socializing. In fact, I consider myself an extroverted introvert. I've met a ton of people on trail, and while traveling, because I'm a conversation starter. Giggles, smiles, and laughter are my medicine, but nature's beauty is my drug of choice.

## Attributes needed in order to be a successful long-distance hiker?

- Love of walking, hiking, and moving
- Independence to make personal gear choices
- Enjoy a minimalist lifestyle
- Know how to dig deep and keep going
- Committed to completion
- Embrace the imperfect

## And when the going gets difficult

My limitations are mostly based on fitness level or hiking solo. I've needed to cope with exercise-induced asthma; to accept that I'm slower than others, especially while climbing; and to learn that it's better to go solo than stay home or go with an incompatible partner. Because I started hiking later in life, I haven't had to compare current performance with a younger version of me, however, there are places that I'd love to have hiked when I had better balance, flexibility, and less concern about consequences.

My mantra: One step at a time. You can do it! Yes, you can! Take a break. Drink, eat, reevaluate. Sometimes that means turning around, or making camp early, or taking a day off, or just taking an hour to go swimming.

## Frightening experiences and challenges

I had one of those push-through-it-or-die-trying experiences. I was snowshoeing at Great Basin National Park; I was solo and the only person on the trail. I decided if I could make it to the point where the trail intersected the road, I'd make a loop by returning on the road. It was 4 p.m. by the time I reached the intersection. I'd had to break trail most of the day mucking through some seriously deep snow as I reached the top. I didn't want to go back the way I came and figured the road would be shorter, and even though unplowed, easier.

*Wrong!* For some reason, I didn't look at my mapping app in advance to see that it was a 'scenic' road, much longer than my earlier route. Once discovered, I had no choice but to continue my forward momentum. It was really cold, and no one knew where I was—well, except for the waypoints I left on my inReach. I kept seeing lights, worried that the rangers were out looking for me as my car was the only vehicle at the trailhead. Later, I learned the lights were road reflectors.

I was tired, hungry, and cold, but knew if I stopped, I'd freeze. I pushed forward for more hours on snowshoes than ever, finally reaching my car at 11 p.m. I learned some valuable lessons: 1) Study your map in advance—duh. 2) Perseverance pays off. Luckily I had plenty of clothes, food, water, and an emergency blanket with me. The temperatures dropped into the teens that night.

### Another time

In the summer of 2018, I was nine days in on what I expected to be a three-week jaunt on the PCT in Oregon. After hiking about five miles that morning, I found myself falling down a slope. I have absolutely no idea what caused me to fall. The trail was in good condition—flat and wide with no real obstructions. My wrist took the full force of the fall and I knew I was in trouble.

I was one of the lucky (or unlucky) ones who pushed the SOS button on my inReach. I was hiking solo, and the spill dislocating my wrist. (I later learned I had fractured it in three places requiring major surgery.)

Several nearby hikers came to my aid. One had recently taken a wilderness first-aid course. He jumped into action, making a sling out of my rain jacket. Another knew I was in shock and encouraged me to push the button. With no other injuries, I was hesitant as my legs were just fine. I finally conceded and began the long wait.

Meanwhile, a couple of hikers, 'Hot Lips' and 'Caveman,' sacrificed their day to tend to my needs. They kept me comfortable and, according to SAR [Search and Rescue], did everything right! I was reassured multiple times by SAR that I did the right thing by pushing the button.

However, it took four hours for an EMT to arrive via helicopter. Search and Rescue volunteers and the EMT helped me hike eight miles to the nearest trailhead, where an ambulance was waiting for me. I arrived at the hospital a full 12 hours after my accident and 10.5 hours after activating my SOS. [After receiving care and being released], I made it back to Redding just as the Carr Fire erupted, with 38,000 homes evacuated, including mine, and 1,000 lost, thankfully not mine.

Surgery and rehab followed; hiking and backpacking were resumed. [Jan's blog post about her fall and subsequent rescue on the PCT trip: jansjaunts.wordpress.com/2018/09/12/ life-interrupted-forever-grateful-for-the-sos-button]

The biggest takeaways: Carry an emergency beacon (which I've done for many years), have your emergency contacts set up on their website (my niece met me at the hospital within 15 minutes), and have your emergency details with you (handing over my paper with allergies, surgeries, insurance info, etc., expedited my care.)

**Advice for women who want to start hiking or backpacking regularly, or who are nervous about going on a new and more challenging trail**

You can join a group to shortcut the learning process. You'll find out about gear preferences, skills, and routines for both overnighting and hiking. Take a class and gain skills in map reading and navigation. Track your hikes to become more familiar with how you perform in various terrains. Learn how to monitor stats such as water usage per mile given temperatures and elevation gain so you'll know how much to carry. Find your tribe through group events.

Read blogs and watch videos, but don't get stuck in the overwhelming possibilities. Start small, and your world will open if you so choose. Close your ears to naysayers. See for yourself, but be smart. Be prepared with knowledge, skills, and the right equipment.

As Nike says, "Just do it!" Define your own limits—don't

let others set them for you. You can always turn back. Lean on a trusted friend to help you conquer fears. Test yourself regularly, and become your own best resource. Don't be afraid of failure. Speak up if you need to go slower or need coaching—99 percent of hikers enjoy the mentoring and teaching experience. We all started as beginners.

## On gear

My $5 DIY hiking skirt was a favorite find because it was a game-changer. My body weight, in particular my lower half, fluctuates dramatically, which means needing several sizes of pants. When I developed a contact allergy to the synthetic fabrics common in hiking pants, I decided to give a skirt a try. Because of chub rub, I typically wear men's boxer briefs or leggings underneath. I made tall gaiters to wear when cold, buggy or hiking in 'stickery, prickery' areas, and I use snow gaiters at other times.

I'd say my Gaia app is my most important piece of gear. I love maps and tracking my hikes. It's helped me become more confident with my navigation skills. These maps are so much more than topos; they also show air quality, snow conditions, and burn areas—and greatly enhance my ability to plan on the fly.

## Bad advice I've been given:
- Pack a gun—um, no thanks, I'll pack my brain.
- No need to treat water—that's okay, I'll skip giardia.
- You only need to carry x amount of water—know *your* needs.
- This is an easy hike!—maybe for *you*, do your own research.
- You don't need maps or navigation aids (i.e. on the PCT)—there are plenty of junctions, creeks, and dead-fall-causing detours, and getting to and out of towns is a challenge of its own.

## Next hiking and backpacking trips

I'm interested in seeing new and different views, vegetation, geology, etc. My mind is most stimulated hiking new-to-me trails where I don't know quite what to expect. I love the anticipation of wondering what's around the next corner or over the next hill. Because I enjoy blogging and photography, I think of my readers as I hike, wanting to share my experiences.

Feeling my personal time clock ticking, I'm motivated to find *wow*-per-mile trails. I mark my maps with those must-see places and choose my travel/hiking itineraries accordingly. While this requires a bit more planning than hiking a long trail, I find more joy than I do walking roads or hiking through less desirable terrain.

Several factors eliminate places from my list or at least move them down the priority list. Those include complicated permits, technical skills, shuttles, and long water carries. Obviously, weather and conditions are another consideration.

For example, rather than hiking the full PCT primarily to experience highlights like the Sierra and the North Cascades, I'd rather skip the in-between and go directly to the Sierra and then to the Northern Cascades. Rather than hiking the CDT through the Winds, I spent six weeks hiking from each of the trailheads there.

I use a digital map to flag future points of interest (POIs); this tool makes it easy to plan on the fly. For example, I was in Idaho hiking the Sawtooths and White Clouds followed by a trip to visit friends in Boise. I used my Gaia app to track current wildfires and smoke, and checked the weather forecast and found the Rubies in Nevada on my POI map, only three and a half hours away. When I finished there, I went back to the map, found Great Basin National Park was another three and a half hours away.... That's how I roll!

### It's tough dealing with COVID-19

[May 2020, Northern California] As for the lockdown, I've ridden the rollercoaster of emotions going through the stages of grief. Writing and sharing my thoughts on my blog has been therapeutic.

It's been a struggle to balance the black-and-white state and county orders against the reality of my personal situation. I felt extreme conflict and envy when I saw photos of others out adventuring when we've been told to stay within our neighborhoods. Forests and parks added to the confusion by inviting safe recreation. As the weeks wore on and nonessential travel and outings became the norm, I had to ask myself why I was staying home. I wasn't going shopping or exposing myself to any social environments. Walking or biking on my local trails wasn't a good option as social distancing wasn't possible. The streets weren't healthy for my body or mind.

Eventually, I gave myself permission to drive 10 miles to a dirt trail. That transitioned into driving 50 miles for a few overnights in the wilderness. That became my new norm. Drive 50-100 miles, then backpack for a few days in my backyard wilderness areas where I might see only a handful of people. Drive home, resupply, do laundry, grab gas, repeat.

At first, I felt guilty, but then I felt so much relief and happiness. I was aware of the risk I was taking should an accident occur on the road or trail. For me, the balance of that risk was much more acceptable than that of virus exposure.

As my community opens to some kind of temporary or new normal, I feel increased corona risk. I also feel the ticking time clock of fire season, so I'm motivated to continue visiting my wilderness areas where I can avoid transmission.

My travel plans are on hold, and I can only wonder when it will be wise and safe to travel again. Until then, I'm happy to have a safe home base and local outdoor options.

**Susan:** Jan frequently posts as 'Jaunting Jan' on Facebook with current information for hikers and backpackers. She is also administrator of the PCT Section Hikers Facebook group.

Her website has a collection of graphs and annual reports at jansjaunts.wordpress.com/graphs illustrating the percentage of time she spends driving to trailheads all over the West (currently), percentage she spends backpacking, and percentage hiking long trails. For the rest of us, utilizing Jan's visual way of showing how she spends her time could be a useful tool for seeing if how we actually spend our time aligns with our stated ways of how we want to spend it. If one of our priorities is to spend more time outdoors hiking, setting concrete goals and keeping track of our success is more motivating than wishful thinking.

**Jan McEwen**

# Karen 'Butterscotch' Najarian

**Susan:** The more hiking and backpacking you do, the more people you learn about who are part of the hiking community. This community doesn't necessarily require you to pay dues or attend meetings—it mostly just requires that you hike and/or support those who do!

Over the years, I've learned about certain individuals who I would consider role models—not because I necessarily want to follow in their footsteps, literally or figuratively, but because I admire what they are doing in the greater outdoors. I've long looked up to Karen. She has a passion for hiking, backpacking, and camping and has over the years found numerous ways to combine those activities and share them with others.

In her story that follows, I think you will find that Najarian is a leader in more ways than one.

**Karen Najarian:** I hiked as a young Girl Scout—always out in front, ignorantly cutting switchbacks, flying up hills like a wild child, thirsting for thinner air. One time, I went to a weeklong day camp at Sunol Regional Park, California. The first thing I saw as I got off the bus was that rocky ridge. We all voted to go climb it.

Eventually, adult leaders and girls peeled off at various points on the way to return to camp. I didn't understand: Wasn't our goal to climb to the top? A few of us made it almost to the top on that hot and sunny day. Satisfied, we decided to turn back at the suggestion of the CIT [counselor-in-training] that there might be rattlers in the rocks. I was probably 10 years old. Fifty-six years later, I remember it like yesterday.

Rick and I met at U.C. Berkeley. Afterward, he went to grad school at U.C. Davis, and I went to Southern California for a medical technologist training program. Rick started backpacking the Sierra with his research director. I couldn't wait to join in when my yearlong internship was completed.

My mother decreed that I couldn't backpack (re: spend the night with a man) unless I was married, so at 23, I got married. We started with overnights in Desolation Wilderness and moved on to four- to five-day trips in Yosemite.

## Where I hike

California's High Sierra holds my heart, and each summer I made it my mission to explore as much of it as possible: Yosemite, Kings Canyon, and all the wilderness areas from Desolation near Lake Tahoe to Golden Trout in the south.

I met adventurer Roland Carlson in 1994. He introduced me to cross-country travel (hiking off-trail) and taught me skills and instilled a comfort with the landscape that expanded the area I could hike 100-fold. Now, it wasn't just what I could experience on trail but the whole of the range—little-visited lakes, loose rocky passes leading to another wonderland, creeks and rivers with no fishermen's trails.

For decades, I'd backpack the Sierra in the summer and lay fallow in the winter. It was always a chore to get in shape for each summer, be it for guiding or adventure. Then I met Scott Williams and Larry Fong. They lead hiking groups here in the Bay Area hills all winter long. In the cool of fall, winter, and spring, I began to love hiking the trails of Mt. Diablo, Mt. Tamalpais, and the East Bay Regional Parks—Briones, Las Trampas, Diablo Foothills, Tilden, Chabot. I discovered a whole new set of friends and low-altitude wildflowers.

## The richness of hiking

For me, hiking is a lifestyle that fills a hunger to find *home*. Moving on foot through the landscape is such a natural and basic way to intimately get to know the places one hikes through. And for me, that is the main reason I hike—to make the acquaintance of a place and have a relationship with it. That level of intimacy cannot be reached by plane, train, car, horse, or even the seat of a bike.

And for me, intimacy with the landscape makes me feel like I'm home. I get to meet Muir's 'gentle mountaineers,' the wildflowers, face to face in their native environment, where they grow the best and have since Muir's time.

It's like shaking hands with eternity. I get to step through fields of granite born millions of years under intense pressure three miles below the surface of the earth. I get to step over the aplite [an intrusive igneous rock] that glues the broken chunks together. I get to hear the story that the landscape has to tell. I get to sit on a comfortable rock and notice, by the obsidian shards at my feet, that someone else found it comfortable hundreds, if not thousands, of years ago.

The more I know the Sierra, the more I feel as if the mountains, lakes, creeks, flowers, animals, and even the weather and I are family—the more I feel that I belong. The mountains and I have a common bond of hardship, struggle, fury, gentleness, beginnings, endings, beauty, and tragedy.

While doing a big chunk of the John Muir Trail, a friend asked, "Well, aren't you here for the challenge?" Shocked, I screamed, "No! I want to experience new territory in my Beloved Sierra."

Then there is the unbelievably wonderful perk of experiencing the mountains with people of like mind—My Tribe. Some of my favorite moments are in our circle-shaped kitchen with everyone sitting on the ground making their meals, telling stories, recalling previous adventures and misadventures, cracking jokes, and telling embarrassing stories about each other. These are group meals our society does not have enough of. It fills a need we all have of belonging to a tribe of like-minded people.

What I like most is that my senses are heightened. Without the din of everyday life, every color, sound, movement, smell, texture, photon of light is noticed with crystal clarity. In this way, I feel most alive. The next best thing is reliving it through storytelling and writing.

## The greatest accomplishment

I would consider thru-hiking the Sierra High Route in July and August of 2014, at the age of 61, my greatest accomplishment at any age. At the suggestion of a friend who also wanted to do it, I had first contemplated it in my forties. Life, breast cancer, and then guiding got in the way. Then with maps out and dreaming of doing a weeklong section, one of the newer and younger members of my tribe flippantly remarked, "We should just do the whole thing."

I remember slowly turning my head and looking at her as if she was a child suggesting we all go play on the freeway. But, we got the mule resupplies coordinated and completed the 33-day, 210-mile, mostly off-trail route traversing the spine of the Sierra as outlined in Steve Roper's Book, *Sierra High Route, Traversing Timberline Country*. It's truly wild country with few footprints or trails linking 33 rocky passes across the roof of the Sierra. It required everything I had: superb navigational skills, strength, endurance, experience, knowledge of the land, of self, of partners, and a love of the range. Without that love, it would have been only arduous and meaningless. This trip showed me that I had what it took. I felt like I had earned the mountains' regard.

## Solo hiking vs. with companions

I've day hiked solo in order to stay in shape when no one else was available, and I've backpacked solo to have real solitude. I stay aware and act smart. I've never felt afraid.

No. Not true. One time near Point Reyes National Seashore, I had a feeling I was being stalked by a mountain lion. I never saw one, and it might have been an overactive imagination, but I was definitely scared.

I usually backpack with friends. There's the perfect balance of alone time and group time, and I never laugh as much as when hiking with friends. My trailname, 'Butterscotch,' came about because I always teach people that Jeffrey Pines smell like butterscotch.

As for others critical of solo hiking, I've never given it a thought. I hold to the adage, 'What someone thinks of me is none of my business.' After I got married and satisfied my mother, I thought I was done with explaining anything to anyone.

I take safety measures. I tell someone where I'm going, even sending pictures on the way if I have a signal. My husband and I have an agreement, "If I haven't checked in twenty-four hours after the appointed check-in time, call Search and Rescue." Luckily, he's in charge of our county's mountain rescue team. He even knows my boot print! My biggest fear is the total embarrassment I would feel if I needed to be rescued. But, I get that extra 24 hours in case something goes wrong or something goes well.

**Long-distance hikers' attributes needed**
- Trip-tested, excellent gear that meets *your* needs
- Physical preparation, including breaking in your *feet*
- Curiosity of what's around the corner
- A fascination with what's at your feet
- A love and care of your body—great self-care
- The ability to push through pain without injuring yourself and knowing that boundary
- Feeling at home with only what's on your back
- Fearless of dirt, hardship, discomfort

My favorite piece of gear is my Long Western Mountaineering Antelope GWS sleeping bag with a three-ounce overfill. It may be overkill for some, but it has enough insulation to keep me warm in the teens in my hammock. The GWS (Gore Windstopper) fabric shell keeps me dry under my 8x10 Cuben Fiber (now known as Dyneema Composite Fabric) tarp when cold rain is blowing sideways, and it repels frost and snow. The collar and hood keep me snug and warm. It's my survival cocoon and main piece of shelter.

**Further advice**
For those starting backpacking, there are so many resources online. Facebook groups will answer any question you have and have information on things you haven't even thought of. Join a local Meetup hiking group and ask questions. Hanging with a group will open the door to regular backpack trip opportunities.

For new or more challenging trails, do your research, get a buddy, and just go do it.

## How to keep going

How do I keep going when everything in my head or body is begging me to stop? I know that part of the price for the privilege of being out there is discomfort, and I accept that. While the pack is heavy, the trails steep, and the air thin, I don't purposely wish to suffer. I prepare in advance so that I have the right gear and I've done the right training to make it as comfortable as possible.

My boots don't blister, I have warm-weather gear and rain gear, and I sleep in a hammock for a very good night's sleep. I plan the trip so that I'm doing mileage within my comfort zone, knowing that my personal comfort zone will include a bit of suffering in it, too.

When I find myself pushed to my limits, I check to make sure I've had enough to eat and drink. I might take a rest for a few minutes. I make a conscious attempt to stay in the moment and notice the little things: the light bouncing around, the crunch of gravel, the shadows, clouds, flowers, animals. I pace my breathing with my pumping legs and move like a tractor in low gear—ever forward.

I have the experience to know that this will pass, and soon enough, I'll be sipping something strong with friends by a creek or lake at five o'clock.

## Challenges to meet and unexpected events

The biggest challenge I've had to overcome is finding boots that fit. I have big feet with bunions that get bigger every year. The doc won't operate on them because they don't hurt. I just have a hard time buying shoes. I wear an extra-wide 10.5 men's boot that I take to a cobbler to get stretched for a week. If I find a pair that fits, I will often buy three pairs.

The most frightening situation I've encountered was when a group of eight of us was two days from the end of a trip. We were deep off-trail in a rugged canyon west of Mt. Ritter [California] when Rick slipped and, grabbing his poles, dislocated his shoulder. Of the seven guys and me, I was the only one with any wilderness first-responder training.

With my husband's screams filling the canyon, six guys stood around with their hands in their pockets not knowing what to do. I was able to get him stable on the 45-degree slope, treat him for shock, give meds that relaxed him, and eventually reduce the dislocation.

Afterward, the guys started mentioning that they were diabetic or allergic to bee stings, and I just lost it. "We need to know these things, you guys!" The incident taught me that in a moment things can go very bad, very fast, and that first-aid knowledge and skills are vital in addition to medical history forms.

### Hikes change and evolve

When I was guiding, I led mostly three-day trips for beginners, and I'd throw in at least one weeklong trip each summer to explore a new area of the Sierra. Some summers, I was even too busy with my business to do that one longer trip. You only get so many summers, and I viewed that as a huge loss.

When I stopped guiding after 2012 at age 59, the door was opened to long-distance hiking and exploring as much of the Sierra as I wanted. Many of my trips became more rigorous and longer with multiple resupplies. I even left the Sierra to do a week in Wyoming's Wind River Range, and a month to hike 200 miles of the Camino in Spain.

It was in my 60s that I was only starting to see how really strong I was. Last summer at 66, I reached a limit—we could not make it over the cross-country pass I intended. It might have been because I missed the pass by about a quarter-mile in very steep, loose, rocky terrain.

It might have been that I unknowingly had metastatic breast cancer rearing its ugly head again after 20 years. My condition is in flux right now as I'm receiving treatment to beat it back and extend my life, so it's hard to know what the future holds. But I know that I've led an extraordinary life, and I have friends who will carry me into the backcountry if need be.

**Of women and physical abilities**

I came from a mother who told me, "You can do anything." But she also told me, "You can't do *that*," if it didn't serve my reflection of her. I saw my brother having way more fun than I did. I listened more to the 'You can do anything" statement and ended up amazing her with my skills and abilities. There are so many Instagram pictures of women doing awesome things and outfitters marketing to women now that it would be hard to underestimate your abilities. The only question, as Mary Oliver put it, is: "Tell me, what is it you plan to do with your one wild and precious life?"

The worst advice I've been given echoes my mother's admonition, "You can't do *that*"—and that is the advice given by rangers that there's too much snow, the rivers are too high, it's too wet and muddy, it's too cold, the bugs are too bad, the lakes are frozen. So *what*?! My advice: Know your strengths, your limits, your passion, and your desire, and go live your life.

**And next?**

[May 2020, SF Bay Area] As for the quarantine, I got double-whammed with the diagnosis of cancer in late January. My medication, which I started in late February, knocks my white cells waaay down, leaving me with a pretty weak immune system, so I have to be very careful about exposure to anything, let alone COVID. The radiation treatments I had from February 24 to April 1 left me too weak to even want to leave home. It's only been since mid-April that I've wanted to get out. So I've been walking in the neighborhood, and last week took that great trip to our cabin at Donner Summit. It felt like I could breathe great chunks of fresh clean air up there. I plan on spending a lot of time up there during the summer.

Oh! I made reservations in January 2019 for a May 2020 bucket-list, all-inclusive, 16-day Grand Canyon rafting trip. It was canceled because of the virus, but it turned out that my doc nixed it anyway because of my fragile spine that's been eaten away by the cancer. I'm on some bone-strengthening drugs now that are supposed to help that.

I'm hoping Yosemite opens the backcountry because I have a permit for mid-June to Cathedral. I have a month to work on getting strong enough to do the trip and friends who've offered to share my load. We'll see. One of my meds also lowers my hemoglobin, which won't help at altitude. I get a PET scan later this afternoon to see if and how much the tumors in my spleen and liver have shrunk. My labs look great for the condition I'm in. Pain is being managed. Fingers crossed.

Rick says that our failed attempt at Lucy's Foot Pass in August 2019 cannot be my last backpack trip. At this point, I will settle for a one-mile walk in with friends or even car camping—just to be out there under the stars and in the arms of my friends.

[August 2020] Yosemite opened up the park two days before my permit date for the Cathedral Trip: three and a half miles and 1000 feet of elevation gain at altitude.

I had trained gradually and consistently, starting with walking around the backyard, slowly adding distance around the neighborhood, elevation gain, and then pack weight, and altitude. Rick packed in my food and eight of us friends spent five glorious days exploring every nook and cranny of the area, discovering new spots even though most of us had guided clients there for years.

I followed up with three more backpack trips and am planning trips for next summer. While my cancer treatment affects my stamina making my trips shorter and less rigorous, I'm very grateful to be out there at all communing with the Sierra and My Tribe.

**Susan:** Karen's battle with this reoccurrence of cancer has been extremely difficult, including long bouts with the inability to eat, much less respond to my request for her story. I feel extremely grateful that she took the time to share her vast knowledge and experience with all of us during some of the brief periods when she could manage to sit at her computer and write.

**Karen Najarian**

# Sylvia 'amaWalker' Nilsen

**Susan:** Though I have never met Sylvia—largely because she lives in Durban, South Africa—I've known of her for decades because of our mutual interests in the Camino de Santiago and writing. Syl worked as a research agent and editor for a UK-based travel guide publisher and produced several African country and city guides.

She is a Spanish-accredited *hospitalero* volunteer trainer in South Africa, has trained 120 new volunteers, and has served as a volunteer hospitalero in Spain.

Sylvia was the regional co-coordinator for the Confraternity of Saint James in South Africa from 2003 to 2010. She founded amaWalkersCamino and accompanies groups of pilgrims on the Camino Francés to Santiago de Compostela.

The times that I have asked her advice on travel arrangements or other things, she has been quick to provide helpful information. I've always appreciated her comments on Facebook and other forums, and enjoyed her lively sense of humor!

**Sylvia Nilsen:** My trail name—amaWalker—is a giveaway as to what role hiking plays in my life! It shows that I am more passionate about walking than adventure hiking. 'Ama' is a noun prefix in isiZulu, and the word amaWalker means 'the walker' (singular).

I started hiking when I was 52. In 2001, when I was 54, I took it up seriously with a walk on the Coast to Coast across England. I never dreamed that I would ever hike across a country from one ocean to another! But that walk gave me the courage to try the 779-km/500-mile Camino Francés in 2002. After that, I was hooked on long-distance walking. I've also walked to Santiago 12 times and from Switzerland on the Via Francigena pilgrimage to Rome twice.

Now, at age 73, I continue to hike locally and in other countries. Here in South Africa, I have recently established a new hiking trail called the Trappist Trail. It's a 300-km/185-mile trail linking eight historic Trappist Missions. My husband Finn and I lead groups on our local Abbot Pfanner Trappist Trail, which is all cross-country. There are rocky river sections on that one that I would avoid if I could.

### Not a fan of camping

I have a confession to make. I am an imposter—big-time! Even though I have hiked many local trails and more than 4,000 km/2500 miles on pilgrimage trails, I am not a 'real' hiker/backpacker. Really, I'm not.

I also don't like hiking through dense, muddy forests such as those on the Piemont/Aragones between Sarrance and Borce on the way to the Somport Pass [the pass over the Pyrenees when crossing on the Arles (French) route]. Geez, I get nervous on the roller-coaster trail from Roncesvalles to Zubiri on the Camino Francés in Spain!

I also no longer like camping—especially in South Africa where we have an abundance of creatures like scorpions, snakes, spiders, frogs, etc., that seek shelter in tents.

Long-distance walking has become a way of life. In the past 20 years, holidays changed from upmarket package tours to hiking across different countries.

### What do you like most about hiking or backpacking?

The outdoors, the simplicity of sauntering. Meeting locals.

### Solo hiking

I admire women who hike solo. I have only hiked solo once and decided that I prefer to have 'compañeros'—people to share the path with and to break bread with.

**'When the going gets tough, the tough get going'**
I believe that the mind dictates and the body follows. When I'm having a hard time keeping going, I sing! It could be campfire songs, marching songs, anything that will keep the rhythm going.

I have some challenges I have to deal with physically—I have osteoporosis and am asthmatic. I don't like hiking down hills, especially rocky, slippery slopes. I suffer from vertigo in high places, so I don't like clinging onto ledges above precipices. So, I've faced some real challenges!

Though I have hiked trails like the Coast to Coast in England, from Paris to Spain, crossed the lower Pyrenees from St. Jean and Somport into Spain, and crossed the Alps at the Great St. Bernard Pass, I really don't like mountaineering.

I really, really don't like scrambling over rocks and boulders or clinging onto ledges on mountain slopes. My close hiking friends who are like mountain goats love those situations, but I am known to freeze on downhill trails, especially on rocky paths like the one from San Juan de la Pena down to Santa Cruz. I still have nightmare flashbacks to that one!

In 2006 on the Via Francigena in Switzerland, we were on our way up to the Great St. Bernard Pass, stuck on a 30-cm/12-inch ledge, clinging onto a chain in the rock face. There had been a landslide, and locals had shored up the scree and stones with long logs impaled into the slope. I nearly died! I couldn't move forward, I couldn't go back, but had no option but to keep going with jelly legs. Thereafter, nothing was ever quite as scary.

**Changes**
In 2002, walks were between 25 km/15.5 miles and 40 km/25 miles per day. Now, I don't like doing more than 15 km/9.5 miles in a day.

**Words of wisdom**
Your body evolved to walk upright and to walk long distances. Join a hiking club, and train to hike. Start off with easy-graded walks, and build your confidence until you are comfortable with longer distances or multiday hikes. [Keep in mind that] everyone

is different, and not all of us are adventure, or extreme, hikers.

My favorite item for walking is culottes (divided skirts). I don't have to roll down shorts or trousers, or remove my back-pack to 'go in the bushes.'

## An upcoming significant hike

I hope to soon be able to walk short distances on the Camino de Santiago with my 11-year-old granddaughter, Emily.

## And then plans had to change

[May 2020, South Africa] I'm especially missing hugging and being with grand-daughter Emily!

[August 1,2020] We are going into day 126 of our lockdown. Finn and I moved to a retirement village a year ago after living in the same house for 50 years, and because the residents fall into the vulnerable group, we are restricted to exercising within the boundary walls of the village. For three weeks, we were restrict-ed to our garden. The next level allows for exercise outside, but only between the hours of 6 and 9 a.m.

We have been planning for two years to do a walk-and-ride Camino in June 2020 with Emily and her parents, our son and daughter-in-law. (It would have been my 13th walk into Santia-go.) We booked to fly to Paris (three days stay-over) then fly to Biarritz (one-night stay-over), pick up our hire car, drive to St. Jean, then over the hill to Roncesvalles. I have planned flattish walks of 3-5 km (2-3 miles) every day on the Camino for two weeks between Roncesvalles and Santiago. Then the virus hit, and we had to cancel our plans.

Anyway, I decided to adapt our itinerary and walk the Camino around our garden! We have been on the Camino for 19 weeks, and last night we arrived in Carrion de los Condes. Last month, a journalist friend, who is writing weekly articles on how people are coping under the lockdown, interviewed us for the Saturday newspaper. His interview is here: iol.co.za/ios/behindthenews/clocking-a-buen-camino-in-spain-in-their-pine-town-garden-47759139.

**Susan:** Sylvia, who appeared on Ivar Rekve's "Camino Conversations" at caminodesantiago.me/camino-conversations-sylvia-from-south-africa, is the author of six books on the Camino de Santiago. You can follow her at amawalkerscamino.com and check out her books at sylvianilsenbooks.weebly.com.

Sylvia's books include *Your Camino: On foot, bicycle or horseback in France and Spain; Camino Lingo—English-Spanish Words and Phrases: For Pilgrims on el Camino de Santiago; Slackpacking the Camino Francés; Pilgrim Footprints on the Sands of Time; and Pilgrimage Trails (a three-part series including Three Short Hikes on El Camino de Santiago; La Via Turonensis from Paris to Spain, and La Via Francigena—Five Pilgrims to Rome).*

**Sylvia Nilsen (on right) with Nancy ONeill — Via Francigena approaching Gr St Bernard Pass (photo credit: Tom ONeill)**

# Marcia 'GottaWalk' Powers

**Susan:** I learned about and started following Marcia's trail reports when she and her husband Ken were hiking across the United States on the American Discovery Trail. How can one not be impressed by someone having the guts to walk across the continent on a barely marked route! And that was just one of her major long-distance hikes—and firsts!

**Marcia Powers:** Gear matters. Over my hiking years, I have changed out or eliminated many pieces of gear. At this point, my gear is curated so that it all works together in a minimalist backpack. The one item that I had swapped out, then came back to, was my tent. For a while, I used a tarp tent that was fewer ounces than a tent, but it wasn't smaller in my pack, took more time to set up, needed a larger setup area for the lines to stake out, and seemed colder to me because it was ventilated at ground level rather than overhead. I am now back to carrying my Black Diamond Wasabi Firstlight tent. It is freestanding (can be set up anywhere without being staked), so it is fast to set up and take down. I pay a price for carrying this tent, but the few extra ounces are worth it for the gain in warmth, time, and convenience every day. I may swap out other pieces of gear but will keep this tent!

## Hiking can grow on you!

I hiked at my local summer camp as a preteen, ambling along in a line of fellow campers, but I wasn't really into the experience. But later, as a mother of two sons in Scouts, I was envious of their weekends away and their gear, especially their tiny stoves. Tom Stienstra's book *California Hiking* (Stienstra is Outdoors editor for the *SF Chronicle*) has a list of top ten 'butt-kicker hikes.' The hardest hike is a day hike of Mt. Whitney. That was my goal for my 50th birthday. When I saw the Sierra backcountry and was told it was a backpacking area, backpacking rather than day hikes became my goal. Within months, I borrowed a backpack and thru-hiked the John Muir Trail. I was smitten.

### My style

I am an avid thru-hiker, hiking a trail end to end. When I was 52, my husband Ken and I thru-hiked the Pacific Crest Trail followed by annual thru-hikes of the Tahoe Rim Trail, the Continental Divide Trail, and the Appalachian Trail.

The following year we researched and planned a thru-hike of the American Discovery Trail. The coast to coast trail had not been thru-hiked, so we needed to figure out resupply points, timing of miles per day, and a weather window before our attempt. In 2005, we completed the first continuous through-hike in 231 days.

That epic hike was followed by thru-hikes of the Arizona Trail and the rarely hiked Idaho Centennial Trail. We also enjoy multiday hikes on routes of our choice. When we don't have large chunks of time, we work on our projects of reaching the high points of each state and each of California's counties' high points.

### The hiker community

I am part of a group of women walkers in my town. One time when I was back in town after spending a summer on a long hike, one of my women friends said that my hiking life was my primary life and my town life was time between hikes. She was right! Each of my lives enhances the other so that I more fully enjoy where I am in the moment.

I don't hike with a 'trail family,' but I really enjoy meeting and talking to other hikers on the trail. Normal social differences of age or education or careers or religions don't seem to separate hikers, so I get to have interesting and meaningful conversations with various people—young or new backpackers full of questions about my gear or hiking style, or how I manage my finances to allow my frequent hiking.

## What is important

There is nothing better than being in nature. I love the scenery, the adventure of not knowing what I will see around the corner, the challenges of solving different problems, and navigating. I like the feeling of independence and living happily, healthily, and safely with the contents in my pack. I like organizing my gear and my system of each piece of gear meshing with the others.

## My biggest accomplishment

*Backpacking 4,922 miles from the Atlantic to the Pacific on the ADT at age 58 was an amazing adventure.* I felt strong and fit and didn't think that my age impacted the hike.

*But my greatest accomplishment was hiking the Idaho Centennial Trail northbound.* As far as I can tell, it was the first northbound thru-hike and the second thru-hike. The route had been established on maps for Idaho's 1990 statehood centennial but remained unpopular as a thru because of a lack of services and hiking information in the wilderness areas.

My hiking experience definitely made completion of that hike possible while my age did not slow me down or make the hike more difficult. The following year, I re-hiked some of the trail solo going south, looking for routes that existed on the ground rather than [as indicated] on maps as 'heritage trail' that had been burned, flooded, or overgrown out of existence.

## Solo hiking

By choice, almost all my day hikes are solo. While solo, I can choose my location and route, hike my pace, and soak in my surroundings. When I walk quietly, I see and enjoy more animals. I also enjoy backpacking solo because I am completely enmeshed in nature without the distraction of other people. I do enjoy quick conversations with other backcountry travelers.

I carry a SPOT locator when hiking, biking, or backpacking by myself. I use it on 'tracking mode' or to send an evening location. If questioned about the advisability of my solo hiking, I can honestly say that I have never had a scary encounter with animals or people.

I also tend to be a little more conservative when solo hiking by choosing, if possible, a route with less exposure or a stream crossing with less forceful water. When crossing notorious Kerrick Creek in the Sierra, I teamed up with another solo hiker. We parted as soon as we were across. I don't hike with music or an audiobook so that I can be aware of my surroundings.

**Does hiking require more mental or physical strength**

I agree that hiking has a large mental aspect. Planning is important, but flexibility may be even more important. Fuming about yesterday's problems is wasted energy, but learning from them is important. Likewise, worrying about tomorrow's challenges is useless, but examining options creatively is helpful.

If I am falling apart physically and emotionally I always try to get back on track with a quick rest, snack, and drink. At home when I am not hiking, I love reading accounts of adventures. When lagging or feeling completely wiped out, I imagine hiking with Jennifer Pharr Davis or pick up my pace by thinking about the ultra-runners who go 100 or 200 miles.

I hiked with a Search and Rescue hiker out of Mammoth, and he complimented my 'mojo,' so I dig deep to find it. There are so many accounts of distance runners, hikers, and explorers who I can imagine trying to keep up with.

I also tell myself that the hard endeavor right now is worth the effort because it is training for the next challenging time.

**How to handle challenges**

Finding a balance between my hiking life and my at-home life is difficult.

**Frightening moments**

Getting caught in quicksand in Utah's Dark Canyon was a shock. As I struggled, my legs slid farther into the red sandy mud. My first thought was who was going to get me out. My second thought was that I was on my own. I remembered reading that struggling causes a person to sink and that a person can float out of quicksand. I spread out my arms, rested my face and torso on the surface, and gradually pulled myself to the edge of the muddy pit. That was my best lesson of self-reliance.

We were on the American Discovery Trail and had dropped into Dark Canyon from Trail Canyon. The designated wilderness area was briefly part of Bears Ears National Monument and feeds into the Grand Canyon. It all seemed remote and infrequently visited to me. I love remote, and this had spectacular red rock and intermittent water that was also red and thick with silt.

We battled willows sometimes. Other times we pulled ourselves up the walls of sandstone layers to hike down canyon unimpeded. When a layer ran out, we would climb down or farther up to continue by running another layer. We would also cross back and forth across the creek to hike another short segment. We exited the canyon by climbing slick rock to Sundance Trailhead near Hite as we were westbound.

Long-range navigation wasn't a problem. The slow part was the jungle gym workout and figuring out where to place the next fifty steps. Because this was our first canyon experience, I assumed we were unknowingly hiking the hard route, but I have since learned that there is no easy way.

The experience was worth every step!

## Adapting to change

I am probably a little slower hiking than I was decades ago, but I ignore that idea. I may slow down a little, but my experience offsets that slowdown. My pack is lighter due to new, lighter-weight gear. I also feel comfortable carrying less so that backpacking is easier weight-wise.

## Advice to others

Getting out on any trail is fun and a way to learn how one's body will respond. Reading accounts of adventures is inspiring and informational. I have an enormous list of books. Now there are online videos and blogs. Reading them before a day hike is inspiring.

It's hard to know if women underestimate their abilities. Title IX should have made a psychological difference, but I can't say. Knowing what women like 'Anish' or Jennifer Pharr Davis accomplished makes me think that mentally they set a goal and expected their bodies to follow through.

### Risky vs. wise advice to follow

I think the biggest risk from other hikers or backpackers is the danger of 'groupthink.' Hiking with a group or trail family is fun and rewarding, but so many times we hear post-hike regrets due to going along with a group decision rather than crafting one's hike to personal needs and wishes.

One rewarding aspect of hiking is self-reliance. Another important aspect is really learning who you are and what you want and how your body works.

We have hiked through so many states and such varied topography and ecosystems, but every location has locals who tell us, "There are dangers out there, especially in this area, where there are snakes, bears, no water, big storms. If they don't get you, you will probably fall off the mountain."

Listen, plan, but don't be convinced that you can't cope with future problems.

### The next hike will offer...

Solo time in the outdoors.

### When the impact of COVID-19 hit

[April 2020, SF Bay Area] Ken has been a part of Kaiser's Impaired Cognition program since early last year. Much of daily life is now a challenge for him, so we are on a journey of a different sort, similar to the ups and downs of a thru-hike that we take day by day, learning new skills along the way. Ken prefers home to longer hikes. These are more reasons to appreciate the lessons I learned while thru-hiking!

**Susan:** During their walk across the United States, Marcia and Ken posted on their blog not only to let others know what they were doing but to provide other hikers with information on everything from route planning to obtaining needed permits.

Years later, Ralph and I borrowed their strategy of caching water in areas where distances would have been too great between water sources. Ralph buried water in one of S. California's most arid PCT sections (and before the time of numerous trail angel caches) before we set out to hike it. Then with GPS, and photos he had taken, we located our caches and made it through the challenging stretch. discoverytrail.org/the-trail/trail-tales/gottawalk

**Marcia Powers — Moose Creek Landing Strip ICT**

# Nancy Reynolds

**Susan:** Nancy is a guide and longtime pilgrim on the Camino Francés, the best known of the Camino de Santiago routes. In 2013, she founded a company, The Camino Experience, to lead pilgrims on the Camino from Saint Jean Pied de Port in France. When Nancy is not walking the route with others or alone, she lives and works at the Hi-Point Reyes Hostel (hiusa.org/hostels/california/point-reyes/point-reyes), a member of Hosteling International, in Point Reyes National Seashore in Northern California. I interviewed her at a nearby coffee shop in February 2020.

Nancy did her first walk on the Camino de Santiago in 2005. Like many who walk the pilgrimage routes, she was in a period of transition. She had been laid off from the corporation for which she had worked and was newly divorced.

The seeds for the journey had been planted when she read about the trail in Shirley MacLaine's *The Camino* and nourished when she heard more about it from a fellow traveler while in India. Thus, she had the time, was footloose and fancy-free, was used to independent traveling, was curious, and hoped that this would be a time to find answers to her question, 'What is my purpose?'

Though the answer to that age-old question eluded her, she was captivated by the trail. So much so that since 2007, she "has returned to walk parts of the Francés every year—sometimes twice a year." Even now, she says, "The irony of it is, I am not a hiker." However, she does believe in the power of travel and finds the Camino unique because it "brings together an international community and is holy at the end."

Having seen that many people who want to walk the Camino have tons of questions about it, Nancy saw a need and an opportunity to support other pilgrims. She wanted to help others but also needed to earn an income. She pondered her strengths. She decided that she was "an expert at getting started." So, she developed a program that would help people navigate the process. It provided such information as the history of the Camino, who walked it, and where to start the hike. It explained how to "book your airline ticket, pack for the journey, and prepare physically, emotionally, and spiritually for the walk."

Nancy began taking small groups of pilgrims to launch their Camino walks. She meets them in St. Jean Pied du Port to cross the Pyrenees from France into Spain and travel onward. The group reaches Pamplona in four days, and then most continue on as independent pilgrims.

There are several benefits to participants of traveling under her guidance, says Nancy. "They are starting with a small group for support, gaining confidence as they go, and are able to reassure family members and others at home about their ability to take this big step." There's also practical support. Nancy teaches the pilgrims the process of finding accommodations, whether it's in pilgrim or private albergues or small hotels—information they will need to continue their journey as far along the Camino as they want to go.

## A successful hike

Learning to enjoy hiking sometimes involves a steep learning curve. On her website, Nancy shares her experiences becoming a long-distance hiker on the Camino. thecaminoexperience.com/meet-your-guide

Before she undertook her first Camino hike, Nancy thought she was prepared. "I had traveled a lot, and I had even lived out of a backpack for six months on a round-the-world trip. But carry my backpack every day, four to six hours a day for a month? Oh no.

"Back in 2005 there wasn't much information available, so I had to just go and work it out as I went. Which I did, and I survived. But I made a lot of unnecessary mistakes. For example…

- My backpack was way too heavy.
- I had the wrong clothes, the wrong shoes, and my rain

gear didn't work at all.
- I had no idea where to find food, so my first day on the trail was a hungry one.
- I had one trekking pole instead of two, which made my knees sore and had me off-balance.
- I hadn't trained at all, so after two days on the trail, I got sick—and needed a trip to the doctor and two rest days to get back up to speed. *I was even carrying my full-sized pillow from home in my backpack!*"

### Why Nancy cherishes the Camino

Besides the spiritual rewards of walking the Camino, Nancy finds many reasons to return year after year. "It's the amazing scenery, the ability to have conversations with others whenever you want. Pilgrims are approachable. You share a common goal in a way not found in many other places.

"And the rewards are also physical and psychological. About a week in, I feel strong and fit. I feel powerful—like don't-mess-with-me strong—a badass... I like those freeing moments. Your pace allows you to notice the breeze on your skin, to pick up trash, to observe... 'Did you see that tree?'"

### Going solo and handling challenges

When Nancy is not leading a group, she prefers to walk solo on the Camino; it's what she calls "my home." And she's very comfortable traveling alone. "My father raised me to be independent!"

Each time she returns to the Camino, she sets an intention. One time, because most of her life she had seen herself as an introvert, her goal was to connect with others more easily by being more friendly and outgoing. When she feels she isn't being as tolerant as she might be, she likes to examine why she feels as she does. She enjoys being with other pilgrims in the albergues or wherever she stays in the common rooms, but because this self-described introvert needs downtime, she always arranges for private time in a private room at night.

"You know," she says, "it's an urban myth that early pilgrims shared dorms while on their pilgrimage. It was only thirty to thirty-five years back that albergues [as we know them now] were created. Before that time, people stayed in inns—or hospitals if they were sick."

## Which leads to her advice for others

Nancy feels it's very important for people to know why they are doing the Camino—to seek what's calling them and to make their goal their own. Doing so helps them plan their trip and to carry on when things get tough. She's encountered people who have become very upset or disappointed because they wanted more than one thing from their walk—things that don't always work together. They might want, for example, to stay with a particular person while traveling but also want to go at their own pace. They might want to stay with a certain group but also want to stop earlier or later than the others, or take an extra day in a specific city. In one case, Nancy explained, a woman who had not come to terms with her priorities ended up injuring herself because she tried to walk faster than was comfortable in order to stay with others.

"The problem is often FOMO—the fear of missing out."

## Underestimating oneself

"Instead of grasping at every moment—seize the moment. Listen to your body," she says, "You can push yourself, but respect your ability."

However, we agreed that sometimes we do underestimate ourselves or others don't believe in us enough. One of Nancy's clients told her, "My daughter didn't think I could do this. She said, 'Mom, you walk to the mailbox and back!'" But, Nancy said of her client, "She had spirit—and she walked the entire way to Santiago."

We both agreed with the expression, 'Never leave the trail on a bad day.' There will be ups and down—nothing lasts forever!

**Susan:** You can find out more about the Camino de Santiago at thecaminoexperience.com and you may cross paths with Nancy at Point Reyes National Seashore or on the Camino Francés.

**Nancy Reynolds**

# Lisa Robinson

**Susan:** Lisa Robinson leads a busy life as a commercial pilot, but her frequent travel allows her to hike in far-flung places. When she is not traveling, she enjoys hiking in the San Francisco Bay Area where she lives.

**Lisa Robinson:** When I was young, I hiked with my parents on camping trips; camping was their favorite vacation. I hiked more seriously in my thirties and forties. Hiking regularly would be a better description. I'm almost 54 and strive to keep up my hiking stamina so impromptu treks won't be a problem. That doesn't mean I hike every week. I am working full-time, but I try to get at least a few hikes in every month.

My favorite hiking gear is probably my hiking poles or my Buff (the best easy-to-carry, cold- or windy-weather accessory you can find).

I've hiked in the U.S. in California, Arizona, Washington, and Utah. I've also hiked trails throughout Europe, Hong Kong, Australia, New Zealand, Southeast Asia, Mexico's Copper Canyon, and South Africa.

My most recent hiking adventure to another country was doing the 'W' route in Torres del Paine National Park in Chile's Patagonia region.

I'm a day hiker and have gone on long or short hikes on nearly every vacation I've taken (and I vacation often). I've hiked the Inca Trail to Machu Picchu in Peru, part of the Te Araroa in New Zealand, hiked/climbed Mt. Rainier and Mt. St. Helens in Washington, and backpacked the John Muir Trail.

## The role of hiking

Hiking for me is both exercise and exploration. I prefer to walk to a destination if it's an option. Hiking can also become a fun treasure hunt—looking for wildflowers during blooms and foraging for mushrooms. My work involves international travel (I'm a long-haul pilot), so I am often combating jetlag, and any physical activity that involves being outdoors in sunlight is very beneficial. Finally, having a sedentary job is all the more reason to pursue physical hobbies.

I like the camaraderie of other hikers, getting out into nature, and appreciating the flowers, wildlife, plant life, and scenery. On longer trips, I like that my pressing concerns on the trail are what flavor ramen to cook each night and considering how dirty can your hair really get?

## Greatest accomplishment

I feel my greatest accomplishment is probably climbing Mt. Rainier with my brother and sister-in-law. They had encouraged me to join on their annual trek for years. I finally said yes and started training in earnest with Scott Williams, a Bay Area resident who sets up group hikes for those looking for great camaraderie, trails, vistas, and training. His hikes pushed me to train harder and carry more weight up the steeps trails of Mt. Diablo. It also gave me an excuse to spend more time outdoors.

## Becoming a successful long-distance hiker

Successful long-distance hikers need flexibility and lots of time off. Again, I'm more of a day hiker than a long-distance hiker, so I cannot comment much on epic, multiday hikes. I've not made the time to undertake these kinds of trips, and only in recent years have I become inspired to consider multi-week trips. I was able to do the JMT—three weeks through the Sierra with friends—because I had built up my stamina carrying weight in my pack on local hikes. In hindsight I wish I had been regularly carrying 28 pounds (my pack weight on the JMT) rather than the 18 I had been training with.

I keep going by not wanting to quit. I've always believed that

I'm a team player, so when I've encountered challenging hikes, the desire to not let others down has been a strong motivator.

## Challenges

My biggest challenge has been inexperience, but I have become stronger and more confident with each hike. If I had one piece of advice to pass along to other female hikers, it would be to seek out other experienced hiking women. I have been so blessed to have been able to learn backcountry camping skills from Karen Najarian and long-distance skills from Nancy 'Why Not?' Huber [interviews from both earlier]. More accurately, I was chasing after Nancy on one segment of her Te Araroa trek. She is such a fast hiker, but I eventually caught up to her by the end of each day (sometimes with the help of a passing motorist). Nonetheless, she was willing to let a newbie tag along, and I am forever grateful for her trail hospitality.

My friend Pam gave me some sage advice to "cast a wide net" and be willing to connect with women whose skills are far beyond my skill set. Through the hiking community, I've met some wonderful women (and men) who have further encouraged me to try things outside my comfort zone. Sometimes, a friendly push is what's needed.

## Looking ahead

I am looking forward to hiking longer trails when I am retired and can devote more time to all my favorite outdoor activities. I've become more adventurous as I've grown older (or grown up) and realize there are so many destinations to add to my ever-growing list.

I'd like to hike solo, but I haven't yet tried. When I become a solo traveler, I'll have more flexibility in hiking/travel plans as I'll have only my schedule to work around. I am looking forward to going solo because I am unaccustomed to traveling by myself, but now that I am newly single, I'm learning to be more comfortable traveling without a companion. It's a process.

**And with the shelter-in-place orders**

[May 2020, SF Bay Area] I've been fortunate that although I'm not currently working (I'm on partial-paid leave), I've been hiking on our local trails like never before. All the exercise has helped me drop a few pounds and explore new trails on Mt. Diablo and in Briones, and I've made some new hiking friends to boot (all groupies of Scott Williams).

**Susan:** Lisa may have limited time to hike, but when she does get out there, she does impressive ones. In April 2020, she joined a small group of friends to hike nearby Mt. Diablo for a 19-mile day hike that involved climbing four peaks and 6,700 feet of ascent.

Lisa Robinson

# Dami Roelse

**Susan:** Dami, founder of WalkingWomen50plus, is a firm believer in walking and hiking as a means to 'dynamic aging.' I was lucky enough to catch her when she was doing a book tour for *Walking Gone Wild, How to Lose Your Age on the Trail*. Her talk, interspersed with hiking stories, was geared to women 50-plus, but all hikers could benefit from Dami's experience and knowledge.

**Dami Roelse:** I grew up walking. My family didn't own a car until I was 16, so walking, biking, and public transportation were our ways to get around in Holland. My first hikes were dawn trampings through the dunes of the island where we lived.

My first big hikes were when I was in my early twenties. I was in Nepal and trekked to Mt. Everest base camp. Hiking didn't become a regular outdoor activity until I lived on the West Coast of the USA, but [initially] was limited to family outings. I became a serious hiker in my sixties when life took a turn and I lost my husband. The outdoor life has been my go-to place for connection and joy since then.

**Where hikes take me**

In the U.S., I've hiked all over the West Coast (including 2,000 miles of the PCT), in Arizona, and some on the East Coast. In Europe, I've hiked in Scotland, Iceland, France, Germany, and Switzerland. In Asia, I've hiked in Ladakh (part of India), Nepal, and Tibet. Australia and New Zealand are next.

I love that I can hike locally in Southern Oregon right out of my front door. No need to get in my car—just walk across town and I'm in the woods and mountains.

**Why hiking matters**

Hiking has played a big role in my life in the last 10 years. It's been like a life companion—I get reflection and confidence from it. Hiking and especially long-distance hiking fuels my life and keeps me fit. Even at age 73, I don't have to step away from adventure travel because my body and mind are resilient and can handle some extremes. I recently trekked at 16,000-18,000 feet and kept up with hikers 20 years younger.

Although I also love hiking solo, I find belonging hiking with others. The result is health and purpose. I've become a published author and maintain a website and a Facebook page and group to inspire others. I lead hikes locally and occasionally backpacking trips in the U.S. or abroad.

**A great achievement**

For me, a great accomplishment was hiking the Washington section of the PCT—a month-long backpacking trip I did at age 69 with steep climbs and descents on an almost daily basis. My hiking companion and I faced high temps, low temps, rain, snow, narrow ledges, and blowdowns for miles (we climbed over 63 trees in one afternoon!), plus dangerous river crossings. I kept my positive outlook in part due to the stunning views and amazing flora (old-growth forests, flowers everywhere, mushrooms) but also because of meeting other hikers. The oldest was an 86-year-old woman finishing her last section of the PCT—inspirational!

Though my hiking trips in the Himalayas (including Mt. Kailash, which I did recently) and High Sierras were hard in their own right because of altitude, I consider the PCT hike through Washington a greater accomplishment because it took longer and required more stamina and fitness than those shorter stretches.

**Solo or not?**

I always say that if you want to do a hike, short or long, be prepared to go solo if no one wants to join you. If you wait for others to go with you, you'll go out much less and cheat yourself out of an experience of finding connection in nature, building confidence, and enjoying the elemental domain of our planet.

I've not met people who were critical of hiking solo. I've read many posts online questioning the safety, but I think that if you prepare properly and hike on known trails where others hike, you can minimize safety issues. If you hike with someone and you injure yourself, they can possibly help by setting off your PLB [personal locator beacon] or wrap a bandage, [but these are] things you can do yourself or ask a passing hiker to help you with.

I've encountered day hikers in trouble on the trail and helped them with the basics I always carry in my pack. I found that they were not fit enough to attempt the hike and not prepared enough to help themselves. It's more the idea of not having to face difficulties alone that [makes] people feel safer teaming up. Team hiking, however, is fraught with its own difficulties.

**To be a successful long-distance hiker...**

This requires 60-percent training and 40-percent planning and preparation. Training both physically and mentally is essential for success on a long trail. Physical training means aerobic and anaerobic exercise, hiking up hills with a pack, strength-training exercises, and flexibility exercises. Hikers should follow a rigorous daily training plan for two months before they go out on a long one. Mental training means the ability to calm yourself through regular centering/meditation.

Planning your hike with a map and guidebook and preparing for your needs—i.e. clothing, shelter, food, and on-the-trail entertainment (books, journal, music, etc.)—can make or break a long-distance hike.

**When you need a break**

Just like with any difficulty in life, take a step back, and give yourself a break. A zero day (on a long trail) or a trail break (on a day hike) let you rest and reevaluate what you're after. Consider how much you've achieved and how much you want to accomplish the hike.

Boredom happens, doubt happens, body aches and pains happen, but they pass with a change of scenery, a day in town, and a rest.

However, pay attention to the nagging feelings of *I'm done with this, I'm not finding joy in this anymore or this pain isn't going away with ibuprofen or rest—there's something wrong.* You can push yourself too hard physically and end up with an injury that needs time off the trail to heal or you can beat yourself over the head for not accomplishing what you set out to do, i.e. the whole hike. *There's a balance between setting a goal and understanding that you've had enough. Long hikes can teach you that balance, and it will help you create a better life for yourself off the trail as well.*

**Getting underway** (related to hiking/backpacking)

One of my challenges is facing pre-trip anxiety—getting everything prepared and lined up before I can take off on a long hike. After 24 hours on the trail, I relax. It happens every time, even after many years, and I know it's part of mastering living with the unknown.

Another challenge is the logistics of getting to an out-of-the-way trailhead. I'm learning new and smart ways of finding my way around. Trail angels are superb!

**Frightening things do happen**

One time, a hiking buddy slid 30 feet down a snowy slope, and I had to stop her and save her from sliding farther. It taught me that keeping calm and making fast intuitive decisions can save lives. I yelled at her to swing herself into a tree well [depression around a tree], which stopped her slide; normally you try to avoid going into a tree well in snow. I was then able to hike down to her safely because I had micro-spikes (she'd lost hers) and could help her out. I then cut steps in the snow for her to follow.

On that hike, I started using GPS to stay on a trail that had become invisible. There's always more to learn. This skill has saved me many times from getting lost and/or getting me out of treacherous situations.

**What time has brought**

My hikes have become longer. I've discovered the benefits of long-distance hiking. As I've aged, I've had to shorten my hiking days by a few miles.

I wear knee sleeves to protect my knees, and I do more specific flexibility exercises when I'm off-trail.

After experiencing a few foot problems [now healed], I pay a lot of attention to my feet. I exercise them and hope they'll keep serving me on the trail.

As I've hiked longer distances, higher mountains, and crossed rivers, I've found that my comfort zone has expanded, and I can tackle new and different adventures. I just tackled the Mt. Everest base camp in Tibet and the Mt. Kailash Kora.

It was physically very demanding to hike at that altitude, and I see less-demanding hikes in my future. I want to keep enjoying the outdoors, and doing a less strenuous hike is just fine with me.

I may use support animals more as I age to go places I still want to explore on foot.

### Good gear helps

My Clark jungle hammock is my favorite piece of equipment. It's 2 pounds, 10 ounces, including ropes and rainfly. My tent is lighter and wins out when weight really matters, but nothing beats swinging in my hammock at the end of a hard day of hiking, legs elevated, snug under the mosquito netting, reading a book, and watching the sun set or the river flow by.

I sleep like a baby, on my side, curled up, no need for much of a pillow since I can adjust my head height with the ropes. I've slept in freezing conditions, muggy, bug-saturated forests, and rainy Pacific Northwest forests. You need trees, although with trekking poles you can set it up as a tent shelter, which I've done occasionally. Mine is six years old; they have made some nifty changes since then, but the durability and versatility of the product hasn't changed.

### Other ideas for women

For those who want to start hiking or backpacking regularly, or who are nervous about going on a new and more challenging trail, find support if possible. Start small, add more miles, then gradually break into overnight backpacking until you start feeling confident. There are a lot of details to learn to be comfortable and safe on the trail. Talk to someone who can coach you or go with someone who's experienced. You may have to pay to get the skills, but it will be worth it to you later.

Some women underestimate their physical abilities. I try to inspire and encourage women over 50 in my book *Walking Gone Wild* by giving them specific training schedules. My advice is, "Give yourself a year to become a confident hiker. Hike at least once a week, and increase your mileage slowly. Walk, walk, and cross-train between hikes."

I don't recall ever been given bad advice by experienced hikers. I guess I've been lucky. I've figured many things out on my own and learned from my mistakes.

### The next hike

I'll be looking for the sense of rhythm and ease that comes after days of hiking, an expanded mind that comes with living in nature 24/7, and new challenges that the unknown trail certainly will bring. I hope to do three or four consecutive weeks on the PCT and explore some new trails in Europe. I want to listen to my body and treat it with respect so it will serve me for a long time to come.

### And then came the lockdown

[May 2020, Central Oregon] and Dami wrote this:

## A trek into the unknown
### ~ Dami Roelse

The days in social isolation have a rhythm of their own. A rhythm determined by the body, the weather, and the immediate environment. This is similar to when I trek in the mountains and my body, the weather, and the terrain determine my movement. Now that it's May, the days are long and sunny from sunrise to sunset in my part of the world. Nature is showing itself in all its glory.

I have a garden that needs tending a few hours each day. The first harvest of artichokes and lettuce, spinach and greens adorn my kitchen counter. A May turnip offers its taste of sweet white flesh inside its purple skin, a delight for the palate. Cooking with these fresh delicacies brings forth new recipes. Today, it's sourdough pizza with greens, artichoke hearts, and the pesto left over in the freezer.

Each day, something new grabs my attention. Today, I wanted to make pizza and build a squash-plant bin, a wire tube filled with compost, manure, and a dripline to water the contents. The plants will grow long tentacles outside the bin as the ingredients decompose inside and feed the squash's roots. Life changes I can see right under my eyes, nudged by my hands. I can't wait to see how big they'll get and all the different winter squashes that will appear!

Life is happening right here, right now. My weeks are no longer scheduled full. I make up the day's doings as my mood requests, and my basic needs demand. As the weeks go by, the world news has become a hum in the background, a litany of data and uncontrollable changes in people's lives. It's as if I live on an island ruled by a faraway government that presides over my living circumstances. The strife between maintaining a lockdown and opening the world up again with all the contingent risks is not my struggle. As a privileged elder living on a pension, I'm not waiting for the outside world to move my life along.

Living in isolation reminds me of hiking solo on the long trail—cut off from the buzz of news and media, surrounded by nature, and tuning in to a body that walks, eats, sleeps, and rests. Hiking lets you experience life at two miles an hour. A pace that allows your senses to take in and process the environment. A pace your brain can absorb.

Life in lockdown affects the brain in a similar way. Life is slower, not so jam-packed; there are no places to go, no one to entertain. Zoom get-togethers lose their charm quickly. So it's me and the daily routine, determined by my bodily needs and nature's offerings. Each time I think up a project and what it entails, I soon realize that only essential stores are open, so I have to improvise, make my own, or go without.

When I eventually do go to an essential store, I find most

of what I need. The times of having what you want at the click of a button—now!—are a thing of the past. I don't know if I want that time back again. I like this simple living. Each day, my awareness expands a little more. I take time to sit, think, observe, and be. I hear a bird singing at sunset and it may take me three days to learn its name.

My birthday balloon, a mark of the beginning of the lockdown, is still half-inflated after eight weeks. The air/gas contained in flowered plastic dances lower in the breeze from the ceiling fan. How long will it be before it is totally deflated?

How long will things last when resupplies aren't coming? We may run out of pork on the grocery shelves, I hear. I can be a vegetarian. We may run out of toilet paper. I can create a bidet. Water is still flowing, rain will come again, wind and water can drive our turbines to make electricity. And haven't I lived without electricity before when I was on the trail? I feel like a child again—a child who doesn't know yet what can be had and entertains herself with what is within reach.

This may be a yearlong journey, a trek into the unknown. I look forward to what I will discover about life. For now, the change feels expansive. The heat of this day is winding down. While the pizza is baking, there's weeding to do in the shady part of the garden.

**Susan:** Dami's newest book, *Fly Free*, a memoir about love, loss and walking the path, covers not only why and how she became a long distance hiker but takes you with her on a trek in Ladakh in the Himalayas. Her *Walking Gone Wild, How to Lose Your Age on the Trail*, is also available online. Learn more about her hiking life and book at transformation-travel.com. Follow her at facebook.com/walkingwomen50plus, wordpress.com/view/walkingwoman50plus.com, transformation-travel.com, or twitter.com/dami97520.

**Dami Roelse**

# Donna 'L-Rod' Saufley

**Susan:** Mention Donna in any PCT hiker circle and there is likely to be a moment of reflection and then an outpouring of stories. I had heard of trail angels Donna and Jeff Saufley and their Hiker Heaven from the moment we first entertained the idea of section-hiking Southern California's arid lands. Because Ralph and I initially were doing section hikes of the PCT for only a couple of weeks a year—and because we had started from the border of Mexico—it was a couple of years before we would get to mile 454 to experience their hospitality at Hiker Heaven.

We walked through the small town of Agua Dulce then turned off the trail to walk the paved road a mile up to the low-slung ranch house. The Saufleys' was a two-acre spread with a few horses on their wooden-fenced property—similar to their neighbors' places. We entered a gate and immediately were greeted—not by our soon-to-be hosts but by a lively and friendly mishmash of dogs.

After Donna came to rescue and greet us, she gave us a short tour. If we had been there in mid-May, we would have found dozens of other hikers, but since we had started this section in April of 2007—years before *Wild* captured the interest of thousands—we had arrived just ahead of most of that year's thru-hikers. We were among only a half-dozen other guests.

The first realization of what a well-organized and complex enterprise this was came when Donna led us to the garage. We wanted to pick up our resupply box that we had mailed ahead of time to their place. The garage was filled with rows of shelves, all carefully addressed to hikers c/o Hiker Heaven for future collection. Donna also gave us an empty laundry basket. We were to put everything we wanted washed in the basket.

Meanwhile, Donna showed us to the most extensive hiker box system we had ever, or would ever, see. On tables, on racks, and in clearly labeled plastic bins were hundreds of items that hikers were free to take. Clothes (organized by type, size, and gender); freeze-dried food packages (including the notorious corn pasta); half-full canisters of fuel; sections of trail guidebooks; utensils and more. There was also a rack of clean clothes for hikers to wear after they showered and while waiting for their laundry to be returned—folded, at the door to their room.

The next stop was a trailer. The living room had a TV, a sofa, overstuffed chairs, a guitar hanging on the wall, and bongo drums. The kitchen was stocked with spices and other staples. A telephone was available—free for local calls.

I was very happy to see the bathroom shower—and to be shown a private room for the night. That we were able to sleep inside was largely due to the year we were there. If we had shown up 10 years later, we would have been put up on folding cots in one of the six open tents that were brought in to accommodate the later-arriving guests when the number of people hiking through soared.

When Ralph and I stayed at Hiker Heaven, which we did twice, the number of hikers on the PCT was much lower than it is these days. In 2007, 101 people reported they had completed the entire trail. In 2019, there were 919 recorded completions. Though these figures don't show the complete picture because many more people hike only a portion of the trail in any given year, it's an indication of just how amazing an accomplishment it has been that the Saufleys have been hosts to tens of thousands of guests free of charge (though donations of money and time have provided help) during the two decades they have operated Hiker Heaven.

And as you will see, Donna is also an accomplished hiker and backpacker!

**Donna Saufley:** I had a used a 20-degree bag for all of California and Oregon on the Pacific Crest Trail, and it had been sufficient, though on freezing nights in the Sierra, I had to wear all my clothes to stay warm. Crossing the Bridge of the Gods over the mighty Columbia River on September 1, 2016, Washington welcomed me by pelting rain in my face exactly where the official welcome sign was mounted on the bridge, reminding me that I was late and freezing temps would soon arrive along with fall's mind-blowing blazes of color. Then, my beloved friends, stalwart Hiker Heaven volunteers, benefactors, and 'in the mountains' accomplished hikers Lucy 'Early Girl' and Larry 'Water Boy' Mann offered me a zero-degree sleeping bag they had no use for.

These two former Washingtonians coached me about hiking the PCT. They warned me about 'sucker holes' and not to let them fool me into hanging my laundry out to dry. [The term 'sucker hole' is quite useful in the Pacific Northwest. It's a small patch of blue amidst a gray sky that can make you think the skies are going to clear only to have the hole disappear and the overcast reappear.]

They told me about the places not to miss and smart tactics like putting quarters for laundry in my resupply boxes. In many ways, their voices accompanied me on my grand adventure in this state that I both loved and feared for its wild, rugged remoteness and staggering climbs. I contacted them and asked if they could send the bag, which they did posthaste.

The bag arrived while I was holed up at the Trout Lake cabin belonging to two other kind and longtime hiker friends, Chris and Dawn Rinehart. We'd had such a lovely visit, but they had gone back to their lives and work in Portland, leaving me alone in the beautiful cabin my friend built with his own hands. The rain fell outside as I did my final prep for the trip along the flanks of Mt. Adams, over Cispus Pass, and into the Goat Rocks Wilderness, location of the subject of my most recent bouts of fear and trepidation to be gotten through and overcome—the famed Knife's Edge.

The bag almost exploded out of the box, the sheer luxury of its fabric and fill taking my breath away. I had seen bags like this but never used one. It was love at first sight. The poor 20-degree bag was instantly discarded and sent home.

There is nothing in my pack that I treasure more than my luxurious, silky-soft, dreamily billowy, zero-degree sleeping bag. It is more than a useful piece of gear. It is the love and spirit with which it was given, a tangible comfort that wrapped around me on icy nights while gales blew. It was and is the caring hands and helpful words that helped me along the way. It made me safe. I was warm and dry, surviving and thriving in the face of the mountains' changing seasons. It is a piece of softness and comfort in stark contrast to a world of rocks and hard earth. Alone in the wilderness, it is a beautiful friend. It is my 'Wilson.'

### The planting of a seed

A fondness for long walks and a sense of freedom as a child melded with a desire to backpack when I sat in my middle-school auditorium at age 13, listening to an afterschool presentation on backpacking presented by a man who went by the name 'Gizmo.' I believe he owned a local gear store, and his ploy to hook youth in was genius.

Gizmo gave us each a cardboard cutout of a '70s vintage backpack, which showed the items you needed and how to pack them. He taught us about space blankets and how you should never go out into the wilderness, even for a day hike, without certain items—like the space blanket, waterproof matches, and a whistle. He gave some important advice: If you ever got lost in the wilderness and hoped to be found, get to a safe open area, make large signs with found objects that could be seen from the air, and do not wander away—stay put. While this may not work in every scenario, it rings true.

### Building a life

All that desire was largely forgotten as the years sped by and life happened. I had a career in secondary mortgage finance that was the antithesis of the wild world. I married, had a child, divorced, and remarried. Jeff and I bought a house and filled it with animals and responsibilities.

Along the way, there were moments that reminded me of that fleeting desire to do something outside the comfort zone.

Reading a newspaper article about the trail. Being awestruck seeing backpackers during an auto tour in Yosemite; they had found a way. I tried some classically over-packed and uncomfortable backpacking, but it never led anywhere.

**The seeds begin to grow**

The change began in 1997 when Jeff and I stumbled into hosting PCT hikers at our home. I fell in love with the notion of the journey but kept saying I was a hotel and bubble-bath kind of girl. But there they were—the ones who were doing it, or trying to. I could pepper them with questions and see their gear.

But being close to the hikers still didn't immediately make me want to shuck my life and go backpacking. In fact, some things were offputting. Especially their feet—toenails blackened or missing from injury or removal horrified me. I did not want my feet to look like that. A bad hair day you can get over quickly. But this looked much more long-term.

The shift came gradually. I could not help but notice that despite the state of filth, tiredness, hunger, cold, hot, or injury that hikers arrived in, each and every one of them longed to get back to the trail. No matter how difficult their outward appearance made the journey seem to an outsider, they couldn't wait. They would grieve if they had to leave the trail.

My curiosity was given an open door when I found two hikers sitting on the sofa in the guesthouse with perfectly beautiful feet, untouched by blisters. The girl had nail polish on her toes, and her feet were something I hadn't seen on any other hiker. They were pretty.

**An unusual gateway drug!**

This was truly exceptional, and I had to know why. I thought they had just begun the trail and hadn't done any miles. No, they had come all the way from the Mexican border. They credited their choice of footwear—hiking sandals—for not destroying their feet. Fewer points of friction, thick protective sole, adjustable (unlike shoes), and amphibious. That was it; I had to give them a try. I tried them, and a hiking addict's first step toward dependency began. The sandals were my gateway.

The first hikes were test runs and training for ascending Mt. Whitney. They involved increasing distances and pack weight, then elevation gains. Overnight trips were test runs; I kept lists of what did and didn't work and made the gear changes between trips. I learned what I did and didn't like. I studied and did research. After one failed attempt at Whitney's summit, I was successful on my 47th birthday in 2003. Now I knew that I could do miles and carry weight. And I loved it.

The real 'getting serious' moment came when I decided to give the John Muir Trail to myself as a gift for my 50th birthday. I could not think of anything I wanted more, so I asked for and was granted a leave of absence from work and the supportive okay from my husband, and then began in earnest to prepare, even making some of my own gear. I spent 30 glorious days living along the Pacific Crest Trail from the southern Kennedy Meadows and completed the John Muir Trail in July 2006. I celebrated my 50th birthday with Jeff in Mammoth Lakes, who had met me for several rendezvous along the way.

### The importance of hiking

The trail represents to me the way we are mean to live on the earth, what we were built for, and how our ancestors traveled and experienced the world. It is a return to simplicity, where all that you want or need can be carried, and less is more. This culture doesn't care about any of the pretenses that the rest of the Western world seems obsessed with; your bank account, position, car, and address does not matter at all. No one out there is impressed with any of that B.S.

All of your external layers fall away, like an onion being peeled. The very heart of you is exposed. It can make you fall to your knees with gratitude for the privilege of being alive and experiencing the earth's wonders. It can make you cry and wonder why you chose such a difficult path when the softness of the familiar routines of home beckon. You will do battle with every fear imaginable that humankind has concocted about the wilderness from bears to bogeymen. Confronting and overcoming those fears can also make you incredibly strong, resilient, and confident. I have faced challenges in a different way because of what I have gained on the trail. Obstacles are measured differently now. Being on the trail makes me view the rest of life quite differently. I am unimpressed by money, fame, and possessions. I do not see any of that but only the true nature of a person when put into difficult situations and the kindness (or lack thereof) in their soul.

### The appeal of hiking and backpacking is...

In two words, trail life. Being a happy vagabond with a smile on my face in the most beautiful places on earth. Seeing wildlife and becoming a part of the natural world. The simplicity and rhythms of each day. The uncomplicated nature of walking until you want to rest, eating when you want to eat, making camp when the day is done. *Knowing that no matter how far the goal may seem, if you just keep putting one foot in front of the other, you will get there.*

### Accomplishments and favorites

To me, the biggest accomplishment was completing the entire PCT in 2017 after 11 years of chipping away the miles. But my favorite year was 2016 when I hiked 1,500 miles as my 60th birthday present to me. I continue to frequently hike the PCT locally and am currently revisiting stretches of the trail I loved the most.

### Pluses and minuses of solo hiking

It's really hard to say whether hiking with some of my favorite hiking partners is better or worse than hiking solo. Each has its rewards. The screaming laughter when I hike with my BFF, Michelle Turley. The joy of sharing the experience with my husband, who always lets me set the pace.

I much prefer solo hiking to being in the company of others I am less fond of. Certain personality types can grate on the nerves and rob your precious time on the trail, making for less than pleasant memories or even resentment. Some people prefer the social nature and security of being in a group; I don't like being forced into group dynamics. You stop, start, and act by the consensus of the group, not by your own choice. My time out there is too rare and hard to come by to let it be dominated by others. In a life where I must do what my responsibilities dictate, my hiking time is a way to counteract the effects of a busy life.

## Life is meant to be lived

As for the critics, I always consider the source. Most of those spouting about one fear or another have little or no experience actually doing the activity; the truth is that people fear what they don't know. And people are fear-manufacturing machines who love to obsess on worst-case scenarios. We worry, we fret. It's what humans do.

I have often told the story of my mother's best friend growing up, Marion Vine. As a young mother, Marion put her four-year-old son down for his afternoon nap after lunch and then laid down for a little nap herself. While she rested, a small plane crashed into her room, killing Marion and the pilot. The little boy was spared. The idea that death can find us in the safest place most of us know—in our own beds—I find oddly inspirational. Why not climb the mountain, swim in the ocean, blaze a new trail? Death will find us all whether we adventure or not. I just happen to relish the view from the mountain and the taste of the sea.

## Knowledge and flexibility

Research and do your homework about the conditions you are going into and then get prepared with the right gear, skills, and good judgment to get through whatever you encounter safely. Have a good understanding of your skillset, your physical and mental limitations, and how they compare to the challenge you are considering,. Make good decisions around that, i.e. take care of yourself along the way.

Flexibility means adapting to a new plan even if that plan means it's time to stop. The challenge ahead can be faced another time, under different conditions. There are times when you should simply listen to your body and follow its instructions. It may be trying to tell you something. Rest is restorative and should be incorporated into your hiking plans. Allowing no time for zeros or rest is a formula for physical and mental burn out.

On the other hand, sometimes your brain is pretty damn whiny and has to be told to shut up and suck it up. It is human nature to take the path of least resistance, and your brain has been conditioned to this regime. It will protest and protest that your body doesn't like working so hard, that you should stop when really you are *fine* and physically capable in every way to continue on. You kind of have to have a little talking to with yourself and set some reasonable parameters, such as, *I am not going to stop until I get to that tree up there.* When you get to that tree, give yourself a pat on the back for making it, take a momentary rest, and then repeat the process.

You may have to take every difficult task and break it up into many smaller, doable bits. But if you persist, you can travel a great distance. With enough practice, you will find it gets easier, like anything else you practice.

### Dealing with challenges and fears

I am, or was I should say, absolutely terrified of heights. The PCT is renowned for its lofty heights and exposures. By facing my fears and getting through them successfully, I have become less fearful and more confident in what I am capable of accomplishing. I will confess to scooting on my behind on a few bits of the Knife's Edge because I was too afraid to stand. But I scooted and walked the entire stretch despite my fears. Twice now.

On another hike, Michelle Turley and I were hiking in Northern California on the PCT, and as evening drew close, there were no places to camp. We finally reached a remote dirt road and found some suitable flat spots nearby. We broke our rule of never camping or hanging out near roads, believing that we were deep enough into the woods that it was unlikely anyone would be driving up there at night, which actually proved to be true. Early in the morning, I woke first and sat on a log near our tents enjoying my morning tea while Michelle still slept. That's when I saw him.

He was dressed in camouflage from head to toe. On his feet,

he wore something that muffled the sound of his footsteps, making his movements silent. His face was covered by a camouflage mask, though I could tell he had a long beard. As though his attire, silent movements, and lack of a recognizable face weren't disconcerting enough, in his hands he carried a loaded crossbow.

While his entire appearance and weapon were disconcerting, I knew (and was grateful) he wasn't after us but some poor deer. In sympathy for that deer, I said (very loudly to scare away any game nearby), "Is it deer hunting season?"

The faceless man only nodded slowly yes and kept walking up the road away from us. Michelle awoke to my noisy question and said, "I don't know, I think so. Why?"

After that, I never felt the same about skinny-dipping or pooping in the woods.

## Gratitude

I have come to terms with being a section hiker—rather than a thru-hiker—and I am okay with that. The mind writes checks the body can't cash, but I know if I start slowly and build up gradually, take rests and days off to recuperate, eat good foods, and hydrate well, I am strong and resilient and can cover great distances at my own pace.

I believe there comes a point for all of us when we become more aware of our mortality. For some, it is the loss of loved ones that brings this realization. It makes one face the fact that there are only so many really viable hiking years ahead and to get while the gettin's good.

The time will one day come when more sedate pastimes may be all that are possible. Until then, I will cover however much ground my body and soul and time allow. I am a true believer that being physically strong is beneficial to seniors, and I want to live what I believe.

I am just extremely grateful for the gift of good health that I have enjoyed that has allowed me to experience a long trail end to end, albeit over 11 years. Not everyone is so fortunate, so I do not take this gift for granted.

**Women's self-perceptions may be changing**

Though this may be too complex a concept to generalize, in my opinion, there may be generational differences in women's self-perceptions about their physical abilities. [It may be true that the younger generations are feeling] far less reined in by the gender stereotypes that older generations more often than not bought into and believed. I think you would have as difficult a time convincing a young woman today that she can't or shouldn't do something adventurous as you would have trying to convince a woman of an older stereotypical mindset that she actually can and should do something she believes she cannot do.

As much as I am a hiking enthusiast, I am well aware that the taste for adventure and the willingness to live out of a backpack for weeks or months in remote areas is simply not for everyone. It is perfectly okay to desire other pursuits. But if someone does have the desire and the physical ability to train and adapt, the truth is this: Only you can make it happen. No one will do it for you. If you want it, find the way to achieve it. Stay focused. Have fun. Life is a gift; make the most of it.

**What works for one person may not work for another**

Everyone, and I do mean each and every one of us, sees experiences through our own filters. What is easy to the hiker who holds a speed record and trains in the mountains year-round is extremely difficult for the average hiker just getting off the couch or away from the office. I found this to be true when Scott Williamson told his wife Michelle and me about a water source below Benson Hut [near Anderson Peak/Donner Pass Road], making it sound easy-peasy because to him it was. For me, at least, it was a death-defying downhill slide that made me cling onto branches and roots to keep from falling. I didn't get far and never made it to the water source, deciding that I, for one, was definitely not in Scott's league. I would not call it bad advice—just a failure on my part to see it through Scott's filter.

I have learned to just not listen to anyone giving unsolicited advice about what's ahead because they are conveying their own view of that experience, which might have been horrible or great but may have nothing to do with my own experience level or comfort zone. That "horrific stream crossing" may turn out to be routine for you.

You have to assess and take a good look at every obstacle yourself to make judgments and decisions about how difficult or easy it is. Take everything you are told with a grain of salt and know that people do mean well when they tell you things. Conditions change. Others' perceptions just aren't always right for you.

**Next stop!**

I am re-hiking sections in Washington because I lost 10 days of photos from my hike in 2016 (my own dumb move with the delete key) from Trout Lake to Snoqualmie, including Goat Rock and Mt. Rainier. Those are must-haves for my photo collection. The Sunshine Coast Trail in British Columbia is on the list, but the list is long!! So many trails, so little time. Meanwhile, we are engaging in other life changes, moves, and such.

**Susan:** Donna and Jeff hosted hikers in 2019 but then announced late that summer that they had some big changes ahead. Plan A was to move to the Upper Olympic Peninsula in 2020. Hiker Heaven was going on the market, and so the future as a respite for PCT hikers was dependent on the buyers. However, the place did not sell by the end of that year, requiring Plan B. In late December, Donna announced that they were considering postponing the move north, and turning their place into an Airbnb. This would require they "pimp-out the guesthouse to make it a special offering worthy of good ratings. We want to be ready to please our guests on a whole new level!" she wrote. And then COVID-19 arrived and all plans were put on indefinite hold.

Being rather outspoken, sometimes Donna does get herself in trouble. Of that, she says, "I am like a 'Lightning Rod.' A lightning rod stands on the roof and takes the heat to protect what it serves." And indeed, Donna had to take the heat when she took a stand by boycotting the ADZPCTKO (Annual Day Zero Pacific Crest Trail Kickoff) and leaving the event's organizing committee because it was causing, many said, a logjam.

The Kickoff has been a weekend event held annually in mid-April at Lake Morena, California—mile 20 on the trail. The event was packed with informative meetings, reports on water sources on the trail, inspirational slide shows, and good food and camping. It was also the first opportunity for many hikers to meet others also starting out on their long journeys, and the camaraderie that developed was a highlight for many.

Donna's vocal opposition caused a backlash from many hikers who had previously enjoyed, or looked forward to enjoying, the event. But as Donna maintained, local businesses were impacted by more people showing up at the same time than they could handle, and many of the small towns and businesses along the way were complaining.

Donna said, "If it means the trail towns will be happier, hikers will see more smiling faces." She added, "What works for a few doesn't always work well for many. Though the event itself was a wonderful gathering of hikers, it caused a human tsunami on the trail, which became known as 'The Herd.'

"The event's impact was not limited to towns and businesses—it was also apparent on the trail itself. Large groups of people trammeling fragile environments damaged vegetation as hikers made new campsites. It also violated LNT ethics."

To no avail, Donna advocated for the event to happen later in the season, and further up the trail ala Trail Days in Damascus, Virginia on the Appalachian Trail. These changes would spread out the hikers rather than creat a herd. It was versus a starting event that had the effect of a starting gun with everyone beginning their journey on or near the same time.

With time, the Kickoff began to struggle. Attempts were made to minimize the number of people setting off at the same time. In 2016, the delay in the permitting process for use of the park caused the event to be canceled. In 2017, the organizers decided to change things monumentally—discontinuing all the Kickoff activities and instead featuring only a few trail angels gathered at the park to offer coffee and advice to any inquiring hikers. It was the end of an era beloved by many.

**Donna Saufley**

# Patricia Schaffarczyk

**Susan:** I have hiked more with Patricia than anyone else except my husband Ralph. Until COVID-19 arrived, we were all tackling the Nifty Ninety Peaks (which she describes below), then we switched to hiking spots where we could walk and social distance nearer to where we live. Though I know that Patricia has had various injuries and surgeries, her sense of determination and joy always keep her in the lead.

Besides hiking and volunteering with the Museum of Local History in Fremont and other local organizations, Patricia has gone on 29 trips (and led about 20 of those) with Wilderness Volunteers in Alaska, Arizona, Arkansas, California, Oregon, Texas, Utah and more to join others in giving back. The earlier trips required backpacking, now she does the car camping ones.

**Patricia Schaffarczyk:** I was 43 when I started hiking. I had always wanted to hike more than my schedule or perceived obligations allowed. Then in 1991 after my divorce, on a trip to Oregon with my son Frank, I decided to hike and camp more.

That trip was a life-changer for me. I remember that one day my son wanted to hike straight up a hill. At first, I thought, "I can't do this; it's too steep and too difficult." Then I decided not to listen to that negative self-talk. I changed my attitude and said, "Yes, I can do this. Let's go." That motto was the beginning of my adventure into the hiking world. On our return from that trip, I stopped at the Sierra Club office in Oakland before we even went home. I purchased a hiking schedule and started going to hikes in the Bay Area.

### Hiking here and abroad

I hike in the East Bay Regional Parks around home and on hiking trails anywhere I travel. In the SF Bay Area, there are many trails near me. I have hooked up with my friends, Susan and Ralph, who like to set goals of different hiking adventures. We have had a great time discovering many new places in the Greater Bay Area by checking off hikes on the Sierra Club's list of 'Nifty Ninety Peaks' in the Bay Area.

In 2001, at age 53, I took a leave from the Fremont Unified School District and decided to fulfill my dream of hiking. In that year, I hiked the Francés route of the Camino de Santiago, trails on the Greek island of Kythera, the Pyrenees of Spain, and the Annapurna Circuit. (I hired a guide to take me on those trails, and we walked for 20 days in the most awesome landscape in the world, going over the Thorung La Pass at about 17,700 feet.) Much of that year, I hiked daily, somewhere. I still live with that incredible memory of a dream come true.

Since that time, I've also hiked in Mexico's Copper Canyon. However, most of my extended hiking has been camping or backpacking in the Sierras. In 2003, I discovered Wilderness Volunteers and immediately fell in love with the weeklong trips doing trail maintenance and other activities in wilderness areas. I have led and participated in several trips throughout the years that have taken me from Alaska to Hawaii to Maine. I usually add on some extra hiking before or after while I am in the area.

### The importance of hiking

I love the fresh air, the challenge, and the feeling of knowing that I can accomplish something that I might not have known I could. I relish the beauty of the outdoors and the many places I can step on a trail. When I began hiking, a new world opened to me.

Hiking is a big part of my life. I have slowed down, so I do not hike every weekend like I did years ago, but I feel obligated to take some kind of walk every day if I can. It feels so good mentally and physically after I get back from a walk.

I once did a solo backpacking trip from Sonora Pass to Echo Lake then on to Truckee, California. It was a real challenge for me to backpack alone. I had to overcome my fears of being alone and of being vulnerable to outside forces. I just told myself, *I am as careful as I can be, thank you.* Once I finished, I had a great sense of accomplishment.

When I was younger, I felt more confident. I was stronger, so I had no worries. Now, I still hike alone (with my dog) on shorter hikes on trails that I am familiar with or that are not so isolated.

**What it takes**

To be a successful long-distance hiker, you need the confidence that you can do it, one step at a time. Hiking is just taking that journey in increments. As long as the hikes are not technical and don't take you into dangerous places—like crossing rivers at the wrong time—you just have to do it.

I stop the negative self-talk. I figure I will get there when I get there, so I just make the best of it. I give myself pep talks: "Okay, I am not there yet, and complaining won't help, so just focus on getting to the next hill." Take breaks often if necessary, and push on.

**There have been challenges and frightening moments**

I was set back for a year from hip surgeries, and then a few years later, I broke my ankle. It took about a year before I could hike the same as I did before my operation/injury. I have to admit that I walk slower, and some trails are more challenging than they were 25 years ago.

When I first started hiking, I thought I had a good sense of direction. After getting lost for several hours a couple of times, I learned to be more attentive to my surroundings and to be sure I always know where I am. If I discover that I made a wrong turn, I go back to where I knew I was. From that experience, I also learned to research more to make sure I know where I am going and what the possible challenges of a trail may be.

On my solo backpacking trip, I had not totally prepared, and my pack was too heavy. Luckily, I ran across a fellow hiker who took my huge bag of nuts/snacks.

One day on that same trip, I knew I would be approaching

an area where my trail would cross a parking area, but I didn't know how far ahead this would be. As I continued on, I noticed that I was walking parallel to a road, so I made sure to make myself inconspicuous and crouched in the bushes whenever a car came by.

Maybe an hour before I arrived at the crossing, I heard shooting. I did not know where the noise was coming from, but then the shooting stopped. I thought it just might have been someone hunting.

So when I came upon a pickup truck parked where the trail crossed the road, I didn't know what to expect. Maybe a family was there? It wasn't until I walked closer while crossing the parking lot that I saw the bullet cartridges on the ground next to the pickup truck. Then I saw two drunken guys—passed out, sleeping in their truck. *What if one of them woke up?* I did not want that! Heart pounding, I passed as quickly and quietly as possible onto the trail, across the side of the mountain and out of sight of the parking lot and road. It was a relief to be in the wilderness again!

Though this was an alarming incident, the trip was amazing. I became more aware of my surroundings and physical needs. I noticed more sounds, silences and beauty in nature. I was constantly re-evaluating my progress and I spent much time thinking about where I would get water, and where I would eat and sleep. I loved the feeling of being a minimalist knowing that everything I needed to survive for a few days, I had with me.

### Advice for those beginning or wanting to try new adventures

Join hiking groups, and be consistent when you begin. I got my experience by joining Sierra Club hikes and a couple of other hiking groups. The leaders I went with were always cautious and made sure that everyone was safe. I went every chance I could get and hiked with people every weekend. I started to get to know the others, and that opened up to being invited to participate in backpacking trips.

I went on a number of private and Sierra Club backpacking

trips with friends. It was through those clubs that I learned how to backpack, and I learned about new places to explore by talking with the people and studying the hikes. A trail or hike is not as daunting if you are going with someone who has done it before. Negative self-talk can stop you before you start. Start with a slight challenge and increase to more challenging hikes in increments.

As for gear and equipment, my favorite is probably my wide-brimmed hat; it really keeps the sun off my face.

### Looking to the future

Some things have changed. I hike less in distance and time per week than I did before, and I would not backpack solo now. I see changes associated with my limitations because I am not as active as I was.

However, my next trip will be a weeklong service trip with Wilderness Volunteers. I had signed up as a co-leader in Carson-Iceberg Wilderness in eastern California in 2020, but that trip was canceled, so I'll just wait and see when things open up again.

I'm looking forward to the chance to explore a new national forest and a place where I have not been. I'll get to work with fellow hikers/campers, and I'll feel stronger physically and mentally after the trip. Each trip is another adventure and an exploration of place and people. I test my abilities, mentally and physically, and tap into my own sense of accomplishment.

**Susan:** Having gone on four Wilderness Volunteers trips and dozens of local day hikes with Patricia, I've seen firsthand her tireless activity—totally amazing considering that she does all this with two hip replacements. She is always the first to sign up for any worthwhile project and the last to stop for the day—always without complaint. And I cannot keep up with her on the trail!

**Patricia Schaffarczyk — Mojave Wilderness Volunteer trip**

# Diane 'Piper' Soini

**Susan:** Diane was referred to me by our mutual friend Scott Williams, who wrote, "Author and long-distance hiker, she keeps up the best blog for the Santa Barbara Mountains and is a lovely person. Hiked the Winds and Glacier together with her."

**Diane Soini:** My dad took me and my sister hiking when we were in elementary school. I still remember there were lots of naked hippies in the woods back then. One time, we backpacked the almost two miles to the meadow on Rattlesnake Trail, a local front-country hiking trail in Santa Barbara, and camped there overnight.

I got interested in the Pacific Crest Trail in 1975 when I was 10 years old and my uncle gave my dad a National Geographic book about the trail. I looked at the pictures hundreds of times. It became a dream, something I would do 'someday.'

## It got wilder

When I was in junior high, we went on six-mile backpack trips in the Sierra with my church. We kept a griddle and a grill hidden in the forest, which we would hunt for once we arrived. My dad would bring a pancake machine, a volleyball with net and pump, a folding chair, and a fishing pole in his 100-pound pack. We'd catch fish and skinny-dip, and sing songs around the campfire at night!

When I was 16, my friend Tonja and I decided to go on the church 55-mile backpack trip on the John Muir Trail. It was us two girls and four guys, one of them the leader. Girls against boys! When they hiked faster, we hiked faster. When they ran, we ran. They could not lose us.

When we got down into Yosemite Valley and boarded a shuttle bus, the first person to talk to us tried to sell us drugs. "Hey, do you get high?" he asked. "Yeah—11,056 feet high!" we replied.

But the thing that stayed with me the most from that trip was the first night at Shadow Lake. After dinner, the leader said it was time for Bible study down at the lake. We sat on boulders with our feet in the water and watched the fish. The alpenglow was making beautiful mirrored images on the surface of the lake. We got out our Bibles, looked at the lake, looked at each other, put our Bibles away, and went skinny-dipping instead. We never took them out again!

When I was a senior in high school, I did a backpack trip in the backcountry near Santa Barbara. It was five high school girls and five dogs. Four of us were seniors and one was just a freshman, but she was strong and tough. The creeks were very high because of all the El Niño rain and we counted 35 creek crossings on the hike—70 total there and back on the eight-mile hike. My poor springer spaniel got swept away at one of the creek crossings and the freshman ran down the bank of the creek, grabbed my dog, and hauled her out of the water. She could have drowned under some tree roots. That freshman was a hero!

I went years without hiking at all after my high school years, but I was inspired when I was in my 30s by a story the *Los Angeles Times* ran about a 66-year-old woman, Sandra Johnson, who hiked on the PCT with her goat every summer and lived in a van with her goat through the winter. This! This was my goal! This is what I wanted to be! (The goat lady story is still out there: latimes.com/archives/la-xpm-1998-jul-12-me-3017-story.)

Then I met a coworker's friend who gave a slideshow of the trekking in Nepal she had done. Back in the '90s, trekking in Nepal was not as commercialized as it is now. She was so brave! Some of the people she stayed with lived in woven, basket-like huts. Then I finally got serious about hiking.

During the slideshow, she announced she was going to celebrate her 40th birthday in Nepal and was looking for hiking partners. I asked her if she'd accept me. She told me that I would have to get into shape. So I started hiking our local trails at least four times per week and going on overnight solo backpacks. I never did go hiking with her in Nepal. She canceled the trip and then moved away.

## Hiking destinations

I live in Santa Barbara, so I've hiked mostly in the Los Padres National Forest in Santa Barbara County and in the Sierras around the John Muir Trail. I have hiked the entire Pacific Crest Trail and spent many days hiking the Continental Divide—five days with some other hikers through the Wind River Range in the Rockies and on my own through Glacier National Park. I also hiked the Kalalau Trail on the Napali Coast in Kauai. [This trail is 22 miles of great scenic beauty, often rated as one of the most dangerous trails in the U.S. because of the narrow trail alongside steep terrain, flooded creeks, and high surf.]

I started hiking with the Sierra Club, which is how I met my current partner. In 1999, he took me to Nepal. I got to hike the same route as in the book *Into Thin Air* and experienced all those trail towns. I hiked the Khumbu trek in Nepal to Kala Patthar, an 18,519-foot (5,644.5 m) peak directly in front of Mt. Everest. I got to see Everest with my own eyes!

When I hiked the PCT, I was 43. I was frustrated by my job at a software company. The room was kept in the dark, and the air-conditioning was so cold that all the women in the office wore ski hats, puffy jackets, and gloves. I took an adult education career exploration course to see if I could figure out what to do with my life. The course was geared toward getting in touch with your inner self. My inner self was screaming 'wilderness!'

Sunshine! Wildflowers! I asked myself, *why the heck am I working so hard and saving all this money if not to make 'someday' be 'today?'* So I quit my job and gave myself six weeks to get ready to hike the PCT. My plan was to hike only the state of California because I don't like rain and my guidebook showed a lot of foggy, rainy pictures farther north.

I imagined the PCT would be a solo wilderness experience, and I was surprised that it wasn't. It was more like a linear party;

I met a new person every day. It was more about the people than the wilderness much of the time.

I did not meet my goal to hike the whole state of California then; I quit in the Sierras. I couldn't take any more of the snow and the moonscapes at high altitude. The moonscapes were worse than the deserts of Southern California. It was too scary. I felt panicked as if I was running for my life. Why was the trail up so high all the time? Didn't John Muir like woods and meadows and wildflowers? The guidebook kept talking about Evolution, Bear, and other horrible creeks where you could die.

I just couldn't do it anymore, so I bailed out at Bishop Pass, rented a car in Bishop, and drove home. My boyfriend drove me back to the trail a week later and dropped me off at Sonora Pass, where there are no more moonscape high passes to hike through. He told me I had to finish my story. I still didn't make it all the way to Oregon because my feet failed me. With spasms of pain running up the backs of my legs, I got off in Dunsmuir and quit.

At a Christmas party that December, a neighbor walked into the party and made a beeline to me. She said she did not understand why, but she felt something was commanding her to give me a message. She said that there was something in my life that wasn't finished, and I had to go and finish it. Oh my god! I knew what it was. I had to return to the PCT and finish the rest of the trail.

## I decided to make the hike mine

I came up with an idea to connect my front door to the PCT, then once on the PCT, I would first complete the part of the Sierras that I chickened out on and then complete the trail all the way to Canada. I mapped out a route through the Los Padres Forest that followed a section of the Condor Trail, a newer and undeveloped route that so far only one or two people have managed to thru-hike. This route would take me to Interstate 5 near Gorman. I would have to road-walk 22 miles on Highway 138 to Hikertown [trail angel stop near Lancaster] to reach the PCT. I stashed a bicycle in the wilderness to make that last part easier. I put a Canadian flag on my pack to tell myself not to quit.

That spring, I set off from my front door to walk to the PCT on my route. I got horribly lost once, but I ended up in the right place. I found my bicycle, but it was too hard to ride with a big backpack, so I got a ride from my partner from Pyramid Lake to Hikertown.

Later, I completed as much of the Sierras and Northern California's burned zones that I'd missed the previous year as I could, got a ride to Dunsmuir, and then continued walking all the way to Canada—1,800 unbroken miles. I consider this my greatest accomplishment.

I eventually cleaned up nearly every bit of trail that I missed, so I am now the proud owner of continuous footsteps from Mexico to Canada. Reaching Canada was the saddest day of my life. It was over. *What on earth will I do for the rest of my life?* I've thought about the 66-year-old lady with her goat. The only thing I can do now is to save up as much money as I can to become her.

As you can see, I was not a thru-hiker. The adventures I have had have not been diminished in my own mind because of the lack of such a label to put on them.

### The personal value of hiking

I think hiking has always been a part of my identity or the aspiration for my identity. I wanted to see myself as adventurous and independent. I am not an athlete. I was the girl they picked last or second-to-last if the girl with the back brace was there. When I learned there were sports you could do solo, where it didn't require playing a game with a ball and you only had to compete with yourself, I was all in. It was liberating. I have enjoyed both hiking and bicycling. These are things you can do alone or with others. They don't require a lot of expensive gear or skill. You can compete with yourself or not at all.

I feel when I'm out hiking solo that I'm not a girl or a woman or a female anymore. I'm a person. A full and complete person. I get to make all my own choices. I get to follow my intuition. I get to play with my gear. Nobody is explaining things to me or barking orders at me or making decisions for me. I don't have to think about how ugly I am, how fat, how slow, how unladylike.

I can just be me.

I guess I also always hope that big backpacking trips will make me not fat anymore. It sort of works for a little while, but I never get as thin as most women, even after three months of solid hiking. I'm always going to be fat. At least when I'm out there, I stop thinking about that so much and start feeling proud of how strong and fit I can be. I begin to see myself as an athlete.

## Women underestimating their abilities

Everyone underestimates their physical abilities. They also overestimate the physical abilities required to go backpacking, especially long distances. It's just walking. If you can go for a walk or a run of a few miles, you can do it. You just do it for more hours per day than you would normally do. I always tell people, *"You don't have to go fast to go far. All you have to do is add hours, not speed or effort."*

## Hiking's rewards

Hiking is a great exercise that you can do your whole life. It doesn't take a lot of training.

I have never felt safer than when I'm by myself or with trusted friends out in the wilderness. Once you get three miles from a parking lot, you're not going to meet any murderers. Once you get about five miles away from the parking lot, you're going to leave the noisy Boy Scouts behind. Once you get about 10 miles away, you're not going to see any people at all.

I also like that it doesn't take a huge amount of gear to get started. I've learned not to go too cheap on gear; I spend money for the best gear. How much money is wasted on things you don't really need that you could instead spend on things that matter like a really warm down sleeping bag? If as a kid you ever had to camp freezing to death in that sleeping bag with the flannel cowboys on the inside (you know this sleeping bag), a warm down sleeping bag changes everything about camping!

## A favorite piece of gear

One of my favorite pieces of gear is my Jacks R Better wearable sleeping quilt. It's rated to 45 degrees, which isn't enough for the conditions I normally hike in, but it worked great in Hawaii. It has a little hole you can put your head through so you can wear it like a poncho. It occurred to me that the quilt is about the same weight as a down puffy, so what if I left the puffy home and brought it as a second sleeping bag? I tried it, and oh my god, I've never been so warm and toasty at night or sitting around camp. I now never go without it. When worn, it falls below my knees, so while sitting around camp, I can tuck my arms and legs in completely. At night, I layer it as an extra blanket either over or inside my 20-degree quilt. I will often pull it completely over my head. On cold mornings, to ease my way out of bed, I can slip it over my head and wear it while I pack up and get ready. Such luxury!!

## What we learn

When I was first getting serious about hiking, I felt like I was getting an education just like college, only it was college for my body. My body was learning, and I was learning about my body. I felt on my longest hikes that it was not healthy. I needed to eat so much, but I did not feel like I could carry enough food to eat healthfully. My body began to break down from overuse injuries.

Near Timberline Lodge in Southern Oregon, someone asked me if I felt like my metabolism was blazing fast, and I honestly sensed that it had slowed to a crawl. I not only couldn't eat enough to stay healthy, if I ate any more than I was eating, I gained weight pretty quickly. In some ways, I felt like Superwoman because of what I could do, but I also felt physically worn out.

At times on both of my longer hikes, I felt I was breaking down from depression—from being hungry, scared, and in pain. I often felt regret that I passed side trails leading to places like waterfalls that would have been interesting to see. I frequently felt bored and angry that I couldn't do other things that I enjoyed. The hiking felt like a job, and I was the meanest boss I ever had.

Toward the end of my 1,800-mile segment of the PCT, I was ready to be done. I might have tried to hike too many miles each day, but I was not sure that a thru-hike was the best way to do a long trail. Still, I loved every minute of it. I felt so close to nature, so free-spirited, so powerful despite feeling so worn out and so superhuman—even though I didn't do anything most other people could do even better than me. I loved it, and I would do it again tomorrow. I don't regret any of it, and as someone on the White Blaze [FB group for A.T. enthusiasts] forum put it, it was like I found the little chink in the wall of the prison we all normally live in. Now that I knew where it was, I could escape whenever I wanted.

People revere thru-hiking, but it's not necessarily the best way to hike. My five-day hike in the Winds was to help four thru-hikers. I had to meet up with them. It required keeping tabs on their trail journals for weeks in advance, then placing the most strategic vacation request I could with my boss, then filling all their trail resupply orders at the grocery store (so many Pop-Tarts!), then driving three days to Wyoming with their resupply, then meeting them at a lodge in literally the middle of nowhere (it was like hitting a moving target, and I almost missed them), then going on the hike with them and struggling but somehow keeping up with them, then tearily saying goodbye five days later and driving three days home again. They may have felt like the five days in the Winds was a blip they can barely remember, but for me, it was an adventure I'll never forget.

## Amazing feats

I was 44 when I invented the route through Los Padres National Forest from Santa Barbara to the Pacific Crest Trail, and then I hiked it. Then, in 2019, when I was 54, I returned to my trans-Los Padres route to the PCT for another go at it. There was one trail I had missed back then because I got lost: the Buck Creek Trail in the far eastern Los Padres N.F. The trail haunted me just like the PCT had haunted me. I had to return.

This time, I started at Nira campground in the San Rafael Wilderness and traversed Los Padres National Forest eastward to Buck Creek, followed the Condor Trail for much of the way. This time, I was determined to find the Buck Creek Trail.

Trails in the Los Padres are not as well-traveled as the John

Muir Trail or the PCT. The trail is often overgrown and faint. Sometimes, the only footprints you will see for days are of bears or mountain lions. It's rare to meet any other hikers. There were fallen trees everywhere. I sometimes had to take off my pack and drag it under fallen trees. It was difficult but also very beautiful and solitary.

This time around, because I was armed with a GPS on my phone and lots of notes I had taken from online research, I managed to find the Buck Creek Trail, but I still got lost near the top. I've heard some people call it the "Buck Creek Triangle," so I think I'm not the only person to get lost in the area. Being lost was only temporary. I camped lost for one worried night, but then I found my way in the morning and made it to my destination on time.

I was proud of myself for making it this time. I still have not managed to make it from the Pyramid Lake area to the PCT without driving though, so I am not finished unspooling the unbroken ball of invisible twine from Santa Barbara to the PCT.

### What about going solo?

I always tell women who are planning to do one of the long trails to go solo. It's the best way. If you go solo, you can make all your own choices. You will be liberated from not being able to do the things you want because of other people's schedules. You also won't burn any friendships. Not everyone hikes well together. You can meet new people and make new friends. This is especially important for people who tend to hide behind more outgoing friends or a spouse.

When it's just you, the gorgeous sunset is a gift just for you, the trail magic is a gift for you, the achievement is yours. When I was solo on the PCT, I often thought to myself that I wished my partner could be here to experience this alone like me. Years later when he went to solo-hike the PCT, he got to be alone out there like me. And then he knew intimately what it was like. In that way, I believe we shared the experience more deeply.

There are people who are critical of hiking solo. The most vocal tend to be males who seem compelled to give unsolicited warnings about wild animals and the dangers of the wilderness. As soon as they start their harangues, I sort of roll my eyes internally. Not this again. I try to laugh it off, or contradict them with stories of my thousands of miles solo-hiking in the wilderness, or just blow by them on the trail hiking in a skirt and sandals as if to make fun of all the fears they've packed in their giant packs, or just thank them and find a way to extricate myself from the conversation. But it always hurts a little bit.

People who are critical of solo hiking don't know what it's really like and probably don't understand that sometimes it is scary but that there really is a difference between fear and danger, or danger and discomfort.

Another thing that I think hurts women is the idea that they, in particular, have no business hiking alone. To have some know-it-all guy mansplaining how you shouldn't be out there alone is incredibly harmful because you start to doubt your skills and intuition, and you start to defer your dreams out of fear. And then you become weak not because you really are weak but because someone else wants you to believe you are. Once you learn you can do it alone, it's incredibly rage-inducing when they start up because it feels like theft. They're trying to take something important away from you.

I spent 44 years of my life believing I couldn't do something like the PCT. As women, we learn to accept limitations we don't really have. Don't listen to these people. Listen to yourself. You can do this!

**Facing fears and challenges**

The biggest fear I had about long-distance hiking was the logistics: planning all the resupplies and trying to figure out the towns and the hitchhiking. I'm not a planner; I'm totally a spontaneous kind of person. Turns out you can hike the PCT spontaneously without a big plan and a bunch of resupply boxes. All you need is a good list of towns and what kinds of amenities they have and the help of the post office. And the hitchhiking turned out to be a really positive part of the experience.

When I first started solo hiking, I had a fear of sleeping

alone. I remember on my first solo trip experiencing that sensation of being awake with something large and dangerous nearby, but being paralyzed and unable to call out "Who's there?" I thought I smelled a gas leak coming from my stove, but I had sleep paralysis and couldn't get to it. In the morning on my hike out, I felt so proud of myself for surviving it. I never felt scared like that on trail again.

Another lesson I never seem to remember is that rain isn't as bad as I start imagining it is. Keeping a positive attitude in the face of adversity would make things a lot better than how I usually handle things, which is to get mad or freak out from fear or anxiety and start running and crying.

It occurs to me that being able to express such embarrassing feelings is another good reason to go solo.

**Lessons to pass along**

To be a successful thru-hiker, it helps to be determined and have a positive attitude. I also think it helps to adjust your definition of success. Too many people are all-or-nothing regarding trails like the PCT. If you don't hike the entire trail in one go, the trail doesn't go away. It's still there. You can return and hike the rest of it. And then you get two adventures instead of just one. There is no failure, only more adventures.

As for a big long trail like the PCT, you're never really going to be alone. There are so many resources to help you plan. And you can throw your plans away and make new plans while you are out there, so the long trails are pretty forgiving as far as logistics. There's really no reason to consider something like the JMT, PCT, or A.T. to be at the top of the list of challenging trails.

**Hikes may change over time**

Planning a three- to five-day trip on some crazy loop of my own design is in many ways just as much of an adventure as hiking the PCT. It's just shorter, that's all. The planning is an adventure of its own. The anticipation. Planning the gear I'm going to try out. Dehydrating the food. Taking pictures, putting together a story from the pictures, and journaling. On my last trip, I took videos and combined them into YouTube videos. That was a lot of fun.

Near where I live in Santa Barbara, I can hike to many back-country camps that are only a couple of miles from where I can park. This makes it easy for people getting started in backpacking (and for me) to do gear shakedowns. It may be similar in other places. A quickie overnighter is a good way to get started.

**What's next**
The thing I liked most about some of my adventures was having a peak physical experience—being able to do more miles than I ever thought I could and experiencing the kind of physical invulnerability that convinces me I can do anything without limitation. I would like to say that I'm looking for that experience again, but I'm not sure I will ever feel that way again.

So, now I am looking for something that is a combination of the physical with the inner peace of enjoying the experience. I know that I spend too much time worrying and being mad at things I can't control, like the weather, and that I have lessons to learn there. So my next long hike is hopefully going to be filled with moments of just enjoying the fact that I can experience the beauty and the solitude and the pain and the frustration because that's when you feel truly alive.

**Coping with stay-at-home challenges:**
[May 2020, Southern California] During this whole COVID thing, I still have to work. I work from home on my computer on the same couch I sit on to watch TV and sometimes even to sleep (so I can be next to an open window—hot flashes, you know).

They have not closed trails where I live. I have been doing one-night trips in my local backcountry. I am lucky to live very close to the Los Padres and dozens of trailheads. I have been choosing trails that are less popular than the ones people normally do day hikes on. The Los Padres has a lot of established primitive campsites with picnic tables and fire pits. Instead of aiming for one of those, I choose a dispersed campsite. I just go for one night, and the trip is pretty short. No campfire. It has changed my perspective on backpacking. A backpack trip does not need to be epic.

Here's how I described my experience doing this recently at BackpackingLight.com: "One thing about doing short weekend hikes like this is I kind of feel like a thru-hiker again in a way. The weekdays are the zero days, days of nothingness that kind of disappear in memory because all I do is sit. The weekends are the days when I'm alive and I'm out there living.

"If anything good comes out of this whole COVID thing, it's that I realize in a more tangible way that there is no need to save up vacation days for a big adventurous trip. Small adventurous trips done frequently kind of add up to the same thing as they accumulate in your memories."

**Susan:** From looking at Diane Soini's ("soy-knees") websites, I learned that she has had "parrots since I was a teenager. They live a long time." She plays old-time music on mandolin with the Glendessary Jam. And she "can cook a really good steak."

The route that Diane developed (and backpacked) from Nira Campground in Los Padres National Forest to Agua Dulce on the PCT is recorded in segments on YouTube. To find them, enter Diane Soini Nira to Agua Dulce in the YouTube Search Bar. You'll even get a peek at the Saufleys' Hiker Heaven.

Diane's website, SantaBarbaraHikes.com, not only has a tremendous amount of information on hiking near her home but also much of value to people headed for other hiking destinations near and far. santabarbarahikes.com/gorp/Diane. She also regularly posts on her blog: santabarbarahikes.com/community/blog.

Diane is the author of *Piper's Flight: A Solo Woman's Journal on the Pacific Crest Trail* (2008), *Adventure and Magic: A Solo Woman's Journal from Santa Barbara to Canada along the Pacific Crest Trail* (2010), and *Santa Barbara Hikes: Great Day Hikes* (available from lulu press: lulu.com/en/us/shop/diane-soini/santa-barbara-hikes-front-country-and-camino-cielo-hikes/paperback/product-3878271).

**Diane Soini**

# Diane Spicer

**Susan:** Diane is the author of *Best Tips For Women Dayhikers: Everything You Need To Know To Hit The Trail* and maintains a blog, Hiking For Her (hiking-for-her.com), "because females do things a little differently than the guys! We need to stick together and get it done on the trail by celebrating our differences and maximizing our strengths. Together, we're stronger hikers."

**Diane Spicer:** I was 13 years old when I plunged into the backpacking world via a Girl Scout trip. My friend Tracy and I shared the shelter of a canvas tarp through a week of cold rain. I learned that there are two kinds of people in the world. One kind equates hiking with a suffer-fest. And there are those who can't get enough of outdoor time regardless of conditions. I knew hiking was for me that very first night under the leaky tarp.

Through my teens into my thirties, I was an Upper Midwest hiker. I learned backpacking skills in Isle Royale National Park and the Porcupine Mountains.

However, the Pacific Northwest has been home for decades, so I've explored most of the trails in Washington state. Mt. Rainier and Mt. Baker are my favorite PNW haunts for day hikes, plus I can cherry-pick the best sections of the northern PCT for good-weather windows to do longer trips.

New Mexico is bursting with hiking opportunities. I've tapped out a few in the Gila Wilderness and around Santa Fe and Taos. Plus, I've done remote trips into the wild country of Alaska including the Arctic National Wildlife Refuge (ANWR) and Wrangell-St. Elias NP. My international trips include Greenland, the Yukon (Kluane, Alsek River), and the Northwest Territory.

## My fine obsession

Hiking plays a central role in my identity as a human being. I'm a hiker who is also a mother, wife, microbiologist, and all the other labels we use when we meet new people. Does that make me obsessed? Oh, yes!

Hiking speaks to me on three levels. It grounds me in my physical reality. It provides me space and time for my own thoughts. And it continues to nurture my link to the Source.

What draws me onto the trail again and again is the sense of freedom. As a teenage girl, it was my ticket to freedom disguised as a sanctioned activity with my peer group. I am so grateful to have discovered hiking early in life! Once you savor the time and space to be yourself on the trail, you crave more of it.

As I've aged, I've continued to cherish this freedom. Older women are invisible anyway in our culture, so I blend in well with the forests and rocks. And my family considers it normal when I disappear for weeks at a time and come back with bruises and wild stories.

## My greatest accomplishment

In June of 2019, at age 63, I took a guided rafting/hiking trip on the Alsek River (a UNESCO World Heritage Site). This wild river runs from its source in the Yukon through British Columbia and ends at the Gulf of Alaska. Imagine floating on the icy cold river surrounded by unnamed snowy peaks as far as you can see. Challenging cross-country navigation made hikes to glaciers and ridges a fun puzzle. The highest concentration of brown bears in North America kept campsites interesting.

## The reality of solo hiking

Solo hiking opens the door to freedom as wide as it can go. But here's the reality: A female solo hiker faces into the strong wind of social sanctions. To disentangle from the fear and judgment projected onto her requires a strong effort.

She must also be smart about going solo. Required tools for soloing include meticulous planning and a strong outdoor skill set. She also should know how to keep her balance on the fine line between caution and fear. My response when someone asks "But aren't you scared to go alone?" goes something like this: I offer a gentle pat on the back of the hand along with a half-smile. Then I whisper, "You're missing out on the best-kept secret in the world, my dear." That refocuses the conversation in a hurry!

### What a long-distance hiker needs...

I don't have the temperament of a thru-hiker, but based on my backpacking experience, I do agree with Yogi [Jackie Mc-Donnell, author of *Yogi's PCT Handbook*] about needing the right attitude. Fear can be an insidious and potent deterrent on the trail. The 'what ifs' can discourage you even when your legs are willing and there's plenty of daylight left.

The flip side of Yogi's quote is the "I'm bulletproof" attitude. Thru-hikers who continue to hike with injuries that grow worse day by day until they collapse make me sad. When your body is kind enough to give you feedback but your conscious mind ignores it, where does the blame go? Getting angry at your knee for taking you off the trail doesn't make sense to me.

In a perfect world, a long-distance hiker is a realist who embraces the facts right in front of her. She uses her mind to get off the long slippery slope into hopelessness (mental defeat). She digs deep for physical reserves (conditioning).

And she doesn't ignore her very best tool, the 11th Essential, which is common sense.

### And if you really want to stop?

When I start to give up, I tell myself that this moment, right now, is as good as it gets in life. My boots on the trail, the wind in my face, the raindrops (or sweat) sliding down my neck—wow! I'm fully alive as I push toward my hiking goal. Plus, extra snacks when I get there!

### Some personal favorites:

For me, personal comfort makes or breaks a hike. That's why my self-inflating sitting cushion is one of my favorite pieces of gear. It makes sitting on rocks or damp ground much more comfortable. I also kneel on it when I'm doing campsite chores.

## Challenges are par for the course

As most hikers can attest, there are physical injuries related to hiking. I suffered through a groin pull from descending on a slippery rock face that took half a year to resolve.

I've also developed food sensitivities over the years. I went gluten-free at least a decade before it became trendy. My body also reacts poorly to grains, citrus, dairy, and nightshades [tomatoes, potatoes, and more]. This makes me a pioneer of the gluten-free/paleo/Whole30 diets—and not by choice. It's tough as a backpacker to find reliable food choices for weeks of energy and stamina. I've got things worked out now, but I do come back from long trips feeling depleted.

## And frightening things happen, too!

My hiking trip to Greenland was the most informative of my long hiking trips. It ended abruptly with a helicopter evacuation.

Travel along the Greenland coastline between hiking destinations is by boat. In warmer summer weather, ice chunks that break off the landmass drift around without impeding travel. These huge icebergs make lovely photographs, and it's easy to avoid them in a boat.

However, when sea currents and wind push drift ice together into huge masses, it is referred to as pack ice. Pack ice coming in without warning in July is a rare, not to mention dangerous, event.

On my trip, huge chunks of pack ice began drifting into Karale fjord, which we were using as base camp. This was a sign that we were going to be unable to leave if we didn't act fast.

Navigating boats in these conditions is an extremely dangerous maneuver. Transporting supplies and people grinds to a halt. Hikers get trapped! It took several harrowing hours to reach Sermilgaq, a fishing village with a helipad.

Then it took several days for a helicopter to become available to evacuate us. The villagers were gracious but pretty freaked out about pack ice in July.

I still get shivers when I recall using my paddle to push the boat off the sharp rocks along the shoreline over and over again. Extremely bizarre event for all of us!

When Mother Nature decides to demolish your hiking agenda, you have no choice. Either you learn to yield the illusion of control or you suffer. It's a good lesson to keep at the top of your mind on any trail: No matter how much planning you do, you're not in charge of the outcome. Giving in to the unexpected with grace and humor is my new trail mantra.

### No aging in one place

An aging hiker becomes a wise old fox. That's one of many gifts from the trail a woman receives. As an elder hiker, I honor and trust my body's feedback. I understand and accept my limits. I know how to get the most out of my feet on any given day without expecting the same the next day.

Adopting this 'wise old fox' persona has made me more adventurous. I continue to defy my AARP card's label of senior citizen by tackling 'extreme' trails and trips. Because why not? I'd rather be resting on the toe of a glacier in Alaska, watching hawks wheel overhead, than on my couch back home any day!

### Guidance for newbies and other adventurers

Find virtual and real-life mentors who approach the trail in a way that resonates with you. Remove these toxic words from your self-talk: can't, shouldn't, afraid.

Stretch your definition of yourself by taking on a more challenging trail. Prepare with checklists, gear shakedowns, background research, and skill-building classes to build confidence. Failing to finish a hike is not the problem. It's failing to start a hike that holds you back.

### Women underestimating their abilities

I think women are taught to underestimate ourselves from Day One. Whether we buy into that thinking is up to us. My advice? Delete old fear-based messages. You know what they are—the ones that you hear inside your head when you think about challenging yourself. Replace them with appreciation for your wonderful hiking body. Respect your ability to make good decisions. Be sure to look in the mirror every day with a smile as you create your own version of a hiker.

## Which kind are you?
In my experience, there are three kinds of hikers: alphas, followers, and individualists. In my hiking career, I've played all three roles depending on the situation. One is not better or worse than another. But it has always been the alpha 'leaders' who gave me the worst advice. Why? They seem to resent the time it takes for careful risk assessment before plunging onward. An impatient hiker is a risky hiker to be around.

That's why I don't follow anyone into a swollen stream without my own reconnaissance, upstream and down. I don't ignore thunder rolling closer and closer when I'm on a ridge top. And I never accept a 'shortcut' without a long, hard look at a topographical map.

I'll let you use your imagination to explain how I came up with that list!

## The exciting next trip
On my next long trip, I plan to visit a remote destination teeming with wildlife, plus new-to-me botany and geology. There will be plenty of daylight hours for backcountry navigation and exploration. In a word, freedom. Yee-haw!

**Susan:** Diane Spicer lives in Seattle, Washington. Though the amount of precipitation in the city is 38 inches per year (about average for the U.S.), most of the time it's a light rain. However, if you live there and like to hike, you'll profit before you set out by considering the following observation by Alfred Wainwright: "There's no such thing as bad weather, only unsuitable clothing."

Diane Spicer's book, *Best Tips For Women Dayhikers: Everything You Need To Know To Hit The Trail,* is available on Kindle and paperback on Amazon. hiking-for-her.com. Photos of Greenland's pack ice: hiking-for-her.com/East-Greenland-Hiking.

You can also join the "Over Forty Hiker Community" on that site, and can ask personal questions without being embarrassed or criticized.

**Diane Spicer — Knapsack Pass, Mt. Rainier**

# Jane Toro

**Susan:** Jane says she doesn't have a trail name yet "I'm waiting for someone to bequeath me a name." I met Jane when we were both teaching at Ohlone Elementary School in Hercules, California. Though our schedules were different, we found time to talk occasionally, and I always found her enthusiasm for whatever project she was working on appealing. And not being a morning person myself, I was totally impressed when I learned that Jane would get up early each day to crew at Berkeley's Aquatic Park before she came to school for her full workday. At 66, her zest for life and love of the outdoors have not diminished.

**Jane Toro:** As a preteen, I yearned for wilderness experiences and heard about Outward Bound. I began counting the years until I would be old enough to go on one of their trips, but life took a turn in another direction when I got into competitive sports before I reached that age. I joined a track team when I was 13 and was training to be a heptathlete (the seven-event female version of a decathlete) when at 15, I was introduced to kayaking.

I was hooked immediately and left the cinder track for the river. I graduated high school early and left Michigan with some teammates in January of 1972 to train in Southern California and try out for the Munich Olympic Games in the single kayak (K-1). I didn't make the cut, though both of my training partners did in the double canoe (C-2).

I started college at the University of Michigan that fall, but after my sophomore year, I married one of my teammates, Andy Toro, and we moved to California, where I started my junior year at U.C. Berkeley. On practically the first day on campus, I saw a flier advertising the formation of a new women's crew team. I was thrilled! I had always thought that I would like rowing because not only would it be a water sport but would use my strong legs from running. Being on Cal's first-ever women's crew was one of the great experiences of my life.

### The hiking life begins

I didn't start hiking seriously until I was nearly 60. My husband and I are paddlers and have spent plenty of time outdoors in beautiful places, but he is just not a hiker. I guess I got to a place in my life where I gave myself permission to do something on my own that I had wanted to do since I was a teenager.

About the same time, my dear friend Donna [also formerly my teaching colleague] was reaching the same place in her life but for a different reason. Her husband had been an avid hiker and they had done many trips together, but when he had a near-fatal bike accident, he became a partial quadriplegic.

Donna and I started by going to the High Sierra camps in Yosemite, but after talking to thru-hikers on the JMT and PCT, I was determined that we would really go backpacking. In the years since, we have equipped ourselves with lightweight equipment and are always trying to go lighter. I feel that I will be able to keep doing this for a long time if I can go ultralight and still be comfortable.

My hiking so far has been in California—the High Country of Yosemite, the Eastern Sierra, and the Trinity Alps. I'm game for any place that calls, but there is so much so close.

### What hiking means

I think about hiking all the time. I often go to sleep planning menus or routes or gear. I think that the elegant simplicity of having everything you need on your back, being self-sufficient, and being away from all modern distractions is beautiful. I feel so 'present' when life is reduced to walking, eating, and sleeping. I feel like I find myself when I am taking pictures of wildflowers, marveling at amazing scenery/wildlife, and pleasantly exhausted at the end of a day on the trail.

## On accomplishments

So far, I would say that my biggest accomplishment was my first backpacking trip. I was the trip leader and planned all the meals and the route. The meals were a fun challenge for a vegan. We were out six nights and seven days. Everything went really well and got me off to a very positive start. I wonder how I would feel about backpacking if that first trip had been a disaster? I haven't done a 'big one' yet. My first long hike will be the John Muir Trail. I can hardly wait!! I plan to do it solo and go NOBO [northbound].

## To go or not to go solo

I haven't done a solo yet, but that's how I will do the JMT. I am a person who often prefers to do things alone. I do expect it will be scary that first night in the dark alone, but I think I will get over that pretty quickly. To help my husband feel okay about this (as much as I can), I am going to get a SPOT tracker or similar so he can follow my progress online. When people express dismay at a woman backpacking alone, I just point out that I'd be more likely to meet with trouble at night in most places in the Bay Area. The statistics are in my favor that I will be fine in the wilderness. I must say that I feel differently about places where there are grizzly bears!

## To be successful

In reading about and talking to long-distance hikers, I think that several things seem to make for a successful long trip. You have to be patient with your body as it gets used to the routine over the first days. You need to have done your homework and planned your nutrition so that you stay well-fueled and have the resupplies figured out. Living off junk food seems to lose its appeal after a while, not to mention that you are not getting quality fuel for your body.

Having good gear that works for you is another factor that can make or break a trip. I think my first trip went so well because I had picked the brains of every hiker who would stop for a while and had sorted through the recommendations to come up with what I thought would work for me. I highly recommend talking to as many different hikers as you can to learn about the whole spectrum of possibilities out there.

### How I keep going

When I know I have to keep going but just want to stop, I break the task down into doable segments with a small reward for each completion. If it's a steep, endless uphill, I will either set my watch timer for a certain number of minutes (the steeper, the shorter) or pick a landmark (tree, rock) and give myself a reward when I make that goal: I get to sit, lean on my poles, have a drink of flavored water, take a bite from a bar, pop another Life Saver into my mouth, or... I'm pretty good at bribing myself along.

### Facing challenges

I feel like I am still working on my biggest challenge, which is how to make time for the trips I want to do. Being retired is obviously a huge plus when it comes to long-distance hiking, but there are still a lot of claims on your time—family and friends and volunteer positions.

Family is the hardest to say 'no' to. We have two children, Kate and Tom, who were both athletic and are now married with children of their own. And, because most hiking happens around the summer months, it is also the time when your school-aged grandchildren are free and their families are asking you to come visit, planning vacations for you to join them on or announcing they will be coming to visit you.

Then there is the aforementioned husband. It takes some negotiation to carve out equitable time for you to do things together and time for you to be away backpacking. My husband is older than me by 14 years, so it won't be long before it may be unwise to leave him alone. It makes me feel an urgency to get in as many trips as I can now and yet it is also the time when we can still do some pretty cool trips together. As someone once said to me, "I thought it would take longer to get old!"

**Getting through what could have gone serious wrong**

I'm lucky to be able to say that I haven't had anything really unfortunate happen yet, but the one experience that stands out in my short career as a backpacker is when Donna and I heeded the signs that bad weather was coming and pitched our tent in a decent spot even though we were nowhere near our goal for the day. Shortly after we had everything and ourselves safely inside, a violent storm came over the ridge and we were lashed with wind and rain for hours! We were both so glad that we were not trying to set up the tent in some random location in the storm. Our tent passed the test with flying colors, too.

**Does age enter the equation?**

I'll have to let you know in a few years how my hikes change as I age. I'm just ramping up now! I'm hoping to do the PCT eventually and maybe more if all goes well with shorter trips like the JMT. As I have mentioned, right now the major obstacle is family obligations.

**Advice for other women**

Some great advice I read in Liz 'Snorkel' Thomas's book, *Long Trails*, is to involve your family as much as possible to help them buy into the idea that you are doing this. They can drop you off, pick you up, meet you along the way, mail or bring resupplies, follow you on tracking devices, etc. I'm planning on getting my family to do many of those things and hoping that some of them actually join me on the trail eventually.

I was able to get started because I went out at first with a friend who had experience. Then I learned as much as I could from other hikers I met. I joined a group of local backpackers on their training hikes in the Bay Area, and of course, most of the casual conversation was about anything hiking related—another great learning opportunity. I went on a Yosemite backpacking trip led by a guide and learned a lot by observing and talking to her.

A wonderful thing happened when I won a free hiking course with Duncan Cheung at a raffle. Duncan [offtrailontrack. com] teaches ultralight backpacking in small groups and tailors the learning toward individual needs as well. I learned so much from him and the others in the class and feel that I have him as a resource on into the future. I would recommend finding a class or going on a trip led by an experienced guide. I plan on learning more about navigation by going to an REI class. Get out there and learn!

### Do women underestimate their abilities?

I do think women are intimidated by all the aspects of a backpacking trip—gear, sleeping on the ground, sleeping in the wilderness, toileting, getting sweaty and dusty every day without showering, wearing the same clothes for days, navigation, first aid, nutrition, cooking...

I didn't come from a family who backpacked nor did I have friends who did when I was younger, so I was starting with a blank slate and wouldn't have known where to begin if it hadn't been for my friend Donna with her background. So, if it's something you want to do, take a guided trip or a class. If you don't already have a buddy who wants to get started with you, make a friend in the class or on the trip!

Once you get started, let your trips grow organically as you become more confident and prepared. It's also okay to be an ultralight camper who only goes on three-day trips. Some women will never sleep on the ground by choice, but if you really want to backpack, you will—and with the right equipment, it will even be comfortable! You will surprise yourself by what you can do without and will find that the reward of being out where very few other people go is tremendous.

### Bad advice and what to try

I can't think of any bad advice I have been given. There have been things that didn't sound like they'd work for me but weren't necessarily bad for someone else.

One piece of information that astounded me at first and which I completely rejected at the time is now something I actually want to try: going without a stove. No cooking! I am someone who can trade off comfort for efficiency, so the more I've thought about going stove-less, the more I want to try it. So, my next short trip will be with cold-soaked food, and I'll see how that goes before the JMT trip. I love the lightness of not carrying the fuel, the pot, and the stove as well as not worrying about how to resupply the fuel on a long hike.

I have been making up my own vegan meals with my dehydrator and will be experimenting at home before going out into the woods. This is my next hiking goal because of how it would simplify and lighten my load. I feel that the lighter and easier I can make backpacking, the more years I will be out there on the trail seeing nature at her wildest.

### And today

I still row for fitness and fun, competing now and then in masters races. I also still paddle with my husband. We now have among our 'fleet' a fiberglass outrigger canoe for two people that has become our boat of choice. We can take it out on San Francisco Bay and the ocean, but most often paddle it four times a week in Berkeley's Aquatic Park.

I have to give a special shout-out to Andy. The 1972 Olympics I mentioned was his third, and he went to one more after that. He competed twice for his native Hungary and twice for the USA, winning a bronze medal in his first Games.

He has written a book, *Chronicles of an Olympic Defector*, about his life growing up in communist Hungary, defecting at the 1964 Tokyo Games and starting over again in a new country with no money, no English, no education past high school.

Andy continued to be involved in canoeing as coach of the 1980 team and then served as the United States Olympic Committee Secretary. Through his involvement, the kids and I had some pretty wonderful Olympic experiences.

### Life's twists and turns

I got a teaching credential in my 40s and had a career as an elementary educator, where I met the fellow teacher who got me up to the mountains where I always wanted to be—just delayed 45 years!

**And as we began to deal with the COVID-19**

[April 2020, SF Bay Area] I notice that it doesn't take far to get away from most of the people out walking. I walked out to the local reservoir again last week. Instead of walking on the old roadway, I tried the Lakeside Trail. Nice, but it disappeared a few times, and I ended up bushwhacking through some poison oak that just manifested on my arm yesterday. Trying not to scratch it!

**Susan:** In keeping with her 'making lemonade from lemons' spirit, when the 2020 shelter-in-place orders were announced, Jane changed her plans from hiking in the Sierra to taking long hikes in the hills and mountains she could reach from her doorstep.

Jane Toro

# Elsye 'Wandering Chardonnay' Walker

**Susan:** Elsye completed the Triple Crown (Pacific Crest, Continental Divide, and Appalachian Trail) in 2018, becoming the first African-American woman to do so. I met Elsye at a 'Ruck'—an informal gathering of hikers and backpackers given by the AL-DHA-West in January 2020. Elsye is a board member at large of the organization. She holds a B.A./Masters in Community and Regional Planning from Iowa State University. Elsye currently lives in Tahoe City, California, where she can ski and play in the snow in winter, and hike and do water sports in the summer.

**Elsye Walker:** I was born and raised in Flint, Michigan, where I had a nature trail behind my house. I moved to Iowa for college and lived there for 20 years, then moved to Colorado where I strolled the mountains. Back then, I didn't consider it 'hiking'—more like just going out for a walk. On to Southern Cal after that where I liked hiking in the desert. Whenever possible, I love hiking the Sierra mountains, and now that I am living near Lake Tahoe, I can go more often.

I did my first backpacking trip at 45 then took off thru-hiking. I thru-hiked PCT 2015, CDT 2017, and AT 2016/2018.

Hiking for me is an occasional outdoor activity that I enjoy. Hiking is just one of the many things I do; I also like biking, kayaking, skiing, and hunting. I am also a 'burner'—a Burning Man regular. I attended for five years, even in 2015 right after completing my PCT thru-hike. Wow, what a shock to the system from solitude to overstimulation! Turns out a lot of burners are thru-hikers and vice-versa. But the two share similar principles, like Leave No Trace and Self-Reliance.

I dive fully into an activity (like hiking all three trails back to back), then I move on to something else. There are so many things I want to try and I'm not getting any younger. Not that I'm done, I just incorporate [hiking] into the next activity. Now I hike up mountains so I can ski down!

### Learning about the trails out there

When I was researching trails to hike in SoCal, I came upon Carrot Quinn's blog about thru-hiking the PCT. It was the first I knew of the trail, and her stories were so exciting. I had initially planned to hike the Camino, but then I thought, well, the PCT is right here in my backyard. Reading stories of other women like Heather 'Anish' Anderson really made me think I could do it, too! Furthermore, not knowing anyone personally who had done it created a level of excitement that I hadn't had since doing Burning Man or RAGBRAI. [RAGBRAI is the registered trademark for the Register's Annual Great Bicycle Ride Across Iowa, a noncompetitive bicycle ride organized by the Des Moines Register.]

### Accomplishments

My greatest backpacking accomplishment would be thru-hiking the PCT at age 45. Before starting that, my longest backpacking trip was two days. If I had actually considered my lack of experience, age, gender, or race, I might not have gone. However, I was too excited about the challenge. I didn't know what I was getting myself into (which made it a true adventure) or that I'd be trying to keep up with people half my age. It taught me I was far more resilient than I realized. *Just finishing was huge and led me to a greater accomplishment—making history.*

### What was it like being on the trail as an African-American woman?

This is always a hard question to answer. Race was not an issue for me on trail, and I feel my experience was like most others. For me, thru-hiking was very much like life; I've always been into activities that many other African-Americans weren't, so the lack thereof did not bother me. My mom used to joke (about my group pictures) that I was her chocolate chip in a sea of vanilla. I do activities regardless of racial demographics; if I had waited till hiking 'looked like me,' I wouldn't have gotten the honor of being first.

At a shelter in Tennessee, I met a woman and her husband out for a weekend camping trip. While unpacking, she said, "Hmm, I never seen a colored person on the trail." I was taken aback by the term but took no offense. We spent the evening chatting over dinner. I told her of another African-American woman hiker on the trail that year.

Moreover, I explained that just because you don't see it doesn't mean it's not happening. It's not about what people expect or think a thru-hiker looks like. It's about what is true. Lastly, just as in life if I ever came into contact with someone on trail that I didn't feel comfortable around, I just kept it moving. It won't help with pack weight, but leave your preconceived notions at the trailhead.

**What has drawn you to hiking?**

I like it for the freedom and adventurous opportunities. My thru-hikes have taken me to places I never would have 'planned' to see. Now, with just a backpack, I feel I can go anywhere! Moreover, I enjoy that hiking has allowed me to meet some incredible people (on trail and in small towns) that I might have never crossed paths with otherwise. There is so much bad news/fear nowadays, however, on the trail I experienced so much kindness and generosity. Lastly, what I like the most about hiking/backpacking is that it allowed me to see/experience for myself the true beauty of this country.

**How do you feel about going solo?**

I love hiking solo! When I hike solo, I feel empowered. All the choices are mine—how many miles, directions, breaks… When hiking with others, I tend to defer to what they want (it's the people-pleaser in me). Bad things happen to good people. Whether you are alone or with a group, things can go wrong. Do your research, make good decisions, and take appropriate safety equipment. Don't let other people's fears rob you of some time to connect with yourself!

### Meeting inevitable challenges requires...

Resilience, a childlike sense of humor, and a good attitude make all the difference in my experience. What's going to happen is going to happen. You can only do so much. No matter how physically prepared you are, it really comes down to how you react or respond to all that the trail will throw at you.

### Challenges for me are...

Time and money. Starting hiking late in life, I feel like there are so many miles and not enough time. Funny that living in the woods for months is not inexpensive. I'm an introvert not seeking attention or the spotlight, so getting sponsors is out of the question. So, not branding myself or selling my soul—I've worked multiple jobs, live in my car (at times), and given up nice things for a walk in the woods.

But the memories are priceless and the stories timeless. There have been times I've wished I had started at a younger age. But I've come to realize that though the younger me was more fit and energetic, the older me is wiser with more experience. Things happen as they should.

### What to do when it gets tough

Music and thoughts of my dad keep me going. Music is that thing that can get me through those last grueling miles. Music gets me outta my head and energizes my body! When a rockin' playlist doesn't work, I draw strength from those who have gone before me, like my dad. My dad worked hard for our family his entire life. After getting us all through college and retiring, he wanted his own adventure, a road trip across the country. He never got that trip because he got cancer and passed. Before he died, he said to me, "Go, Gee, go." So, when my tank is running low, I think of those who made it possible for me to have this opportunity. Their paths were way more challenging.

## One of the hardest times was…

Being injured when I fractured my ankle on the PCT with 1,000 miles to go. I was afraid going to the doctor would end my hike, so I kept hiking (after three days off). After quickly sliding down the mountain, I realized the error of my ways. The small wooded field was by no means small, and there was a steep drop-off between me and said field.

*Doh!* With the sun dropping quickly, I couldn't bring myself to climb back up, so I continued on. I found a way down, but I would first have to cross a stream of rushing snowmelt. After some crying and beating myself up, I forded that freezing stream, wonky ankle and all. Bushwhacking the whole way, I finally made it through that 'small' wooded field and up to the highway. There was nobody to 'save' me. Bad decisions were made, and I learned I needed to listen to my body, put my safety first, and always stay on trail. It's not an adventure 'til something goes wrong!

## Things change over time

I started out thru-hiking, light weight and trying to go fast. Over the course of three long hikes, my pack has gotten heavier as I wanted more comfort. You have to find your own way of hiking. I think it's very important if you're older to just kinda do your own thing. And listen to your body and not get caught up in the hype because it will wear you out. So, my hikes have also gotten shorter as past adventures have taken a toll on my body.

## On the practical side

My favorite piece of gear is my ULA Circuit backpack. Your backpack is an extension of you; mine certainly is. It's my favorite because the weight sits more on my hips than on my shoulders. Plus, it has numerous places to put all the things I need (mostly snacks!). Kinda like that perfect purse that you can always find your keys in. Not only do I hike with it but I travel with it (great as a carryon)! I named her Blackbird. If nothing else, I recommend getting a good backpack.

**And advice for other women**

Do it! Start small and work up to what's comfortable for you. You are stronger than you think you are. With every step, you become stronger. Those nerves are just your spirit wanting to soar—you have what it takes to fly, siStar!

I think women underestimate their physical abilities even though we are capable of so much. Luckily, studies have shown that women's confidence tends to increase with age; experience increases confidence! Confidence leads to action, attention, and resilience. Best advice: believe in yourself when no one else does.

**This was bad, even risky advice...**

That no map was needed. When I was hiking the CDT, my phone broke, which had all my maps on it, and I did not have paper maps for that section. The person I was hiking with suggested I have the new phone shipped to the next town (so we could keep moving) and pick it up there. "You won't need it," I was told. "You'll be with us, and the trail is easy to follow."

I opted *not* to take this advice and let them go ahead while I waited for a new phone. So easily I could get separated or take a wrong turn, and that could jeopardize my safety. Best advice: Always have backup paper maps, be self-reliant, and don't put your safety in the hands of others.

**The next big hike or backpack trip?**

[Now that I'm 49], I want my next trip to be more introspective. I know now what I am capable of, making history, when it comes to hiking. I no longer have anything to prove to others or myself. My next hiking trip will take me to what started my hiking interest in the first place—a desire to go on a nice walk with myself.

**With restrictions in place...**

Going through old photos and reminiscing, I came across this poem below. After my PCT hike, I went back to Burning Man and a local regional Burn. I requested a low-income ticket that year (due to all my funds going to the hike). As part of my submission, I wrote a poem as my 'art' requirement. I think it speaks to the connection between the two and how so many burners helped me throughout my hike. Happy to say I was rewarded that low-income ticket!!

## Finding My Flame
### ~ Chardonnay

I am only ordinary
Not special in any way
Not even noticed
As I go on day to day
I went in search
Of something
But the dust made it hard to see
What was truly me
But the voices around me
Said what do you want to be
Confident humble strong
With that I could not go wrong
From the desert city
To the woods I did flee
There I'd find what eluded me
The path was full of obstacles
Night dark as could be
Yet there was light from
The desert community
A flaming fire
Inspired encouraged
and restored my soul
From sunrise at a fence
To sunset on a mountain
I began to see
What I seek
Inside of me

**Susan:** Elsye enjoys most anything exciting and exhilarating that takes her outdoors. Besides having thrown herself full-steam into hiking, she cycles, skis, and more. Indoors, as her trail name suggests, she likes a good chardonnay. On her website, she points out that she is "not a fan of labels. It's the excitement and exhilaration of trying something new" that gets her moving (that and good wine, she says).

Websites
- wanderingchardonnay.com
- aldhawest.org (zoom interview on Hiking While Black)
- tinyurl.com/HikingWhileBlack if you didn't find above

Elyse Walker

# Katie Williams

**Susan:** Katie is one of those people with whom you immediately feel comfortable—open, accepting, and generous, which is also probably a large part of what made her a successful social worker supervisor with Children's Services until she retired back in 2012. She lives in Martinez, California, where she can freely explore the area that was the family home of John Muir—writer, adventurer, environmentalist—for the last 24 years of his life.

**Katie Williams:** I was about 23 when I started hiking. I didn't hike as a child. I began after I moved to California and became interested in exploring the outdoors. Generally, these were short day hikes. I did a few short backtrack trips, a couple of overnights, with women friends.

When I was about 28, I started hiking somewhat more and did a longer backpack trip with my partner, Scott (who I later married), who had a lot of experience backpacking. Generally, my hikes would be around six to eight miles; a 10-mile hike was a milestone. I stopped hiking for a long time, largely due to being overweight. I returned to hiking at about age 58. I really became a serious hiker after I retired from full-time work at age 62.

## Hiking destinations

I have hiked a lot around the Bay Area close to my home in Contra Costa County and also in Marin, Berkeley, and Oakland. Point Reyes in Marin County is a favorite. I have also hiked lots of places around the U.S. where I have traveled, including Alaska and Hawaii. I have hiked internationally as well—Spain, Italy, Peru, New Zealand, and Israel. Some of these are famous places and some are just local hikes. Most of my hiking has been day hikes of varying distances and levels of difficulty.

## Meeting challenges

I don't have great balance, so I have to pay attention to where I am walking, especially toward the end of a hike. I hate crossing streams; I am always afraid I will fall in. I am somewhat better than I used to be, but depending on the difficulty, I can still get freaked out. Being careful, judging the safest route, not lingering on shaky rocks, and at times being willing to walk through a stream have all helped.

My hiking poles have been invaluable. They are my favorite gear because they have allowed me to feel confident in a variety of hiking conditions. They help with balance, which is not my strongest suit, and they help me use my upper body along with my lower body when hiking. Currently, I am just using an inexpensive pair (Cascade) that I bought at Costco for about $40. They have lasted a long time, the adjustment system works pretty well, and I just like their feel.

I don't have [much experience or knowledge of] the skills to hike in snow, but when doing a backpacking trip in the Wind River Range in Wyoming, I had to cross several snowfields (with no spikes because we weren't expecting much snow). With guidance from Scott, I had to just do it—literally dig my heels in to safely cross, and calm my anxiety until it was finished. Crossing the snowfields, while not frightening to many people, was to me. We heard there might be a little snow, but there was quite a bit more than we expected. I learned that despite being afraid, I could balance if I focused, and I learned about digging into snow.

I tend to avoid frightening events by planning fairly carefully and choosing hikes that are known. I am adventurous in that I want to see new, interesting, and beautiful places, and new (to me) cultures, but I am not adventurous in that I don't look for and don't like potentially dangerous or unknown terrain. I will probably never be a mountain climber.

I have grown to love hiking. However, I have been dealing with a back injury that's compressing a nerve, resulting in pain from my hip and down my leg. This became acute in August 2018 and has severely limited my ability to hike. I had surgery in November 2019, and during early 2020 was still recovering.

Before I had surgery, I was able to do moderate hiking in the Dolomites for about seven days (five of which included carrying a light backpack) after working extensively with a Pilates trainer and using something called ENSO (like a TENS unit) to help relieve the pain However, my condition worsened, and I decided to have surgery. My goal is to recover from surgery, return to training, and walk the Ireland's Kerry Way and Dingle Peninsula.

## Why I hike

Being in nature fills my soul. Before this injury, hiking was something I enjoyed doing fairly regularly, sometimes a few times a week. Hiking kept me out in nature and active. I always feel better afterward; I think both the physical activity and being in nature contribute to keeping me feeling good both emotionally and physically. I also enjoy the social aspect—hiking with a friend or with my husband and occasionally with a group.

Seeing places I can't see unless I walk to them, being out in nature, accomplishing a challenge. Being in an environment and seeing what it looks like close up. These are all reasons to hike.

## Accomplishments include...

I walked the Camino de Santiago in 2015, at age 64, from St. Jean Pied de Port, France to Santiago, Spain—approximately 500 miles in 40 days with some days off to rest and/or sightsee. I carried a backpack and stayed in albergues, small hotels, and bed-and-breakfasts. This required walking an average of 12 miles a day with one being as long as 20 miles, several 15-mile days, and a few five- to six-mile days. This was well above the number of miles I had generally hiked and required months of training to increase my fitness. Walking day after day has a cumulative effect and is much more physically demanding [than going out for a one-day hike.]

I had never done anything like this before; it was an amazing trip. I traveled with Scott, who is an accomplished long-distance hiker, but I carried my own backpack, the trip was my idea, and I determined distances.

### When it gets tough

On the Camino, there were days, especially at the beginning, when by afternoon, I would ask myself, "What am I doing here?" But there was no choice, I had to keep going to have a place to sleep, and the next morning I was always ready to go again. Sometimes, just taking a break or drinking some water helped. On the Camino, you can often stop at a café—a real break. I would tell myself I can do it, and of course, I could. Sometimes distracting myself by talking with other hikers helped; sometimes just plodding along alone was all I could do.

### Thoughts on hiking solo

I have hiked solo locally but never overnight backpacking. If I am training, that takes priority, so sometimes it's better to hike alone so I can accomplish whatever goal I have for that day. But I also need to hike with people while I am training because it is usually more fun and helps with motivation.

### Does age matter?

In retirement, I became interested in increasing to longer distances. I had an experience that increased my confidence in my ability to hike longer and more challenging trails. A couple of years ago, I decided to hike with friends doing the Double Dipsea [best-known as a running event that takes place annually in Marin County, California, but its grueling course is also popular with hikers desiring a difficult challenge]. It was mostly because I wanted to spend time with my daughter's boyfriend's parents. This is a challenging 14-plus-mile hike with a lot of elevation gain and lots of steps. With a lot of coaching and support from my companions, I saw that I could do it. It was beautiful and a lot of fun.

But, as mentioned before, I currently have a condition that has drastically curtailed my ability to hike. I am hoping the recent surgery will enable me to go back to the level at which I was hiking before the injury. As a person who has, in later years, become more active, I want to be able to continue that activity. I would like to be able to do more backpacking trips, especially while traveling outside the U.S. I would rather stay inside at night (huts, B&Bs, hostels, hotels) rather than camping but may be willing to do some shorter camping trips. I also want to be able to do day hikes both at home and while traveling.

**Pertinent advice**

Hiking: Just start doing it. Go with friends; check out hiking books and online hiking sites for ideas. Find hiking groups—you will be surprised how many there are. Try hiking poles but learn how to use them so they actually help. Shoes are important; there is a big debate among hikers about whether trail runners or traditional hiking boots are best. I go with trail runners. Start slowly on easy to moderate hikes, and build up to avoid injuries.

Backpacking: If you start hiking, you will find people who backpack. It's a good idea to go with other people, especially at first. There are books on the subject—look for those that focus on lightweight backpacking, which is so much more enjoyable. There are organized group trips that you can do. They often cost money but may help as an introduction.

What helps me meet new challenges is getting information online, in books, and firsthand from people who have done the hike I'm considering. Figure out if you can cut the hike short if need be. If you are going with other people, make sure you are comfortable with how they are approaching the hike and feel you can say what you need. Try to gauge the difference between [the fear of] trying something new and [the fear of] doing something you don't feel safe doing.

Training is essential, even more so if you are older or less experienced. Training means hiking regularly, slowly increasing distance and difficulty, and ultimately carrying a backpack at the weight you intend to carry when on your trip. So, you need a certain amount of persistence and consistency. When training, be realistic. For example, know when to stop to avoid injury while still pushing yourself a little beyond what you have done before.

Wanting to be out there and stopping to look at and appreciate your surroundings help to keep a positive attitude. Having others who support you in your goal is also helpful.

### Confidence in one's abilities

I think women do underestimate their physical abilities; I have definitely underestimated what I could do. Not having been active physically as a child, I often don't have a sense of what my body's abilities are. My years of experience have helped build my confidence. Accepting the level at which I feel comfortable as well as the challenges I am willing to undertake have been important.

If I start thinking competitively, I will often feel negative about my abilities. Sometimes, hiking with other women helps. There are many role models now—women who have accomplished amazing feats—and I think younger women today are less hampered by lack of confidence.

### Advice good and not so good

Being around accomplished long-distance hikers as I am, because of Scott's heavy involvement, I just try to take what I hear with a grain of salt and translate it to my level. Mostly, I have received very helpful advice.

### What is next for me

I have really felt deprived by having to limit or stop my hiking during this period. I want to visit places I have not seen in the U.S. and internationally, and walk some of the most beautiful areas—see the scenery and meet the people close up. For example, I had a trip planned for Spring 2020 to hike the Kerry Way and the Dingle Peninsula in Ireland with my husband and a small group of friends. Then, due to the coronavirus, we had to postpone that trip. But when we do go, it will take about three weeks allowing for some non-hiking days. The trip was initiated by a friend who found a well-recommended company to make reservations at B&Bs and transport our luggage, so we will be carrying daypacks only.

At some point, I would like to do another Camino hike,

possibly the Portuguese or El Norte. We are also planning or hoping to take other trips in the next few years that will include day hiking and possibly some overnights in the Canadian Rockies and/or Nova Scotia, Costa Rica, Iceland, Norway, possibly Sweden, Australia, Bhutan. Someday, I would like to do some hiking in England and Scotland similar to the trip to Ireland.

That's my short list. Who knows what else may come up!

**Susan:** Perhaps foretelling Katie's long-time interest in nature and the outdoors is that she went back to school after she and Scott were married to obtain her Master of Science. She is also quite interested in history, particularly in studying her Jewish heritage.

Not everyone likes planning trips, but Katie enjoys it and is very good at it. Her trip reports and photos are filled not only with images of hiking trails but also the richness of her surroundings—the mountains, sea, flora, and fauna.

Katie Williams — backpack/shakedown for Wind River trip

# Sue 'Leapfrog' Williams

**Susan:** Sue lives in Davisburg, Michigan. She retired from her career as a financial advisor at 57 and decided it was time to fully embrace her passion for the outdoors. She became a ski instructor, learned to windsurf, and continued hiking, camping, and back-packing. Then, wanting to encourage and motivate other Boomers, she and her husband John founded Fiftysense.com, which focuses on "Human-powered Outdoor Activities and Adventure Travel, including geocaching, but [which also encourages] people with experience in areas such as health, aging, humor, to share their advice and stories on any topic."

**Sue Williams:** John and I started Fiftysense.com in 2007 after realizing how many mistakes we had made and [how] some could have been life-threatening. We wanted to share ideas and motivate people to get off the couch. After 50, you don't need to stop, you just need to continue with caution and knowledge.

I have been hiking all my life but started backpacking at the age of 47. Once I met Bill Irwin, the blind thru-hiker on the Appalachian Trail, I decided that maybe an older 5-foot-3 female could do it. [Bill Irwin, 1940-2014, was the first blind man to traverse the A.T. His thru-hike was completed in 1990. Irwin credited much of his success to the help of his seeing-eye dog, Orient, and a deep faith in God.]

I've done around 1000 miles of the A.T.—mostly the southern half, all section hikes—the longest being 17 days. I was planning on thru-hiking it after my last daughter graduated from college, and then John asked if I would wait until he retired so he could do it with me. Then the bottom fell out of the housing market, and we lost two houses and most of our life savings. So now, at 71, he is still working. It was a very hard goal to give up, but I'm fine with it now.

I have hiked all over the U.S. I have really enjoyed the Pictured Rocks Trail, a National Lakeshore Trail on Michigan's Upper Peninsula (actually, anywhere in Michigan is great), the Centennial Trail in South Dakota, and the Bruce Trail in Ontario.

However, my favorite hike was the Annapurna Circuit and base-camp sanctuary in Nepal. This was by far my greatest accomplishment, hiking over an 18,000-foot pass—a trip that took 30 days. Before I did this at the age of 52 with my daughter (we were the only mother-daughter team), I had never even had a passport. It took me four days and three days traveling by myself to get there—I was more nervous about that than the hike! It was life-changing to spend six weeks in their culture.

## It's who I am

Backpacking is an identity for me, an average woman doing extraordinary things! I never thought I could do it and found that when you push yourself, it's exhausting and exhilarating. I teach downhill skiing in the winter and hike the rest of the year, so I don't have to go to the gym to stay in shape.

Nature is my spirituality. I find it hard to be in a bad mood when hiking. I love when I am backpacking. I have all I need to survive and I don't have to go back to civilization at night. The quiet wakes up my other senses.

## Solo or with companions

I have hiked solo. If we're compatible, I prefer hiking with someone else. I have never been in fear of anyone when backpacking. When I get bad vibes, I keep walking. It's important to listen to that.

## My strengths

Being a 5-foot-3, 72-year-old backpacker, most is mental. I do notice I don't have the strength I did 10 years ago, and because

I'm not disciplined enough to get in shape before a trip, I am doing more hikes on easier terrain. I really don't care where I hike as long as I can get out in nature. It's okay to slow down. I usually don't go out for longer than a week at a time now because my husband doesn't backpack, and I want to spend time traveling, camping, and day hiking with him. I still believe that if I wanted to do a long-distance hike, I would start slow, build up my strength, and be fine. I don't see any reason why I should have to give up this sport for a long time.

The biggest attribute I have that keeps me going is my sense of humor. I always say when things are bad, "This will make a really good story someday!" I also take Werther's [caramel candy] to be eaten only on false summits. I have bonked, and that's okay as long as your hiking partner doesn't bonk at the same time.

## Challenges

I think the biggest challenge I have had to face mentally was the initial negative attitude of my husband. At first, he didn't like me spending so much time doing something that didn't include him. We had pretty much done everything together, and I realized I needed my own identity. He is now a great supporter.

Physically, I have fibromyalgia, IBS, hypoglycemia, and migraines. The hiking helps the fibromyalgia. I have to be vigilant with my diet and sometimes have had to get off the trail because of blinding migraines. It's all okay if you're flexible. I know the trip will always have a Plan B at least.

My most unexpected inexperience was when I took a backpacking trip [with a small group] for two weeks in South Dakota. One woman was mad that her friend invited me and decided she was not going to like me. I did not ask enough questions about their hiking style before going, and they were mad because I didn't want to do a three-mph pace. They got up at five in the morning, no breakfast, and did a daily average of 15 miles at a forced march. I was so miserable that I would get into camp, set up, fix dinner, and hide in my tent the rest of the evening. I was glad I drove so I had some leverage.

I now try to do a shorter hike with a new partner before

committing to a longer hike. I think you need to hike with someone who is flexible, supportive, and willing to compromise. This sport can get competitive, and I'm not out there to impress anyone.

### Role models can help

Women definitely underestimate their physical abilities. My mentor was 'Grandma Soule' [fiftysense.com/stories/verna]. She started backpacking in her fifties and thru-hiked the Appalachian Trail at 63 in four and a half months, averaging 14 miles a day. She logged more than 45,000 miles before she died. She was a tiny woman who looked like everyone's grandma and gave me the best advice. When I asked her if she ever thought of quitting, she said she didn't think so. I said I could see myself sitting on the trail sobbing. She said, "Oh, I did that! Then I just got up and kept on hiking!" [Verna passed away in her sleep on September 5, 2007, at age 82.]

For women starting out, do research, join hiking groups, attend gatherings, and try to find a mentor. This sport can be life-threatening if you don't know what you are doing. Knowledge and experience are power. There is so much information out there now. Don't be afraid to ask questions. Most backpackers love to help.

### My favorite gear

My favorite hiking gear is my Montbell liner jacket. I use it in all weather and for my pillow. Some of my favorites that people may not know about—the Geigerrig pressurized hydration system that you don't have to suck [the system sprays water into your mouth with a simple squeeze or bite of the valve], Farm to Feet socks that are the only wool socks I'm not allergic to, Leki hiking poles, and a Western Mountaineering sleeping bag.

When I started, lightweight backpacking did not exist. I would hear that a pound or two didn't make a difference. It does! On the other hand, ultra-lightweight can be life-threatening to a beginner. Be reasonable with the weight. Dry weight (everything but food and water) should be under 20 pounds. With three liters of water and five days of food, around 35 pounds should be max. Listen to your body. Electrolytes are key, and hiking poles are the bomb!

### And next time...

Every time I hike, I look forward to slowing down, finding my center, remembering my blessings, and challenging my body. I also enjoy taking inexperienced women out so they can start with a good trip and empower others to do the same.

### Changes with COVID-19

[Michigan, May 2020] John and I are doing well; he even learned to cut the back of my hair! My husband is wonderful. We were going to celebrate our 50th anniversary with our daughters' families (all 14 of us) for a week in the Smokies. We had to cancel, but I'm glad everyone is safe. We have our health, our three daughters married well, and we have six wonderful grandchildren.

Because we camp, we are used to doing without. Since my Nepal hike, I have believed that we all put too much emphasis on material things, so I'm not concerned about going places or buying things.

I think sometimes it's easy to lose balance in one's life, especially with what the world is facing right now. The hardest is not hugging my grandchildren. We are walking, day hiking, gardening, and making tons of facemasks. I hadn't sewn in 40 years; I started making them in April, the first one taking 3-1/2 hours! It has really helped my mood doing something positive. It's gotten so much easier. My goal was 10/day, 300 for the month of April, and so far I've made almost 400. [As of August 2020, she had reached 1,300.]

When I can't be active physically, I have to be active mentally. My philosophy of life: If I keep on walking, I can walk all day.

**Susan:** In Sue's Column Sense (2/28/20) she wrote, "My new family physician asked me what makes my fibromyalgia worse, and I was taken aback. I never think about what makes it worse but what makes it better. I ski at least four days a week, and once the days get warmer, I try to hike at least that often. When time and opportunity allow, I still love backpacking. I have noticed I don't ski as hard, becoming a recreational skier versus attacking the hill. I have also found easier hikes are more fun. I just don't have the strength in my legs that I did 10 years ago. That doesn't mean I should stop, just adjust. It's all about the attitude!"

**Sue Williams**

# About the Author

Susan 'Backpack45' Alcorn

We who like to hike know that being outdoors has many rewards—views, fresh air, new discoveries. Those who like hiking with groups or a buddy often report that the time on the trail flies when you are chatting with compatible partners. Those who hike solo often report a sense of pride at being able to meet challenges using their own wits and skills.

All this can improve not only our fitness but also our sense of well-being. Often being immersed in physical activities can release us for a while from all the 'should' and 'could' of everyday life. Certainly, for me, it is a powerful way to be distracted from the depressing and horrific news that media brings us most every day.

In addition, I find hiking valuable because it is full immersion. When I travel to foreign countries, I can travel with minimal clothing and other items and yet be well prepared for changes in weather, unforeseen trail conditions, and time spent in both cities and the wild. I can forgo the shelter of cars and buses, be placed on foot in direct contact with my surroundings, and meet the challenges. I can leave behind some of the barriers to meeting new people—differences in wealth, language, and culture—and be open to learning about other peoples' ways of coping with life.

When I hike near home, my preferences are to challenge myself on new trails, or to enjoy being with friends, seeing wildlife, experiencing changing seasons on old familiar ones.

I credit my ability to hike as much as I do on a combination of factors beyond my genetic makeup and environmental influences. I use hiking poles, have lightened my pack, have had some medical interventions, sometimes choose easier trails, and have added stretching and strength training to my daily routine. Not everyone has the option to ask for help, but because it is necessary if we are to do some of our longer hikes, Ralph usually carries more of our gear when backpacking.

When I am going through a rough patch with back problems or leg pain, I try to adhere to the philosophy of a wonderfully optimistic friend, Jeannine Burk, who has rheumatoid arthritis. Years ago, she said, "I have a choice—I can hike and have pain, or I can sit and have pain. I'd rather hike." Obviously, sometimes people experience too much pain to make this applicable, but many times I have found that when I just get up and out, especially when hiking with a companion or in new and amazing surroundings, the distractions block out the problems—whether physical or mental—and the miles fly by.

Sometimes, in cultures that appear to only value youth, we need to be reminded of the determination, achievements, strength, and wisdom that we who have weathered a few years, have attained.

I hope that the stories that have been shared throughout this book have inspired you to start or continue your own hiking lifestyle. Incorporating hikes, walks, or saunters into our lives is not only good for us in the short term—lifting our mood, improving our self-confidence, strengthening our physical health—but also long term—enhancing our well-being throughout our lives and increasing our life expectancy. You deserve to enjoy all of these benefits.

**Susan's major hikes:**
- **Camino de Santiago** routes between 2001 and 2019: Francés (Spain); LePuy (France); Geneva (Switzerland) to LePuy; Porto (Portugal); Arles (France). Norte and Primitivo (Spain); Mozarabe (Spain, partial); Vezelay (France, partial).
- **John Muir Trail** (section-hiked all) between 1989 and 2001.
- **Mt. Kilimanjaro**, Tanzania, ascent (to peak) in 2007.

- **Pacific Crest Trail** (section-hiked all) between 2004 and 2010.
- **Patagonia Torres del Paine**, Chile, 'O' (circuit) and 'W' routes in 2009-2010.
- **Hiking plans for the near future:**
- Locally: Completing the Nifty Ninety Peak Challenge (90 peaks in the Greater Bay Area as selected by the local Sierra Club). Eleven to go!
  Europe: Completing the remaining 140 miles of the Vezelay, France Camino route.
- **Hikes on my wish list:**
  The Dolomites, Italy; Camino Inglés, Spain; Robert Lewis Stevenson Trail (GR70), France.

**Susan Alcorn — Goat Rocks Wilderness, WA on PCT**

# Glossary

*Change your life today. Don't gamble on the future, act now,
without delay*
~ Simone de Beauvoir

Hiking? Walking? Or 'sauntering' (as John Muir preferred to
say)? One would think that the terms *walking, hiking, long-distance
hiking, thru-hiking, backpacking, trekking, bushwhacking, tramping,*
and *strolling* would be easily defined by those who do any or all
of these activities, but the ways they are defined are quite varied—sometimes rather arbitrarily. Is it walking when you go two
miles per hour and hiking when you go three? What about when
you are climbing a steep grade, does the term change? Call your
adventures whatever you choose and enjoy arguing the point at
the next hikers' gathering.

## Definitions A-to-Z

**ADT or American Discovery Trail**: This contiguous trail
is a network of recreational trails and roads that can be hiked,
bicycled, or (in part) ridden on horseback. Extends from Cape
Henlopen State Park, Delaware, to Point Reyes National Seashore, California. The trail divides in Elizabethtown, Ohio,
and rejoins as the western route in Denver, Colorado. Length:
Northern route 4,834 miles, Southern route 5,057 miles. American Discovery Trail Society, discoverytrail.org.

**AT or Appalachian Trail**: This National Scenic Trail is a
marked hiking trail on the East Coast from Springer Mountain in
Georgia to Mt. Katahdin in Maine. Length: 2,190 miles (~3,500
km). Appalachian Trail Conservancy, appalachiantrail.org.

**Backpacking:** Backpackers generally carry their own gear and camp out. They may replenish their water supply from streams or ponds as they progress. If their trip is to be of any duration, they resupply (collect additional food and supplies) at towns or from someone in a support vehicle along the way.

**Blowdown:** Tree or trees down on the trail, sometimes covering a wide area that has been hit by a strong wind or storm. Hikers encountering blowdowns may need to spend considerable time climbing over, around, and/or under the trees due to the number, the size, and/or the surrounding terrain.

**Bonking (or hitting the wall):** Sudden weakness, dizziness, and fatigue—a loss of energy caused by the depletion of glycogen stores in the liver and muscles. Serious hikers should start the day with complex carbs such as oatmeal, whole-wheat foods, bananas (if you can get them). Mild cases of 'the bonk' can generally be turned around with a break for food and liquids with carbohydrates. Energy bars are generally loaded with carbs. Nuuns and other tablets and powders containing electrolytes can help with hydration.

**Camino de Santiago or Camino:** A network of pilgrimage trails, primarily in Europe, which lead to the Holy City of Santiago de Compostela, Spain. The most popular of the routes is the Francés, which is ~500 miles if started from St. Jean Pied de Port, France, in the Pyrenees.

**CDT or Continental Divide Trail:** This National Scenic Trail extends from the border of Mexico to the border of Canada going through New Mexico, Colorado, Wyoming, Idaho, and Montana. Length: 3,100 miles. Sometimes called the Constantly Disappearing Trail because it does often disappear! Hikers encounter a countless number of alternatives, detours, and shortcuts that add to the other challenges. Continental Divide Trail Coalition, continentaldividetrail.org

**C2C or Coast to Coast:** The Coast to Coast Walk across northern England was devised by Alfred Wainwright. It's 190 miles across from St. Bees Head on the west coast to Robin Hood's Bay on the east, passing through the Lake District, Yorkshire Dales, and North York Moors.

**False summit:** For mountaineers, a false summit is a peak that appears to be the pinnacle of the mountain, but upon reaching it, it turns out the summit is higher yet. For a hiker in the hills or mountains, it's when you think you are approaching the highest point of the stretch of trail, but when you get there, you see there are higher points ahead.

**Flip-flop:** On long trails, hikers may encounter trail conditions—such as snow or other weather conditions or forest fires—that make it difficult if not impossible to continue in a straightforward way to the trail's end. Bypassing a difficult section and then coming back later to do it is a flip-flop.

**Luggage transport service:** Services hired to carry backpacks between accommodations along a route—popular with many Camino walkers but seldom available on U.S. trails.

**Mt. Kailash Kora, Tibet:** An "important pilgrimage site for Hindus, Buddhists, and members of the Bon and Jain faiths. Many pilgrims journey to this remote Himalayan corner with the goal of completing a Kora, which is Tibetan for the circumambulation of a holy place. According to Buddhists, one circuit around Mt. Kailash will absolve the sins of a lifetime, and for those looking for a little more in the way of karmic insurance, it is said that 108 circuits will lead to nirvana and freedom from reincarnation. Because of its sacred qualities, the mountain has never been summited." thehikinglife.com/2020/04/mount-kailash-kora-trekking-around-tibets-sacred-mountain.

**PCT or Pacific Crest Trail:** The Pacific Crest Trail, another of the 11 designated U.S. National Scenic Trails, is a long-distance hiking and equestrian trail that travels 2,650 miles (4,265 km) from Mexico to Canada through California, Oregon, and Washington. Forester Pass is its highest point at 13,153 ft. (4,009 m), the bridge at Cascade Locks its lowest at 140 ft. (43 m).

**PLBs or Personal Locator Beacons:** Satellite-synced devices that send an SOS signal to rescue agencies, along with your location.

**Prominence:** A given peak's height above the lowest pass/col connecting it to a higher peak.

**Section hiking:** As the term implies, it means doing part of a longer trail. However, many section hikers go back repeatedly to a trail in order to complete the entire thing.

**Slackpacking:** For backpackers, slackpacking generally refers to not carrying most, or all, of your pack and its usual contents. Can be achieved in various ways such as planting a vehicle at each end of a trail segment or hitchhiking back to your vehicle.

**Thru-hikers:** People endeavoring to hike an entire trail in one season. On the PCT, for example, thru-hikers start NOBO (northbound) from Campo, California. Those hiking SOBO (southbound) start from the Washington-British Columbia border in E. C. Manning Provincial Park.

**Trail angel:** Someone who goes out of their way to help hikers or backpackers on their journey. This can include such things as providing rides to those needing to reach a town for a resupply of food (or back to the trailhead); leaving a cooler full of sodas and candy bars along a remote stretch of trail (and cleaning up the area regularly); hosting a barbecue for hikers at a campground, and providing a place to stay or set up a tent. **Trail Magic** is what we call these often unexpected gifts.

**Trekking:** Similar to backpacking because it usually means staying overnight multiple times, but trekkers tend to stay in hostels or mountain huts with food available whereas backpackers usually sleep in tents, 'cowboy' camp (out in the open), stay in shelters (on the A.T.), or (occasionally) sleep in hammocks and carry their own food. In some locations, **trekkers** enlist the help of porters or animals to carry heavy packs and supplies.

**Triple Crown:** An award is given by the American Long Distance Hiking Association—West (ALDHA–West) to those hikers who have completed the three major U.S. trails—the Pacific Crest, Continental Divide, and Appalachian for a total distance of approximately 7,900 miles. As of the end of the 2019 application period, ALDHA-West had recognized a toral of 440 Triple Crown Awards winners.

Five of the women in this book have accomplished this amazing feat: Mary E. Davison, Nancy Huber, Naomi Hudetz, Marcia Powers, and Elsye Walker. Jan Barlow, having completed the PCT and AT and 1,000 miles of the CDT, has it in her sights. Also completing the American Discovery Trail gave Marcia Powers (and husband Ken) four major trails, earning them the *Grand Slam* of Hiking.

**Waymark (pl: waymarks):** One of a series of signposts indicating a pathway or trail. A **waymarked trail** is such a trail.

**Zero or Nero Day:** In backpacking terms, Zero means advancing zero miles along the trail in a day, and Nero means nearly none.

# Resources

## The Cover Letter and Questions

*How this book came about:* In late 2019 and early 2020, I sent the following letter (with slight variations) to about three dozen women hikers—all 45 or older—inviting them to participate in this book project. I wanted to collect their stories about hiking that would be inspiring and interesting to others—especially those of comparable age.

Reaching most was relatively easy. I had some women's email addresses because I had met them previously and knew we had a mutual interest in hiking. Others I found by requesting their contact information through social media or others in the hiking community. Other names popped up when I looked online for websites, blogs, or books by women who I thought would have supportive and adventurous stories to share.

I didn't make the selections scientifically. I wanted a range of participants—not just hardcore backpackers who had scaled dozens of notable peaks, but also hikers who stuck closer to home yet had achievements and lessons to inspire readers.

I wanted the stories to be like those that are shared while walking with friends, at a pub after a hike, around a campfire after a long trek, or in a hostel while sharing a meal—open and honest, informative or fun.

So, I held my breath and sent out the following email requesting help making my vision come true.

December 2019
Hi _____,

I'd like to include you in my new project—a book focused on women who hike. It will be geared toward women who are looking for support and encouragement to resume hiking, hike more regularly, hike or backpack more challenging routes, or explore new places. I am sending this to you because I admire and am impressed by what you are doing in the hiking world, and I think others will be similarly inspired by your story. You are leading the way—others can learn important practical and motivational skills from your experience and wisdom.

Included will be the stories of a few dozen women representing a range of hiking abilities and achievements—such as women who hike moderate distances regularly; those who lead groups locally or internationally; those who travel abroad to hike historic trails such as the Camino de Santiago; and those who have earned the Triple Crown by hiking the Appalachian, Continental Divide, and Pacific Crest Trails. I'm certain that readers will not only identify with many of you but will also gain confidence that will help them become even more adventurous in the outdoors.

There will be some similarities to my earlier hiking book *We're in the Mountains, Not over the Hill: Tales and Tips from Seasoned Women Backpackers* and some differences. *Similarities* will be a focus on women hikers who are age 45 and over, and presenting their stories to inspire, inform, and support other women of all ages. *Differences* will include focusing on women who hike and/or backpack, and that each woman included will have her comments and answers featured in her own section (rather than being intermixed).

Attached you will find a set of 16 questions. The questions at this point are rather general, but because each of you is unique, my plan is to follow this set with a couple more questions that would be more focused on *your* personal background or hiking-related interests—i.e. leading group hikes or backpacking trips; overcoming particularly gnarly medical conditions; food preparation for long trips; packing for a long-distance hike; training for hiking, etc. I'll be better able to come up with these focused questions when I know who is going to take part.

This project has been percolating on a back burner for several years, and I am really looking forward to delving into it. I hope you will choose to participate so that the hiking community will learn more about your hiking life and that they will reap the benefits of hiking that we enjoy—including better health and more joy.

I hope this finds you well. Thank you.

Happy holidays and happy trails,
Susan Alcorn

## The questions:
Name _____; trail name if appropriate
_____
Where you live_____.
Age_____.
Phone number so I can contact you with follow up inquiries
_____. (Absolutely will NOT be shared)

The following questions are meant to be open-ended—feel free to shift the focus to make them fit your experiences:

1. Do you have a favorite piece of hiking gear? (People like brands and models, but even more they like to know why you would name a particular item your favorite. My favorite item happens to be a Smartwool top because I can wear it hiking, sleeping, and going out to dinner. And it never stinks!)
2. How old were you when you started hiking? When did you start hiking seriously?
3. Where have you hiked/where do you hike?
4. What role does hiking play in your life? Is it a way of life and important to your lifestyle, or is it more of a thing you do occasionally? (If this helps: Is it an obsession? A physical or mental health boost? Does it fill certain social needs?)

5. What do you like most about hiking or backpacking?
6. What hiking (or backpacking) trip do you consider to be your greatest accomplishment, and why? (Please keep in mind that the focus is on 45+, so while I'd welcome answers related to hikes you did when younger, we need to also relate what is possible at age 45 and above.)
7. What are your thoughts and preferences about hiking solo? IF you do hike solo, how do you respond to people who are critical of it?
8. Yogi Berra is known for being an All-Star catcher and Baseball Hall of Famer, and his quips like this often hit home: "Baseball is 90-percent mental. The other half is physical." What do you think are the attributes needed in order to be a successful long-distance hiker?
9. How do you keep going when everything in your head (or body) is begging you to stop?
10. What challenges have you had to overcome (related to hiking/backpacking)?
11. What frightening (or unexpected) event or experience taught you the most? How/explain.
12. How have your hikes changed over time? As you have aged, have you needed to adjust to any new realities? Become more or less adventurous? Become more or less physically demanding? Do you see changes ahead?
13. What advice do you have for women who want to start hiking or backpacking regularly, or who are nervous about going on a new and more challenging trail?
14. Do you think women underestimate their physical abilities, and if so, what advice would you give them?
15. What bad (even risky) advice have you been given on hiking/backpacking by experienced people? Conversely, what would you advise in similar situations?
16. What are you looking for in your next long hiking or backpacking trip, and why?

Thank you!
Susan Alcorn

### And then came COVID-19 and all of its challenges

When I launched this project in late 2019, little did any of us know that only a few months later, we would all be affected by a pandemic. At first, as we all watched and listened to the news coverage of COVID-19 (novel coronavirus), we thought that this new virus was only of great consequence to those living in far-off Wuhan, China. Little did we know that it was actually a threat to all of us, no matter where we lived, and that we would be told to stay home, not visit with friends, and practice 'social distancing.' If we did leave our homes for what were termed 'essential activities,' we were advised or ordered to stay six feet away from others outside our household, and to wear masks when closer.

Although what were defined as 'essential activities' varied in different states (and regions, counties, and countries), in general people were told to shelter-in-place unless they needed to shop for food and medications or had to leave home for jobs that were considered essential.

The governmental orders that followed required many businesses to allow employees to work from home or to close if that wasn't feasible. Stock markets dropped precipitously in March, millions of people were either laid off or lost their jobs, paychecks were slashed, and economic turmoil grew. The fear of the fast-moving and highly-contagious virus, the heavy restrictions of the lockdown, and the fear of financial disaster combined to cause all of us to be thrown into a time of great uncertainly.

### When would things return to normal?

As time went by, the restrictions that many thought would last only a couple of weeks were extended. We began to be seriously concerned about when things would go back to normal. When would we get our 'old life' back? Would it be in the foreseeable future, would it take years, would it ever happen?!

The added stress and anxiety that arose did not bypass many. For many people, not just hikers, it mattered whether exercise was allowed outside their homes because exercise is a healthy way to reduce stress.

For people accustomed to being outside often, the restrictions posed another set of challenges. If they could leave the house, where could they go? The orders varied: in some areas, one could not go beyond the garden gate; in some places, people could walk their dogs; in other places, they could walk or bicycle, but only in their immediate neighborhood…

Most national parks and monuments in the U.S. closed for a while. Some states, regions, and cities closed all of their parks; others kept them open; still others created a patchwork of what was open and what was not. Some regions and states discouraged travel from other states. Other countries closed their borders, making foreign travel extremely restricted.

**It dawns on us…**

As we watched COVID-19 begin its spread around the globe, we hikers began to wonder if we'd be able to go on our travels and hikes planned for the year. As the months passed—March into April into May and so forth—we realized that this new virus would not soon be controlled. The associations connected to our some of our best-known long-distance hiking trails—such as the Pacific Crest Trail, Continental Divide, and Appalachian Trail— issued statements of concern because of the possible impacts of the virus on hikers, the trail communities through which hikers would travel, and search-and-rescue crews in case of emergencies.

**A new question**

And so I went back to my computer and sent a new request to the women of the book: "How are you coping with the changes in your travel and hiking plans?" I envisioned hearing a lot of sad tales—but as I corresponded with many, I heard answers that I think will inspire you with their creativity, resonate with how you have felt while going through these times, and help you reframe how you are dealing with the big changes we are facing.

May 7, 2020
Hi all,

I hope this email finds you well during these unsettled and challenging times. The book is moving along—and I am at the point where I'll be finding a few readers and getting editorial advice.

I know that most, if not all, of us are sheltering-in-place, in lockdown, or whatever you want to call it, and that most of you had hiking and/or travel plans that have had to be postponed or canceled.

Considering how different it is to be staying so close to home rather than traveling far afield, I have decided to include a section in the book about how people are coping with the changes/restrictions. In our back-and-forth correspondence, several of you have made upbeat comments about how you are continuing to live your life during these times.

Whether you are hiking, biking, or otherwise active in order to stay happy and fit, volunteering, doing home improvement projects, I would love to include additional stories or thoughts about creative ways to handle all of these changes. So, if you have anything you would like to share, please let me know.

I personally have been having my ups and downs. Not often being able to see friends and family (and then at a distance), not being able to hug, having to cancel a major hiking trip—these things have not been easy for me. Most days are good, but a few haven't been all that great.

BUT, there have also been some wonderful things happen that I would have missed if I were traveling! I am finding great pleasure in being home to enjoy springtime wildflowers (now moving into summer!). I'm seeing my garden at its best and enjoying being able to pick tomatoes at their peak. Ralph and I are enjoying our neighborhood walks searching for quirky yard art (and TONS of Teddy Bears in windows!) to photograph. We are still able to take longer hikes in our regional parks. And finally, I have had time to work on this book!

Hearing from each and every one of you has brought so much **JOY**! Thank you all very much!

Stay safe and take care,
Susan Alcorn

# Susan's Ten Essentials for Hikers

Whether you are going out for a short walk or a long one, there are certain items that you should carry with you for safety. The good news for *day* hikers is that their list is not nearly as long, the contents not as heavy as it is for backpackers.

1. **Water/hydration:** The amount will vary depending on weather, terrain, the time of day, the distance you are hiking. If the temperatures will be high, avoid dehydration by carrying electrolyte tablets such as Nuun, or enhanced beverages

2. **Navigation:** Carry a map or directions as appropriate. GPS systems and phone are handy, but can fail or you can go out of range, so have a backup plan.

3. **Sun protection:** Bring sunscreen (most people under-apply), protective clothing and hat as needed. Carry a hiker's sun umbrella if warranted for weather and time you'll be out.

4. **Illumination:** Headlamp or flashlight. Headlamps can be used hands free. Extra batteries!

5. **First aid:** Lists abound on what to include; there are kits available. If you put together your own, consider these items: Motrin (or other pain med), bandages, blister care and/or preventive taping, Neosporin, Swiss Army knife, cortisone (anti-itch) cream, Glide or Vaseline, antacid, Pepto-Bismol. Keep in mind that a bandanna or other clothing can be used as a bandage or splint.

6. **Shelter:** Space blanket, large plastic garbage bag, bivy bag.

7. **Fire:** Lighter and matches.
8. **Food:** Energy bars or similar. RXBAR protein bars, for example, provide essential nutrients, while products such as Clif Shot Blox with sugar (carbs), caffeine (some kinds), and electrolytes can give you an extra burst of energy.
9. **Clothing:** Bring extra—a wind jacket, rain jacket, Smartwool top, and wool hat for unexpected changes.
10. **Common Sense:** As many have said, trust your gut, check the weather before you head out, know where you are going, let someone know where you'll be and when you're coming back, and be wise enough to change your plans if conditions change adversely.

The *original* 10 Essentials was an itemized list (knife, flashlight, etc.) developed by The Mountaineers, a mountain-climbing organization based in Seattle. Over time, their list evolved to 10 essential *systems*. The particular item that you choose within a category may vary on your hikes. Different weather and climate conditions, different trail conditions, your hiking abilities and experience, and personal preferences may all affect your choices.

**The 10 Essential Systems: Freedom 9 Systems***

Navigation: Map, altimeter, compass, GPS device, PLB or satellite communicators, extra batteries or battery pack
    11. Illumination: Headlamp, extra batteries
    12. Sun protection: Sunglasses, sun-protective clothes, and sunscreen
    13. First aid: Include insect repellent (if required) and items for foot care
    14. Knife: Plus repair kit (depends on trip, such things as duct tape, needle and thread, replacement parts, air mattress patches, etc.)
    15. Fire: Matches, lighter, and tinder, or stove as appropriate
    16. Shelter: Carried at all times (can be light emergency

bivy)
17. Extra food: Beyond minimum expectation
18. Extra water: Beyond minimum expectation or the
    means to purify
19. Extra clothes: Beyond minimum expectation

*Based on text from *Mountaineering: The Freedom of the Hills*, 9th edition and quoted with permission from www.mountaineers.org/blog/what-are-the-ten-essentials

In addition: Many would include communication devices if they aren't already included with your navigation system: a whistle, cell phone, two-way radio, satellite phone, unbreakable signal mirror or flare, laser pointer, and/or other items to signal for emergency help. Sometimes it's important to supplement the above with an ice ax or crampons for glacier or snowfield travel.

# Safety Measures for Solo Hiking

*I must be a mermaid, Rango. I have no fear of depths and a great fear of shallow living.*
~Anais Nin from **The Four-Chambered Heart**

As you have read, the women who contributed their stories have differing opinions about hiking solo. Some prefer it, some prefer to hike with a companion or group, and some like doing either. Many women choose to go alone because they like the greater challenge of having to rely almost totally on their own strengths and decisions. They can stop when they want, eat whatever and whenever they choose, go at their own pace, and not have the distractions that others can cause.

Some who choose to go with a partner or group do so because they feel the miles go faster; they like the conversations and sharing that are involved when they're with others; they can learn from more experienced hikers, and they feel safer.

Statistics show that the proportion of women to men on our major trails, including the Camino de Santiago routes, has increased through the years. In many cases, the split is nearly 50-50. That indicates that women are feeling increasingly that they belong on the trail as much as men do. It also means it is easier to find a female companion if you want to.

The women in this book have considered the pros and cons of hiking solo—and have sometimes made different decisions. They've assessed the risks, considered the means and likelihood of getting rescued, and kept the "10 Essentials" in mind.

# Fitness and Training

**Meeting our walking goals**

With increasing age, it also usually takes longer to increase our strength and stamina. Therefore, when we come up with a new goal—whether it's to walk a certain number of miles per day or per week, thru-hike a particular long-distance trail, or something in between—we need to train. It might be possible for those in their twenties to grab a backpack and hop onto a major trail, but for most people, their hike is more likely to be successful if they prepare.

**Start from where you are and make changes gradually.**

Your goal should be to increase your fitness while avoiding injury. If you are only able to walk for five minutes, then do that and gradually add time. If you usually only walk once a week, start walking additional days.

If you have only hiked on flat surfaces, move to hiking in the hills and on uneven terrain. If you want to go backpacking, start adding weight to your empty pack slowly but surely. It's best not to make all of the changes at the same time and to rotate the order in which you make the increases—this week head for the hills, next week add the weight, the next week walk an additional day.

**Use hiking poles.**

As mentioned earlier, hiking poles provide more stability on the trail—especially important when doing stream crossings or descending hills. Pushing off from the ground with poles strengthens the upper body and reduces the load on the lower body.

If you choose to use hiking/trekking poles, it is worth your time to learn how to use them efficiently. Common mistakes include not putting the straps on correctly and not keeping the poles positioned behind you when on level terrain or uphill climbs.

You'll find various videos online that demonstrate how best to use them. For example REI explains pros and cons of using a staff or walking with one pole vs. two poles and the advantages of adjustable poles vs. fixed length ones. rei.com/learn/expert-advice/trekking-poles-hiking-staffs.html

Backpacker online has information from Jayah Faye Paley who often teaches classes. Her *How to Master Your Hiking Poles* can be helpful. backpacker.com/skills/how-to-master-your-trekking-poles

Use rubber tips on your trekking poles on city streets to keep the noise down. They can also be used on other slick surfaces (if metal tips won't grip) and to prevent scarring fragile environments.

**Adapt when you want or need to adapt.**

Keep in mind that there are often alternative ways to enjoy hiking long-distance trails. For example, on some European trails, it is possible to get help for hire. Many people use luggage transport services when walking the popular Francés route (and increasingly on others) of the Camino de Santiago.

Also keep in mind that many more people hike sections of major trails such as the Pacific Crest, Appalachian, or Continental Divide than hike the entire trail. If you later want to do more of these trails, you can return and do other sections—eventually completing the whole thing if you wish. HYOH, Hike Your Own Hike applies!

**So what to do even with your busy life.**

You don't have to be a marathon runner to consider yourself physically active. Walking 2.5 to 3 mph (~ 20 minutes per mile) is considered moderate intensity, but depending on your fitness level, and where you are walking or hiking, this pace could be considered anywhere between moderate and strenuous. If you are able to talk, but not sing, it's considered moderate. If you can only say a few words, it is considered vigorous.

According to the U.S. Dept. of Health and Human Services, these guidelines are key: "Adults should move more and sit less throughout the day. Some physical activity is better than none. Adults should do at least 150 minutes (2 hours and 30 minutes) to 300 minutes (5 hours) a week of moderate-intensity, or 75 minutes (1 hour and 15 minutes) to 150 minutes (2 hours and 30 minutes) a week of vigorous-intensity aerobic physical activity, or an equivalent combination of moderate and vigorous-intensity aerobic activity.

Additional health benefits are gained by engaging in physical activity beyond the equivalent of 300 minutes (5 hours) of moderate-intensity physical activity a week. Preferably, aerobic activity should be spread throughout the week. Additional health benefits are gained by engaging in physical activity beyond the equivalent of 300 minutes (5 hours) of moderate-intensity physical activity a week."

In addition, the following key guidelines are just for older [defined as 65 and older in the cited report] adults: "As part of their weekly physical activity, older adults should do multicomponent physical activity that includes balance training as well as aerobic and muscle strengthening activities. [They] should determine their level of effort for physical activity relative to their level of fitness. [Those with] chronic conditions should understand whether and how their conditions affect their ability to do regular physical activity safely.

"When older adults cannot do 150 minutes of moderate-intensity aerobic activity a week because of chronic conditions, they should be as physically active as their abilities and conditions allow." U.S. Dept. of Health and Human Service health.gov/sites/default/files/2019-10/PAG_ExecutiveSummary.pdf

# Contributors' Books

**Aksamit, Inga.** *The Hungry Spork Trail Recipes: Quick Gourmet Meals for the Backcountry* (2019). *The Hungry Spork: A Long Distance Hiker's Guide to Meal Planning* (2017). *Highs and Lows on the John Muir Trail* (2015). All by Pacific Adventures Press and available in print and eBook.

**Alcorn, Susan.** *Healing Miles: Gifts from the Caminos Norte and Primitivo* (2017). *Patagonia Chronicle: On Foot in Torres del Paine* (2012), *Camino Chronicle: Walking to Santiago* (2006), and *We're in the Mountains Not over the Hill: Tales and Tips from Seasoned Women Backpackers* (2003, updated 2011). All by Shepherd Canyon Books and available in print and Kindle.

**Anderson, Barbara.** *Letters from the Way* (Encanto Press 2015). A wonderfully illustrated book about Anderson's 600-mile walk on the GR653, the Chemin LePuy, a French Camino route.

**Bahrami, Beebe.** *Moon Camino de Santiago: Sacred Sites, Historic Villages, Local Food and Wine* (Moon Travel 2019). *Cafe Oc—A Nomad's Tales of Magic, Mystery, and Finding Home in the Dordogne of Southwestern France* (Shanti Arts Publishing 2016). *Cafe Neandertal: Excavating Our Past in One of Europe's Most Ancient Places* (Counterpoint Press 2018). *The Spiritual Traveler Spain: A Guide to Sacred Sites and Pilgrim Routes* (Hidden Spring 2009). *Historic Walking Guides: Madrid* (DestinWorld Publishing 2009).

**Blanchard, Jane V.** Women of the Way: *Embracing the Camino* (translations in Spanish and Italian: CreateSpace Independent Publishing 2012). *Hadrian's Wall Path: Walking into History* (CreateSpace 2015). *Camino Tips: How to get the most out of 'The Way'* (Amazon.com 2016). *A Peek at the Remarkable Camino de Santiago: A Photo Journey* (Jane V. Blanchard 2016). *Camino Quotes*

*and Poems: The Meaning of the Journey* (Jane V. Blanchard 2016).
**Davison, Mary E.** *Aren't You Afraid* (Vandeleigh Publishing 2020). *Old Lady on the Trail: Triple Crown at 76* (Vandeleigh 2018). Mary takes up long-distance hiking on our major trails at age 60.
**Nilsen, Sylvia.** *Camino Lingo* (Pilgrimage Publications 2013, print and digital): A Handy English-Spanish words and phrases booklet. *Pilgrim Footsteps on the Sands of Time* (EURL Pilgrimage Publications 2013, print and digital): A historical novel of romance and intrigue set on a pilgrimage trail from England to Spain in the turbulent 12th century. *Pilgrimage Trails: Three Short Hikes on El Camino de Santiago* (Sylvia Nilsen 2012): Aragones route from Lourdes to Pamplona, Camino Ingles from el Ferrol to Santiago, and the Fistera route from Santiago de Compostela to Finisterre. Includes a diary of Nilsen's 15-day service as a hospitalera in the San Roque albergue in Corcubion on the Fistera Route. *La via Francigena: Five Pilgrims to Rome* (Sylvia Nilsen 2012): Five middle-aged friends trek 700 km from Switzerland to Rome over the Great St. Bernard Pass. *La via Turonensis: From Paris to Spain* (Sylvia Nilsen 2012): The 1,120-km trek from Paris to Pamplona and from Sarria to Santiago is described. *Slackpacking the Camino Frances* (EURL Pilgrimage Publications 2013): A guide for walking the Camino Francés without staying in dormitories or carrying a pack. *Your Camino: A Lightfoot Guide to Practical Preparation for a Pilgrimage* (EURL Pilgrimage Publications 2011): A planning guide for pilgrims.
**Roelse, Dami.** *Fly Free, a memoir about love, loss and walking the path* (New Sarum Press 2020). How and why the author became a long-distance hiker as she takes you with her on a trek in Ladakh in the Himalayas. *Walking Gone Wild: How to Lose Your Age on the Trail* (Fuze Publishing 2018).
**Soini, Diane.** *Piper's Flight: A Solo Woman's Journal on the Pacific Crest Trail* (Lulu Press 2008). *Adventure and Magic: A Solo Woman's Journal from Santa Barbara to Canada along the Pacific Crest Trail* (Null 2010). *Santa Barbara Hikes: Great Day Hikes* (Lulu Press 2008).
**Spicer, Diane.** *Best Tips For Women Dayhikers: Everything You Need To Know To Hit The Trail* (independently published on

Kindle and paperback 2017). Advice on gear selection, trip planning, and more.

# Recommended Reading

## General Interest:

**Anderson, Heather.** *Thirst: 2,600 Miles to Home* (Mountaineer Books 2019). 'Anish,' as she's known on the trail, writes of setting her Pacific Crest Trail speed record. The title refers to both when she ran out of water while on the trail in the Southern California desert sections and the strength that keeps her pursuing thru-hiking records. She was the National Geographic 2019 Adventurer of the Year.

**Berger, Karen.** *America's National Historic Trails: Walking the Trails of History* (Rizzoli 2020). *America's Great Hiking Trails* (Rizzoli 2014). Beautiful coffee table books to whet your appetite. *Hiking America's Triple Crown* (Mountaineers Books 2001). How-to, in paperback.

**Carvin, Geolyn.** *On the Trail with Boots McFarland* (Geolyn Carvin 2018). Geolyn completed the PCT in 2014, but her cartoon character, Boots, continues to capture the spirit of long-distance hikers—adventurous and fun. From the publisher: "Whether it be our questionable eating habits, debatable hygiene practices, or simply the crazy notion that people would want to walk thousands of miles just for the fun of it, Boots' illustrations are a chafe-and-all celebration of what makes hikers tick."

**Davis, Jennifer Pharr.** *The Pursuit of Endurance: Harnessing the record-breaking power of strength and resilience* (Viking: Penguin Books 2018). In 2011, Davis set a fastest-known thru-hike of the A.T.—46 days, 11 hours, 20 minutes—for an average of 47 miles a day. Her record held for four years. She was the National Geographic 2012 Adventurer of the Year.

**Mann, Barney.** *Journeys North: The Pacific Crest Trail* (Mountaineers Books 2020). In this book, legendary trail angel, thru-hiker, and former PCTA board member Barney 'Scout' Mann spins a compelling tale of six hikers on the Pacific Crest Trail as they walk from Mexico to Canada in 2007. This ensemble story unfolds as these half-dozen hikers—including Barney and his wife Sandy—trod north, slowly forming relationships and revealing their deepest secrets and aspirations.

**Miller, Dorcas S.** *Adventurous Women: The Inspiring Lives of Nine Early Outdoorswomen* (WestWinds Press 2000). The nine women profiled in this book, part of the Pruett Series, "defied the expectations of an age—the 1800s into the early 1900s—which expected women to stay at home. They pushed themselves to their physical limits to explore the beauty of nature and experience the thrill of an outdoor life. They hiked, paddled, climbed, and ventured far from civilization, and in doing so returned to their other lives stronger for the experience."

**Rochfort, Heather Balogh.** *Women Who Hike: Walking with America's Most Inspiring Adventurers* (Falcon Guides 2019) profiles more than 20 of America's most inspiring hikers. Each woman tells her own story accompanied by a map with a favorite trail described—including GPS coordinates to the trailhead, mileage, level of difficulty, and elevation as well as words of wisdom.

**Thomas, Liz.** *Backpacker Long Trails: Mastering the Art of the Thru Hike* (Backpacker 2017). Over the past decade, Liz 'Snorkel' Thomas has hiked numerous long-distance trails around North America. That well of experience, combined with an attention to detail and a knack for communicating ideas in a down-to-earth manner, has resulted in a book that represents an excellent resource for aspiring thru-hikers.

## Guidebooks:

**Honan, Cam.** *Wanderlust USA* (2019). *The Hidden Tracks: Wanderlust off the Beaten Path* (2018). *Wanderlust: Hiking on Legendary Trails* (2017). This trio of books, all published by Gestalten, are odes to the beauty and wonder of experiencing the natural world on foot. Each features about 30 of the finest trails and routes from around the globe, including Tibet's Mt. Kailash Circuit, California's Lowest to Highest Route, Peru's Cordillera Huayhuash Circuit, and the legendary Haute Route between Chamonix, France and Zermatt, Switzerland. The books contain background history, trail descriptions, overview maps, and most notably, scores of spectacular wilderness photographs. Backpacker magazine has called Honan "the most traveled hiker on earth." Follow him at thehikinglife.com.

**Wainwright, Albert.** *A Coast to Coast Walk: A Pictorial Guide* (Frances Lincoln Publishers LTD revised 2003) From the editor: "Born in Blackburn in 1907, Alfred Wainwright left school at the age of 13. A holiday at the age of 23 kindled a life-long love affair with the Lake District. Following a move to Kendal in 1941 he began to devote every spare moment he had to researching and compiling the original seven Pictorial Guides."

# Additional Resources:

**Outdoor Afro.** The reality is that many people of color have not felt welcome on our trails, but some progress has been made. One of the best examples is Outdoor Afro, a nonprofit organization founded in 2009 by Rue Mapp, then an Oakland resident. There are now more than 46,295 members in 37 chapters throughout the U.S. You can find out more at meetup.com/topics/outdoorafro and Rue at her website, ruemapp.com.

**The American Hiking Society.** Here you'll find a page, "Racism in the Outdoors," which includes links to articles, videos, organizations and thought leaders, affinity groups, non-profit and small businesses to support, and more. A good starting place for those who want to better understand systemic racism in the hiking world and for those who may feel marginalized in the outdoors. https://americanhiking.org/hiking-resources/racism-in-the-outdoors/

**Study: Saint-Maurice PF, Coughlan D, Kelly SP, et al.** "Association of Leisure-Time Physical Activity Across the Adult Life Course With All-Cause and Cause-Specific Mortality. "Although long-term participation in physical activity may be important to lower mortality risk, the present study provides evidence that becoming physically active later in adulthood (40-61 years of age) may provide comparable health benefits." JAMA Netw Open. 2019;2(3):e190355. Published 2019 Mar 1. doi:10.1001/jamanetworkopen.2019.0355.

# I hope you have enjoyed this book

If so, please post a review with Amazon or your favorite book review site. You can contact me at backpack45@yahoo.com, visit my websites at susandalcorn.com and backpack45.com, enjoy my blog at backpack45.blogspot.com, and join me on Facebook.

Bookstores, whether independent dealers or online, can order this book from their normal Ingram book sources using ISBN 978-0-936034-07-2. My books are also all available on Kindle.

The contributors' comments and stories have been edited and formatted to meet the constraints of the book, so I take responsibility for any errors you may notice.

Finally, do check out the books of these women adventurers.

Thank you and take care.

*Susan Alcorn*